14

CROSSING OVER
Teaching
Meaning-Centered
Secondary English
Language Arts

CROSSING OVER
Teaching Meaning-Centered Secondary English Language Arts

Second Edition

Harold M. Foster

The University of Akron

LEA
2002

LAWRENCE ERLBAUM ASSOCIATES, PUBLISHERS
Mahwah, New Jersey   London

President/CEO: Lawrence Erlbaum
Executive Vice-President, Marketing: Joseph Petrowski
Senior Vice-President, Book Production: Art Lizza
Director, Editorial: Lane Akers
Director, Sales and Marketing: Robert Sidor
Director, Customer Relations: Nancy Seitz
Senior Acquisitions Editor: Naomi Silverman
Textbook Marketing Manager: Marisol Kozlovski
Assistant Editor: Lori Hawver
Cover Design: Kathryn Houghtaling Lacey
Textbook Production Manager: Paul Smolenski
Full-Service Compositor: TechBooks
Text and Cover Printer: Hamilton Printing Company

This book was typeset in 10/12 pt. Times Roman, Bold, and Italic.
The heads were typeset in Lubalin, Lubalin Bold, and Lubalin Italic.

Lawrence Erlbaum Associates, Inc., Publishers
10 Industrial Avenue
Mahwah, New Jersey 07430

Acknowledgments appear on pages xxx–xxxii.

Library of Congress Cataloging-in-Publication Data

Foster, Harold M.
    Crossing over : teaching meaning-centered secondary English language arts / Harold M.
Foster. – 2nd ed.
        p.   cm.
    Includes bibliographical references.
    ISBN 0-8058-3258-0 (pbk. : alk. paper)
    1. English language—Study and teaching (Secondary)—United States.   2. Language
experience approach in education—United States.   3. English language—Composition and
exercises—Study and teaching (Secondary)—United States.   I. Title.

LB1631 .F67   2001
428′.0071′273—dc21

                                                                    2001040241

Books published by Lawrence Erlbaum Associates are printed on
acid-free paper, and their bindings are chosen for strength and durability.

Printed in the United States of America
10 9 8 7 6 5 4 3 2

*For
Greta,
Jane,
and
Elizabeth*

Brief Contents

Table of Contents

Preface

A few years ago, my wife and I took our two daughters to see the 50th Anniversary edition of the Walt Disney film, *Fantasia*. The theater was crowded with parents, young children, teenagers, and young adults, most of whom obviously loved the movie—from Mickey Mouse as the Sorcerer's Apprentice to the unicorns dancing to Beethoven. After each of the musical and visual segments, applause would break out in the audience, and at the end of the film, a large round of applause echoed throughout the theater. Yet, over 50 years ago, when the film first came out, the public rejection was severe, badly demoralizing Walt Disney and his gifted animators. The film languished as Disney's greatest failure for over 20 years (Solomon, 1990, pp. 3, 92–93). Then something happened. In the late 1960s, the film found an adoring mass audience that continues through today and has made it a popular classic. The film stayed the same. It was the audience who changed.

Crossing Over is about that changed audience, the children and teenagers currently in schools, and the next student generation. It was written to enable teachers to help these young people navigate and interpret a complex world characterized by a sophisticated and multifaceted communications web. It is about teaching English and language arts in today's world—one that includes talk and print but also includes computers and television and film. A world where talk can occur between people 10,000 miles apart connected by telephone receivers and a communications satellite; a world where print may be as fresh as the instantaneous thoughts of the writer and the microseconds the computer or the fax machine requires from sender to receiver; a world where a basketball game ends at 11:00 p.m. in New York and is reported in California newspapers the next morning; a world where television offers 300 channels and thousands of video choices; and a world dominated by computers with instant messages and chat rooms, with the World Wide Web offering immediate home access to commerce, information, and entertainment, creating communication systems undreamed of by previous generations.

The world young people live in today looks nothing like my world did at their age. Many have advantages incomprehensible to my parents, but their world requires knowledge and skills very different from those any previous generation needed. Their schools and teachers face a large challenge to prepare today's students to speak, listen, see, read, and write in this complex environment. And their schools and teachers need to accept this new world and the instructional methods required to bring its progeny successfully into it.

This book is about instructional methodologies that work with the young people who are now in our classrooms. *Crossing Over* is appropriate for a secondary level English education methods course, and as a sourcebook for English/language arts professionals including college professors and instructors in the fields of reading, English education, elementary education, and English; secondary English teachers; and English/language arts supervisors and curriculum specialists. *Crossing Over* will engage readers, writers, and thinkers. Its ideas are examined through both my own experience and through stories and portraits of teaching. Part of my purpose is to actively engage the reader by provoking debate and reflection. This textbook portrays ways in which learning English can be meaningful to students of the new millennium.

Maybe there was a time in America when some students were capable of learning from fragmented, formulaic skills approaches to the teaching of English, but not any more. We have crossed over. All the enriched new, global electronic media have created young people who respond to messages that are instant and meaningful. Classrooms of this century have to compete with this instantaneous communications web. Our students expect classrooms to be at least as meaningful as what they experience outside the classroom. The title of this book, *Crossing Over*, means that English teaching is about preparing students for this new multimedia, communication saturated world where we find ourselves. We have to learn how to teach our young people to survive in this world so different to us. The heart of English teaching in this new world has to be about discovering meaning.

Overview

Part 1 lays down the theoretical foundation of the book. Chapter 1 defines the meaning-centered theories of literacy and their specific applications in secondary schools. Chapter 2 is a personal narrative of what happened to change literacy in the last 25 years to push

English teaching toward this model. Personal narrative is a way of knowing, a path of discovering knowledge and insight. I use my own story to illustrate a major paradigm shift and the concomitant curriculum described is based on my experiences as a student, teacher, and father. It is also based on the ideas of Robert Scholes (1989), Wayne Booth in *The Company We Keep* (1988), Robert Coles in *Call of Stories* (1989), Michael Real in *Super Media* (1989); Louise Rosenblatt's ideas; and the thoughts of Frank Smith, James Moffett, and others who have shaped the ideas of psycholinguistics into the ideas referred to here.

Part 2 features portraits of meaning-centered secondary English language arts teaching, activities for analyzing and reflecting on the stories, and sections on relating meaning-centered teaching to the *International Reading Association/National Council for Teachers of English/Standards for English Language Arts*. The lessons described in these case studies include the following:

- Conducting a reading workshop (Chapter 3)
- Leading a reader-response book discussion (Chapter 4)
- Teaching drama: *A Midsummer Night's Dream* (Chapter 5)
- Teaching poetry (Chapter 6)
- Teaching classic novels: *The Great Gatsby*, *The Adventures of Huckleberry Finn*, and *To Kill a Mockingbird* (Chapter 7)
- Teaching writing: A writing workshop (Chapter 8)
- Teaching the new literacies: film, computers, and television (Chapter 9)
- Grading and assessing, including preparing students for proficiency tests (Chapter 10)

Part 3 is divided into two sections. In the first section, "Reflections on Becoming and Staying a Teacher," Chapter 11 presents a portrait of a tough but realistic first-year teacher. This chapter offers several approaches to surviving the difficult apprenticeship of teaching. Chapter 12 demonstrates how an English teacher develops classroom plans. Chapter 13 provides an example of how a veteran teacher manages to keep his enthusiasm for teaching alive. In the second section, "Resources," Chapter 14 contains three formalized unit plans for lessons portrayed in Part 2 of *Crossing Over*. Chapter 15 is a glossary of essential information for secondary English language arts teachers.

Themes and Issues

A number of important themes and issues are woven throughout this text.

Integrating Language Arts

Crossing Over is about integrated language arts. You will find all of the language arts practiced here and most of them practiced together. There is writing in all the reading chapters and reading in all the writing chapters. Writing has been separated out for reader clarity, but in the classrooms portrayed in this book, writing is not separated from the reading part of the class in any way. The ideas for writing come from the class readings and all the student writings are also read. Almost all of the chapters have listening and speaking included as well.

Of course, you will find chapters on film and television. In these chapters you will find that students read and write as they study these media. And computer use and study are woven throughout this text.

Thus, *Crossing Over* offers you a portrait of integrated language arts. Every classroom portrayed here is a study in many, if not most, of the areas we know as the language arts.

Stories

The heart of Part 2 is stories that illustrate meaning-centered teaching in secondary English classrooms. Arthur Graesser (1981) has distinguished between *narrative prose*, such as stories, and *expository prose*, such as explanation of events or objects. This distinction is important, because there is ample evidence that students are better able to organize and remember narrative passages than expository passages of equal complexity (Mayer, 1987, p. 177).

The reason I chose stories to illustrate English language arts teaching can be found in the nature of meaningful teaching itself. What better way to illustrate principles of teaching than to bring them alive, make them real, build them? Teachers know that stories are one of the best ways to make concepts meaningful. These case studies, stories of teachers, are meant to breathe life into meaning-centered English teaching in secondary schools.

These stories are composites that describe teaching I have seen or done. The teachers in these stories also are composites, shaped by the many teachers I have been fortunate to know and work with. Whenever possible, I use real voices of students and teachers. The compositions are student written; most of the discussions have taken place. These stories illustrate teachers who are committed to meaning-centered English teaching and who attempt to create lessons. The English teachers in the case studies are "trying" to help their students build meaningful language arts activities, building bridges for students to cross over. Do they succeed? All the time? Under what circumstances? You be the judge.

Although these stories represent a wide range of English teaching, they cannot possibly reflect all the potential classroom situations and methods available to English teachers. They are meant to serve as baseline illustrations of secondary English teaching. Thus, I provide stories that have enough teacher-driven structure to be possible in today's classrooms. Yet, these stories are meant to show how teachers of today, of our time, attempt to create secondary English classrooms where students are asked to create language that is meaningful and contextual. Readers of this book are asked to consider how they would teach these lessons, improve upon them, change them. I highly recommend modeling these lessons; try them out if you have a classroom.

National Standards: Performance Benchmarks

The IRA/NCTE Standards are rather inclusive and intentionally vague for good reasons. These Standards are meant to prevent reducing English teaching to its most basic and least effective minimum. However, even if the Standards demanded specific books or correct grammar, effective teaching would be able to meet them. After all, in *Crossing Over* you find Shakespeare as well as grammar and spelling concerns. Once again, the content is only one issue. The larger issue is how the content is delivered, and that is what *Crossing Over* is about. The goal is to provide you with ideas to aid you in structuring your classrooms for the best possible delivery of a complex and exciting curriculum.

Diversity in English Classrooms

Meaningful classrooms encourage students to speak, read, and write with different voices. Such classrooms promote differences in writing styles and topics; offer a variety of texts, many of which describe diverse cultures; and celebrate differences in student responses to texts. Thus, crossing over means embracing a system that promotes and celebrates the diversity of the students teachers now have in their classrooms.

Crossing Over relates to the great variety of students found in American classrooms and deals directly with several issues concerning diversity. It does this by providing:

- A discussion of multicultural literature
- Examples of class discussion on *Roll of Thunder, Hear My Cry*, a book about the African American experience, and *In the Year of the Boar and Jackie Robinson*, a book about the Chinese-American experience
- A list of multicultural young-adult novels
- A sample class discussion of the ethnocentricity in *The Great Gatsby*
- An episode about the racial issues raised in teaching *The Adventures of Huckleberry Finn*
- A story about teaching *To Kill A Mockingbird*
- A sample class discussion of Langston Hughes' poem *Dreams*
- An example of using the film *Glory* in a thematic unit on race
- Teaching plans based on using *Roll of Thunder, Hear My Cry* and *To Kill A Mockingbird*
- A discussion about the impact of dialect in writing

English as A Second Language

Several of the teaching ideas have been used with English as a Second Language (ESL) students. For instance, the writing and reading workshops have been successfully implemented with ESL students. The Shakespeare unit has been done with ESL students in several schools, such as in Texas where students spoke Spanish as their first language, and in an urban Midwest high school where students came from Eastern Europe, Asia, Middle East, and Africa.

Because meaning-centered classrooms celebrate differences among students by providing an environment where everyone's language and responses are respected, all the activities described in the book are aimed at diverse students.

The Teaching of Writing

Meaningful writing experiences are at the heart of effective English language arts teaching and the writing chapter in this text illustrates this. Chapter 8, however, deals with some of the tougher language issues teachers face: grammar and correctness, personal writing versus public writing, dialect issues, grading, and competency testing. The teacher in this chapter concerns himself with such issues, but without losing sight of the larger meaning-centered goals of effective English instruction. Although the writing section takes the reader from freewriting to editing and grading, writing instruction is presented as fluid, recursive. Other features of this chapter include:

- Portfolios as a means of assessment
- Recordkeeping ideas

Computers in the English Classroom

How computers aid in the teaching of English/language arts is presented in three different chapters:

Chapter 8, "The Teaching of Writing" contains a section showing how a writing teacher uses classroom computers in his instructional program.

Chapter 9, "Teaching the New Literacies," shows how a teacher uses the World Wide Web as an instructional research tool.

Chapter 10, "Grading and Assessing," includes a section on how computers and computer labs may be used to help students generate projects for assessment. The website linked to this text provides hands-on experience.

Pedagogical Features

Lesson Examples Embedded within the Stories

Part 2 provides a full picture of meaning-centered English language arts teaching portrayed through stories. Each story presents a complete lesson, including most of the following elements:

- A description of the teacher, the school, and the students;
- An introduction to the lesson;

- Teacher-generated procedures and activities;
- The teacher's thoughts;
- Evaluation methods—some formal, some informal;
- A reflection/summary of the lesson;
- Questions and activities ("Teacher as Researcher");
- Recommended readings.

National Standards Benchmarks

All chapters in Part 2 contain Benchmarks that are correlated to National Standards developed by the International Reading Association/National Council of Teachers of English, showing how the lesson corresponds to the Standards.

Analysis and Reflection

The introduction to Part 2 provides readers with methods and questions for analyzing the stories. Each story is followed by "Teacher as Researcher" sections offering questions and activities that aid reflection and analysis. The point of *Crossing Over* is to develop reflective teachers who read critically; this section is meant to aid in that process.

Planning

Part 3 includes features that will be helpful for new and veteran teachers: a demonstration of how an English teacher develops classroom plans—including unit, weekly, and daily planning as well as workshop planning, and three formalized unit plans for lessons portrayed in Part 2, which provide detailed examples of the planning involved in complex lessons.

Glossary

The terms and issues in the glossary in Chapter 15, "What Every English Teacher Needs to Know," are meant to add depth to the picture of English language arts teaching found in *Crossing Over* by providing a common vocabulary.

Website

A website, *www.crossingoverbook.com*, accompanies this book. This website is a forum for meaning-centered English teaching. Descriptions of lessons are included as are changes and developments with issues and cases from *Crossing Over*. Critiques of *Crossing Over* lessons are included. You are invited to submit your stories and ask your questions, which the author will attempt to answer. This website will be continuously updated and will provide an interactive up to date forum for *Crossing Over* readers. The website will allow *Crossing Over* to always be a work in progress.

What's New in the Second Edition

This book begins with the story of *Fantasia* written for the first edition. As I prepare the second edition, Disney released its second edition of *Fantasia*, first in IMAX Theaters with the screens about the size of half a football field. Although the music and most of the cartoons differ in this new version, Mickey Mouse remains the star.

Like Disney, I have kept much of what succeeded in the first edition, but, also like Disney, I have added and adapted *Crossing Over* in response to changes and developments that have occurred since the first edition.

- Updates. Chapters 1 and 2 have been significantly rewritten to reflect the changes of the past few years.
- Standards and Benchmarks/Testing and Accountability. The *International Reading Association/National Council of Teachers of English Standards for the English Language Arts* have been incorporated into this text. You will find them at the beginning of Section 2. Also, after most teaching chapters you will find a box giving performance assessment measures (benchmarks) for the instruction in the stories.

Many of the changes in *Crossing Over* serve as help on how to work with a meaning-centered curriculum in an educational environment demanding accountability. Testing, performance assessments, and standards are here for a while, although there are critics, particularly of the high stakes testing movement. Teachers need to know how to deal with these issues; therefore, the new *Crossing Over* provides help.

- New Sample Unit Plans. Major new sections have been added to *Crossing Over*. These include: Teaching *To Kill A Mockingbird*; "Testing, Testing, Testing, Testing," a story about a teacher preparing her students for state proficiency tests; "Three Sample Unit Plans," which are just that, sample unit plans based on instructional stories in Part 2.

- Computers. More is included on the use of technology, in a section in Chapter 1 called "Wired"; in stories about using computers in Chapter 8, "Teaching Writing," Chapter 9, "Teaching the New Literacies," and Chapter 10, "Grading and Assessing."

- Glossary. The glossary in Chapter 15 is new in this edition.

- New Bibliographies. The book has been updated throughout, including the Recommended Readings and References.

Acknowledgments

Crossing Over exists because of the talents of Naomi Silverman, senior editor with Lawrence Erlbaum Associates.

I am fortunate to know teachers who inspired the portraits in this book and I wish to thank them.

Patti Cleary and Nancy Brunker, National Board Certified teachers, are continuing sources of teaching inspiration, and I am grateful to have them as models.

Paulette Urycki and Lisa Lin have shared their urban classrooms with me for several years, and I have based many of the portraits here on their fine teaching.

Ann Johnson provided me with a fine model of a teacher who knows how to make Shakespeare come alive to her students.

Tracy Burkholder, Lorri Herro, Barb Baltrinic, and Rob Pyett provided me with substantial views of how excellent teachers teach writing.

I owe thanks to one of the finest principals I have ever known, Harry Jordan, who makes excellent English teaching possible.

I thank Tori Washington, Jane Rasinski, Melinda Nagle, Terry McCrory, and Jody Seibel for allowing me to use their writings in the book.

Karen Gegick showed me the gentle power of an excellent Language Arts specialist, and I thank her for her inspiration.

As always, I owe Stephen Dunning gratitude for his support and imagination.

Robert Probst provided me his wisdom and inspiration, and I thank him for teaching me how young people learn to read.

Kylene Beers taught me how reluctant young readers can become readers, and I thank her.

My wife Greta was a constant source of support and editorial aid. Without her this book would not be possible.

I owe thanks to Roberta Reese, who was instrumental in the preparation of this manuscript through its many drafts. Also, thanks go to Susan Wheeler, Peggy McCann, and Heather Mitchell, who greatly helped me with this book.

I thank Anne Vlosky, James Tamulewicz, and Adam Cohen for their help creating the *Crossing Over* website.

Beth Stroble and Susan Olson deserve credit for their support during this project.

My colleague and friend, Cindy Kovalik, allowed me to use her fine planning rubric, which can be found in Chapter 15.

Lori Hawver and Tracy Napper, along with Jo-Anne Weaver, all contributed much to the life of this book.

I am grateful to Susan Detwiler of TechBooks and to Kelly Peel for her help in the final stages.

I am also grateful for the feedback from the reviewers of this text: Kathy Van Til (Slippery Rock State University), Lawrence Baines (Berry College), and Mark Krabbe (Miami University of Ohio).

Finally, I owe much gratitude to all the readers of the first edition, many of whom contacted me with comments and suggestions that were greatly appreciated and well used for the second edition.

The author is grateful for the following permissions: Standards for the English Language Arts, p. 47, by the International Reading Association and the National Council of Teachers of English, Copyright 1996 by the International Reading Association and the National Council of Teachers of English, reprinted with permission; Newbery Award Winners and the Corretta Scott King Award Winners, pp. 81, and 84, are reprinted by permission of the American Library Association; "Dreams," p. 127, from THE COLLECTED POEMS OF LANGSTON HUGHES by Langston Hughes, copyright © 1994 by The Estate of Langston Hughes, used by permission of Alfred A. Knopf, a division of Random House, Inc.; "Foul Shot," p. 129, is reprinted by permission of Weekly Reader; "Thumbprint," p. 131, by Eve Merriam is reprinted by permission from Marian Reiner; "On Reading Poems to a Senior Class at South High," p. 133, reprinted by permission of the author, D.C. Berry; "June Twenty-First," p. 134, is from JANUARY THAW by Bruce Guernsey, © 1982, reprinted by permission of the University of Pittsburgh Press; www.54thmass.org, p. 251, reprinted by permission of Mr. Ben Hawley, President, B Company, 54th Massachusetts Volunteer Infantry Regiment.

CROSSING OVER
Teaching
Meaning-Centered
Secondary English
Language Arts

CROSSING OVER

Build A Bridge

Introduction

> I see a chasm; a great divide. On one side of this stands the old world, the world where the only real means of knowing came from books and newspapers and magazines. On the other is a new world, the world we all live in now where books exist but are only one of many forms of communication, and for many people, not the most important form.

The old literacy, words and print, has a lot of competition now. Reading, always an acquired taste, is now endangered. Did English teachers 10 or 20 years ago need a rationale as to why reading and writing should exist? No. But now we do, and here it is:

- Reading is the most cognitive communication medium, perhaps the only way to learn difficult ideas and as a result the only way to become formally educated.
- Reading creates empathy, understanding, and compassion.
- Reading gives stories but allows readers to create the images that come with the stories. Imagination plays a huge part in reading, more so than in most other media.
- Reading is satisfying; it is a creative act that allows a person to discover meaning in the complex symbol system of language.
- Reading is the most controllable medium, the one that is easiest to encounter at a pace you desire, the medium that is the easiest to stop and repeat, skip or skim, or put down or pick up.
- Reading is sensuous; books smell and feel a certain way; there is satisfaction in turning pages, marking spots, and looking at covers.

- Books give people the past, the present, the future; any desired time and place.
- Reading is a pleasure in which only those who are skilled can partake. It is one of the great means of both escape and self-awareness—a pleasurable oxymoron that is one of the great blessings of books.

Other media can do some of the above. Ultimately, it is not a contest. A person of the new century will benefit from computers, from movies, and from television. Yet, a person of the new century will be ill-equipped to survive without reading. That same person will need computer skills, but so many of these skills are language dependent. E-mail is writing; the web for the most part is reading. This will not change. If people wanted e-mail to be voice activated they would call it telephoning. The pleasure of e-mail is in the ability to read and write instantly with each other yet allow some delay for thinking it through. The pleasure of e-mail is saving it.

We are the generation of English teachers who have to make a case for traditional literacy. "Why do we have to read and write?" will come at us even more than ever before. I believe: You will wither if you don't read and write. You will die spiritually and intellectually. You will be a victim of circumstances. Your destiny will be in the hands of others, those who don't really care about you, but covet the little money you have. Television will be your enemy, but you won't know it; movies will be your enemy, but you won't know it. Your work experience will be limited, and the money you earn will be threatened by what you do not know.

Reading and writing will remain the basic skills of the next century, but television, film, and computers must also be integrated into our curriculum. Understanding the tools and knowing how to use them are the core of English teaching that has crossed over.

The idea is already out there for the new English teaching. Many English teachers have crossed over and are practicing this kind of English teaching. They are our guides, the builders of the bridges.

The center of the ideas in *Crossing Over* is that language teaching— English—is about building meaning, primarily with words.

Some advocate viewpoints that do not see English teaching as creating meaning. Many of these viewpoints see skills as the essential building block in language learning. For instance, behaviorist theory sees the necessity of building from simple to complex skills in order to learn language.

Crossing Over does not deny the need for skills, but sees the importance of placing skills in the context of the meaning of the texts being read or being written. This is different from the behavioral approach. In other words, behaviorism states that language skills should be built from the part to the whole. This text sees meaning emerging first from the whole and then the details—the parts—are added.

In any case, you, the reader, will make up your own mind. Unfortunately, or fortunately, the debates about English teaching are just that, debates. My argument in this book is that a whole body of knowledge and practice exists that leads us to meaning-centered English teaching. You will read about these ideas and their practice in this book. I do not propose this approach as the only truth. A good English education textbook gives the reader a context for debate, discussion, and thought, which is the purpose of *Crossing Over.*

Principles of Meaning-Centered English Language Arts Teaching

The underlying theories for meaningful English teaching come from many sources (linguistics, English, education, anthropology, psychology, critical theory, and social sciences) but form a uniform picture of how people learn, develop, and maintain language abilities. The basic premises follow:

- People come born with the ability to develop language. That is, babies learn to speak and listen through a natural process of imitation and maturation (Chomsky, 1975).

- Children develop language for communication. Language is, at heart, a meaning-making enterprise.

- Language is a performance art. We learn our first language skills by performing them. This forms the basis for all future language learning. An effective English teacher creates opportunities for students to perform language in contexts that make sense. Thus, an English classroom is an endless search for meaningful, performance-based speaking, listening, reading, writing, and seeing activities.

- Learning language is like learning how to ride a bicycle. Although both activities require many complex skills, it is best to learn them holistically, by trial and error. In fact, errors in language such as in spelling and pronunciation, are often a sign of growth, according to Goodman (1977) and Shaughnessy (1977).

- Real language learning is very difficult to isolate into subskills and hierarchies. It is difficult to separate reading, writing, speaking, listening, and seeing (Strickland, 1991). Therefore, effective classrooms stress integration and de-emphasize categorizing learning skills, scope, and sequences. To some extent, real language growth is so unpredictable it may be impossible to define a language plan that corresponds to any particular grade level, such as "all fifth-graders will know this."

- Yet valid classrooms have structure and have lessons on skills, such as grammar. Also, language assessment does take place in effective classrooms. These activities occur within meaning-making contexts, such as formal public writing (Newman & Church, 1990).

The Historical and Theoretical Roots

In the last century, the principles that undergird meaning-centered language arts have tugged at American schools. In 1911, with the founding of the National Council of Teachers of English (NCTE), the roots of meaning-centered English teaching were planted. Before 1911, English was firmly defined as the study of grammar or correctness, literature as culture, and composition based on prose models and set topics (Tchudi & Mitchell, 1989, p. 13).

In 1917, NCTE, along with the National Education Association (NEA), issued a statement based on this growing movement. This statement called for English teaching that prepared students for "life," as well as college entrance exams. These ideas, which wove through American education in the early parts of this century, are often attributed to John Dewey, and are still tenets of effective teaching, particularly "learning by doing" and education for the "fostering of personal growth." These ideas represented the "other" way to teach English—a persistent voice that would not be silenced, no matter how vociferous the opponents.

NCTE was, more often than not, the banner carrier of this meaning-centered view and in 1935 published "The Experience Curriculum." This curriculum emphasized preparing students for life. It developed thematic literacy units as a form of personal growth aimed at engaging students with literary experiences. This curriculum also recommended the teaching of real-world communication skills, such as letter writing and telephone use. "The Experience Curriculum" was an important practical document in maintaining an ongoing commitment to a "personal growth model of English teaching."

In the 1950s, the triad of composition, literature, and grammar was still firmly in place in American schools. Perhaps an industrial nation enamored with technology had a hard time accepting empathetic and child-centered ideas. Beginning in the 1950s, the entire curriculum, including English, was influenced by a scientism that had been brewing for years in certain academic circles. Behaviorism, with its eclectic form of grammar handbooks and its more structured form of criterion-based kits, such as SRAs (Scientific Research Associates' self-paced reading materials), entered the curriculum. The behaviorist movement claims educators can break all learning materials into discrete observable outcomes that can become the objectives of teaching. The appeal of this is enormous to a society enamored with the clear, pragmatic goals of industrialization. Behaviorists promise that learning can be measured accurately and that the public can know exactly what and how much has been learned. The behaviorist movement would continue to grow throughout the 1960s and into the 1970s with its emphasis on accountability.

However, in 1966, meaning-centered teaching was catalyzed and changed by the Anglo-American Conference on English, often referred to as the Dartmouth Conference. British and American English educators gathered at

Dartmouth College to discuss English teaching. It was here that English and personal growth were tied together. Dartmouth, a watershed event in English education, boosted the credibility of the personal-growth movement.

Of course, the 1960s was a time of turbulence and had an affect on all aspects of life, including English teaching. For a while, schools influenced by "romantic" critics would experiment with a form of progressive education that included:

- A complicated system of class scheduling that allowed for flexibility, giving teachers some power over class size and the amount of class time.

- Elective courses, often with themes such as sports literature or science fiction.

- Increased use of paperback books, leading to a somewhat expanded selection of school literature.

These experiments of the 1960s were largely attacked in the backlash era of the late 1970s and early 1980s. The teachers of the 1960s were accused by many of precipitating a national literacy crisis ("Why Johnny Can't Write,"*Newsweek*, December 8, 1975). The 1980s response was to shun the experiments of the sixties and return to regular schedules, core requirements, and statewide testing.

Nonetheless, meaning-centered English teaching kept growing in definition. The National Writing Project, which began in Berkeley, California, in the 1980s, was a grassroots project aimed at translating the latest research on the teaching of writing into classroom practice, almost all of which emphasized the importance of the learner in relation to the teaching of writing.

In the 1980s, two different trends emerged. One of the trends was state-mandated proficiency testing. Proficiency testing swept the nation where now most states require high school students to pass several high stakes tests in order to receive an unblemished high school diploma. These tests have dramatically altered the curricular landscape because many classes, particularly in the middle school and early high school grades, are dedicated to passing these exams. These tests have led to state-generated report cards where the pass rate for schools is made public and where schools and teachers may be punished for not doing well enough.

Whether these tests are compatible with meaning-centered teaching is a tough question. Most states use a writing sample with topics that would interest teenagers. In many cases, writing about these topics constitute meaning-centered classrooms. However, in most cases, reducing the writing test to a simple formula for students to follow may be the teacher's wisest course of action. In too many classrooms tests have resulted in reducing the curriculum to teaching kids to pass the tests. Fortunately, a backlash against reductive tests is finally occurring. More on this very important subject will be forthcoming in the chapter dedicated to testing.

The second trend for English teaching to come out of the 1980s is "whole language." Education goes in cycles, but the quickness between the birth and the death of whole language is startling. The term "whole language" became an anathema to the public by the mid-1990s. Reggie Routman (1996) in *Literacy at the Crossroads* details what happened particularly in California to diminish the term whole language.

Whole language was never clearly defined in many places where the term was used. For the most part, whole language was associated with elementary education, particularly language arts and reading. Three books appeared on secondary whole language, the first edition of this book being one of them. The critics of whole language blasted it for all the reasons people blast progressive education—too soft, more concerned with feelings than with learning, too relative, no wrong and right, no structure.

In the teaching in *Crossing Over*, all of the criticism is unwarranted. There is structure, there is assessment, there are skills, and students can be wrong. However, all of the learning is contextualized, meaning-based, and most of the learning is project-based. Thus, students write about meaningful issues, but correctness is still a factor, whether in spelling or grammar, as is clarity and power. In reading, students have a great deal of interpretive latitude, but the text must support what they say or write about. The purpose of reading is to discover meaning. Teachers spend an enormous amount of time developing scaffolds or building bridges to help students interpret and understand texts.

Meaningful language arts builds on the stage model of Jean Piaget. Piaget's theories were adapted into the psycholinguistic theories described by Frank Smith and James Moffett.

Psycholinguistics combines psychology, the study of human behavior, with linguistics, the study of language. Theorists, such as Smith (1982), postulate that language cannot be divorced from the growth and development of the learner. These psycholinguistic theories claim that language is a natural human endeavor, akin to walking; that is, all relatively healthy people are born with the capacity to learn language, primarily to create and comprehend speech. From this primal language source, all other language activities, such as reading and writing, are possible. It is incumbent upon the schools to tap into this natural learning capacity and use it as the model for language teaching.

James Moffett (1968) believes that because development of language is meaning-centered—that is, people use the language to create and discover meaning—this is the paradigm that language teachers should follow. In other words, language teaching should be modeled after natural, meaning-centered language development.

Views on reading also changed dramatically. The old behaviorist paradigm of seeing reading development from part to whole has been challenged by newer psycholinguistic models. Kenneth Goodman (1977) even calls reading a "psycholinguistic guessing game," where a reader's strategies are fully engaged at searching out meaning, comprehending a text, rather than attacking words as postulated in more traditional models. In fact, as psycholinguists such as Frank Smith (1982) in *Understanding Reading* point out, word attack skills may slow down a reader, making the central act of comprehension more difficult.

Most recently, reading theories for early childhood have reconsidered the place of skills, particularly phonics in reading programs. Many reading specialists now argue for a "balanced" approach to early reading programs where systematic phonics have a place in reading instruction (Tompkins, 2000). Some theorists argue that children who bring little naturally learned skills from home must learn those skills in school (Cunningham, 2000). However true this may be, I fear for children who may only experience isolated skills. How will these children ever develop the habits of reading that grow from appreciation and love of books? I consider this to be a central dilemma in teaching children to read, particularly those unfortunate children who have not developed the literacy skills at home before entering school. The precarious balance between skills and authentic reading experiences is very difficult to determine. Having too much drill is every bit as bad as having no skills instruction. At least reading specialists such as Patricia Cunningham and Gail Tompkins are trying to place skills in a meaningful context.

Theories into Practice

The influence of any theory on school practice is limited at best. Ed Farrell (1991) points out that teaching practice in this country tends to be atheoretical; that is, oblivious to theory. Yet, the behaviorists have had some influence, particularly in the development and dissemination of curriculum materials such as skills-based texts and expensive criterion-referenced kits. Furthermore, the neotraditionalists seem to hold political power; therefore, many of the state-mandated tests are based on their ideas. These neotraditionalists may continue to influence schools by their advocacy of national testing, and if they get their way, a national curriculum.

Teachers often consider theory impractical, while some theorists consider teachers antitheoretical. Yet, while the theory war rages, public schools are experiencing inextricable changes driven by economics, demographics, social forces, and technology. For example, groups now considered minorities will soon become a majority of students. African Americans, Hispanics, Native Americans, Southeast Asians, and other Asians are now about 40% of our school population and this percentage will increase (Gere, Fairbanks, Howes, Roop, & Schaafsma, 1992, p. 23). Computer and communication technology will make ever-increasing changes in the way people think, act, work, and play. If poverty continues to grow in this country, schools will face more and more students who lack the essentials of home life, such as nutritious food and comfortable shelter, needed to sustain an education. If the moral climate continues to deteriorate, schools will see an increase in drugs, violence, and pregnancy. Therefore, no matter what ideas are in vogue, or what classroom practice looks like, English teachers will be challenged by difficult problems that will not lend themselves to simple solutions.

Read, listen, listen, read. Pay attention. Check out the teaching and, with care and intelligence, reflect and critique. English teaching is not a fixed system, nor an exact science. All one can do in a text such as this is portray English teaching as fully and as honestly and as systematically as possible. The readers of this text are full partners in it, I hope, creating their own version of English teaching based on the stories and case studies presented within this book.

Meaning-Centered Pedagogy

Currently, there is no term placing all the concurrent secondary English directions under one paradigm. Yet, all the following curricular ideas and resources are meaning-centered, performance-based approaches to English instruction. They are as follows.

The Teaching of Writing

A revolution in writing instruction has taken place in the past 15 years. Nancie Atwell's (1987) book about writing, *In the Middle*, is a thorough description of a student-centered, meaning-based writing program. Students select their own topics, write at their own pace, and revise and edit as needed.

Quality writing instruction does not have to be entirely like Nancie Atwell's workshops, but has most of the following elements:

- Meaningful topics. Students write about things that engage them. Yet teachers provide a variety of ideas and writing opportunities for students to select from.

- Free to write. Students, much of the time, are free to write whatever they want without having judgments made on it. Most student writing will remain free and unedited.

- Free to develop voice and discover meaning. Students need the freedom to write uninhibited to develop styles and rediscover the meaning and path of their writing. Young writers can only do this if they are without fear of penalty for grammatical and structural errors.

- Developing public statements. Students select from their free writing to develop pieces into writing statements for audiences beyond the writer. Students get the opportunity to write for a variety of audiences.

■ Responses to the writing. Students receive responses to their writings, which help shape and craft the writings based on the writers' needs and personalities and based on the audience the writing is addressing. These responses help students shape and craft and revise the public statements. These responses come from teachers, tutors, and peers.

■ Editing help. Students get feedback to help them edit their public statements into logical, clear, organized, error-free statements.

■ Use of technology. Student writers are given every opportunity to learn how to use word processors and computers as technological tools in the writing process.

■ Flexibility. Although the composing process may be demonstrated as a method or paradigm for writing, writers and writing needs are different so teachers need to be careful not to apply a rigid set of guidelines to every writer.

Reader Response

Although Louise Rosenblatt published her book, *Literature as Exploration*, in 1938, her theories of reading did not make a wide impact until recently. Her theory that "the reader must, in a real-sense, construct the text" (Rosenblatt, 1978) is a model of how people read all texts, all narratives, including novels, short stories, epics, plays, films, and the storytelling medium of television (Thornburn, 1988, p. 56).

Here is how Louise Rosenblatt (1978) defines the relationship of reader and text:

> "The poem comes into being in the live circuit set up between the reader and the text" (p. 14);
> and
> "A specific reader and a specific text at a specific time and place: change any of these, and there occurs a different circuit, a different event— different poem" (p. 14);
> and
> Poem stands here for the whole category, 'literary work of art,' and for "terms such as 'novel,' 'play,' or 'short story'" (p. 11);
> and
> "Yet, we must remember that once the creativity of the author has ended, what remains for others, for even the author himself—is the text. To again bring a poem into being requires always a reader" (p. 15).

Thanks to her and to derivatives from authors such as Robert Probst (1988) and Purves, Rogers, and Soter (1990), English teachers have a theory that empowers their students to create transactions with texts, allowing students their views and interpretations. What fits more into a meaning-centered view of English teaching than a view of reading that allows readers to create their own meanings from books?

Louise Rosenblatt does not believe that the act of reading is relative. There is a text and there is an author's point of view of this text. Whatever information the reader has to help clarify and make sense of a text is useful. The interpretation, according to Rosenblatt, has to be warranted and reasonable. However, the major supplier of meaning for every text is the reader, and every reader has the right to her or his interpretation as long as the text supports it. Purves et al. (1990) define response-centered reading this way:

1. An individual will feel secure in his response to a poem and not be dependent upon someone else's response.

2. An individual will know why she responds the way she does to a poem— what in her causes that response and what in the poem causes that response.

3. An individual will respect the responses of others as being as valid for them as his is for him.

4. An individual will recognize that there are common elements in peoples' responses (p. 47).

Reader-response is the most meaning-centered approach in responding to narratives. This reading paradigm offers potentially the most motivational methods of teaching literature. A reader-response teacher leads discussions that allow the young reader freedom to discuss the book without fear that the one right interpretation known to the teacher will come crashing down upon her or his head. Reader-response theory allows for the experiences and opinions of the reader and allows the reader to recreate the text (Winterowd, 1989, p. 24). Discussions allow the community of readers to sharpen and focus their individual responses. In honest reader-response discussions, the teacher gives up the sole authority—the know-it-all new critic with the only right answers.

Adapting reader-response techniques to the secondary English curriculum may bring back many young readers. These techniques mirror the new patterns of thought of this new generation of student who interpret movies, television shows, videos, and all other media as Rosenblatt and later Paulo Frieire envision: "Reading the world always precedes reading the word, and reading the word implies continually reading the world" (Freire & Macedo, 1987, p. 35). Our students are continually reading the world in the lively interactions they have with the fascinating array of images and sounds they experience on a daily basis. Reader-response techniques could bring color to their education and place books as a new, powerful medium in their lives.

Books for Young Adults

Fortunately, starting with S. E. Hinton's *The Outsiders* in 1967, exciting new books exclusively for young people have appeared. These books, dealing with modern themes and current issues, have proven to be very popular with young readers, and seem to have made a positive dent in the decline of reading in this country (Cullinan, 1990, p. 17) because they offer powerful reading experiences about subjects important to them. These books foster a lifelong love of reading in many young people. These books are a major source for English teachers who seek relevant, exciting reading experiences for their students. Young-adult literature has a great appeal for several reasons.

- The books are thematically relevant for young people. They deal with subject matter that is realistic and close to the heart of kids. *Jacob Have I Loved* deals with sibling rivalry; *Dicey's Song* concerns living with the absence of parents; *A Wrinkle in Time* describes a young girl's search for a missing father; *Roll of Thunder, Hear My Cry* depicts a black sharecropper family coping with the racism of the 1930s South; and *Tears of a Tiger* deals with teenage suicide. This list could go on and on as titles proliferate.

- These books bridge the child reader to the adult reader and fill a vacuum. Before young adult literature, there was very little for the in-betweener (from 5th to 11th grades) that was interesting as well as readable. This group, which has been the most difficult to keep reading, now can select from the relatively easy and exciting S. E. Hinton novels such as *The Outsiders* or *Tex*, to the more difficult and ambiguous Robert Cormier books such as *The Chocolate War* or *I Am the Cheese*.

- Many of these young adult novels are of very high literary quality. Although we may disagree on any given title, it would be tough to dismiss this entire genre as weak. *The Outsiders* and *The Pigman* are two fine young-adult novels, as is Katherine Paterson's *Bridge to Terabithia*. Karen Hesse's *Out of the Dust* is striking as is Gary Paulson's *Hatchet*, and Christopher Paul Curtis' *The Watsons Go to Birmingham—1963*.

- Kids love these books and they are reading them. They compete with television and film. These books, and the teachers who use them, have recaptured potentially lost readers at a very tender age (Cullinan, 1990).

These books succeed because they are contemporary. They touch the same nerves as film and television. They portray the stories, characters, and themes to which kids growing up now can relate. These books also reflect a community of many cultures and ethnicities, the real world of kids.

Teaching the Classics

The literary core of the secondary English classroom has always been what teachers refer to as the "classics," a parade of works almost unchanged since time began. The typical sequence has been something like this:

Ninth grade:	*Romeo and Juliet*
	Great Expectations
Tenth grade:	*Julius Caesar*
	All Quiet on the Western Front
Eleventh grade (American Literature):	*Huckleberry Finn*
	The Great Gatsby
	The Crucible
	The Scarlet Letter
Twelfth grade (British Literature):	*Macbeth*
	Beowolf
	The Canterbury Tales

I have also come across the following works in high school classrooms:

Hamlet

Oliver Twist

Arms and the Man

Silas Marner

Tale of Two Cities

Sir Gawain and the Green Knight

Death of a Salesman

Paradise Lost

And, of course, I have seen poets from Donne to Marlowe to the British Romantics to Whitman and Frost. I have taught T. S. Eliot and James Joyce and the short stories of William Faulkner, but never his novels. I have seen high schoolers read and study *Brave New World*, *A Passage to India*, *Wuthering Heights*, and Joyce Carey's *The Horse's Mouth*. I have watched, over the years, *Death Be Not Proud* and *A Separate Peace* come and go. I have taught *Oedipus* and *Antigone*, and *The Odyssey*.

It is the above authors and titles that so many English teachers pine to teach. However, these are the books that have come under fire from many directions. "The classics; who says?" critics shout. "Dead white male writers with dead white male ideas." "Not representative of the diversity of our schools," the polite adversaries claim. "Not relevant to kids, particularly our kids; these books just won't work."

This debate is going to continue. Critics of the classics have some strong arguments that need to be aired. The way many of these great books have been taught has "dulled up" English teaching to the breaking point for many non-reading students. These works certainly do not reflect the diversity of cultures and ideas represented in American classrooms.

However, many excellent English teachers use the "classics" with great success in a student-centered, meaningful way. Many readers began with great teachers, teachers who generated enthusiasm for the classics, the "great books." These teachers helped make transactions between students and texts possible. They helped students to appreciate the wisdom and beauty of the great works. The teachers who we remember most made books—old books—timeless, relevant, and meaningful. Perhaps we live in an age where truth seems more relative than it did 50 years ago, but truth seemed to reside in Macbeth's thirst for power, in the hellishness of war in *All Quiet on the Western Front*, in the natural bliss Wordsworth found at Tintern Abbey. I know of high school students who have devoured *Pride and Prejudice* and *Jude the Obscure*. I have watched wonderful English teachers give excellent model readings of *The Love Song of J. Alfred Prufrock* and *Kubla Khan*. I have witnessed reader-response discussions on sections of *Paradise Lost*, and I have seen witty and well-written parodies based on *The Canterbury Tales*. So, the classics can work if taught well with methods that engage young readers. Eliminating them from the secondary curriculum is not what I recommend. Rather, I would like to see the literature in the classroom expanded to reflect the diversity of our students.

Expanding the Canon: Multiethnic Literature

A language arts supervisor in Alaska explained to me why she was so committed to reader-response technique.

> My students come from so many cultural backgrounds that 30 languages are spoken in my schools. My students see life in many different ways and they often comprehend the same books differently. If they are committed readers, they need the freedom reader-response techniques offer.

This text, and the theories behind it, celebrates diversity. Even if a teacher has the class read the same book, that teacher can and should promote multiple and diverse interpretations. Of course, effective teachers provide many opportunities for students to select their readings from diverse and rich sources. As classrooms become increasingly ethnically and culturally diverse, literary experiences should mirror this diversity, not only so that that African-American students can read about African-American experiences, but so that all students can read and learn about African-American experiences, as well as Hispanic, Native American, Laotian, Korean, and so on. The reasons for this are obvious:

- Students will be more interested in literary experiences that relate to their life experiences.
- Students will become more sensitized to the cultures of their classmates through literary experiences.
- Students will acquire a taste for reading and, thus, will become more motivated readers of a wide range of materials.

There is no need to throw the classics out of the classroom; there is every need to expand the literary selections in English classrooms. Young-adult novels have become part of many high schools, middle schools, and junior high curricula. Literature expressing different cultural experiences is starting to trickle in, and as more fine and multiethnic literature is written, this trickle will turn to a stream. Multiethnic literature can enhance and complement the best of the canon.

Therefore, as teachers learn more about the cultural and ethnic backgrounds of their students, they constantly search for books that describe a variety of experiences. Recognizing the specialness of every learner is a necessity in an effective classroom.

The New Literacies: Curriculum of the Future

There is one more curriculum suggestion necessary to make English/language arts instruction effective for our time. For our students to become readers and writers, they need help in interpreting and controlling the multiple literacies and technologies they face. These new literacies are enormously powerful political, social, and economic forces. There is no better place to study these than in English class and no better media to study them in than in reading, writing, speaking, and listening.

Television should be watched, analyzed, and discussed, as should film, music, and popular print. All the modern technologies of computers, jet airplanes, and telecommunications need to be studied, as well as analyzed for their social fallout, including changes in family life, urban violence, use of drugs, shifting values, and so on.

Maybe many English teachers do not feel equipped to teach the new media. Perhaps these English teachers could learn with their students in an interactive learning environment that values collaboration and learning by doing, both major tenets of effective teaching.

Intent and Reflectiveness in the Secondary Language Arts Classroom

Wise advice counsels carefulness in judging what is meaning centered and what is not. For instance, if a visitor walks into an English classroom and sees a teacher instructing a class on subject-verb agreement, does this mean the teacher is not a meaning-centered teacher? What if over half her students are making these mistakes, would it hurt to do a drill? What if subject-verb agreement is on the state-mandated competency test? Is it a bad idea to pre-pare students even for a poor but important exam? What if the teacher just wants her students to have an editing vocabulary to use during student-student conferences? The way to determine if a secondary teacher is effective is by the following two methods.

Intent

Is the teacher intending to teach in a manner consistent with meaning-centered teaching? Does the teacher have a philosophy and is the teacher trying to solve the complex classroom issues in a meaning-centered manner? To determine intent, much evidence must be gathered, including classroom performance and teacher analysis.

Reflectiveness

Teaching English is enormously complex. The right way and the wrong way; success and failure; good lessons and bad lessons are difficult judgments to make. Therefore, thinking about the classroom is an important element for a classroom teacher. This reflectiveness in a teacher can be evidenced by the nature of the analysis. An effective teacher must ask herself the following:

- Are my lessons student-centered?
- Are these activities meaningful?
- Do I provide flexibility for the differences among my students?
- Are my measurements of growth "direct language assessments" and varied enough to provide for differences?
- Do I create classroom situations where my students construct language?
- Do I model meaningful language use?
- Do I create a bridge between my students and meaningful language experiences?

These and many other questions provide insight into the ongoing and ever-present task of creating meaningful language classrooms. Teaching is never a done deal; it is always an act of creation. This text's purpose is to serve as a conduit for reflecting on English teaching.

Teacher as Researcher

A teacher I know refers to teachers who never change or grow as experiencing the first year of teaching over and over again. Reflective teachers have a professional awareness of their classrooms where they gather data and information, and change their classrooms as a result. These teachers are asking the questions found under the "Reflectiveness" section. Reflective teachers are classroom researchers aware of the conditions they find in teaching. These teachers grow, change, and flourish in the teaching profession. Teachers who cross over do so because they are researchers.

Reflections

In this opening chapter, meaning-centered English teaching has been described. But why is meaning-centered teaching most appropriate for our time? The reasons follow. Effective English teaching:

- Is patterned after natural language growth. The theory is based on careful observation of children and adolescents using and developing language in real-life situations. No theory of language development can claim total accuracy. Language development is complicated, but meaning-centered teaching provides a paradigm closer to natural language growth than any other theory.

- Empowers teachers. The decisions teachers make in meaning-centered classrooms are critical. Teachers structure learning environments, act as facilitators and coaches, and create performance-based lessons. Above all, teachers approach meaning-centered classrooms with a consistent view of English teaching. Putting the theory into practice takes enormous professionalism and skills. Meaningful classrooms will never see teacher-proof materials or mastery learning kits that can be operated by technician-teachers. Effective teachers are decision makers who can watch their decisions become the means by which their students grow and develop as language users.

- Empowers students. In effective classrooms, students perform and create language. Students select books and writing topics, interpret readings with freedom, and express themselves openly.

- Promotes diversity. Effective classrooms are places where different backgrounds, cultures, and languages are celebrated and studied. Diversity in reading and writing is honored. Language use is considered situational. This means the way language is spoken or written depends on the audience. Students are not committed, chastised, or demeaned because of the way they speak or write.

■ Develops fluency and literacy. Students write and read constantly in effective classrooms. Writing and reading well is a continuing goal promoted by a variety of meaning-centered writing and reading experiences of growing complexity based on student abilities, interests, and needs.

■ Stimulates a love of reading and writing. Effective teachers, by example and through classroom activities, model and promote full participation in the bounty provided by wonderful literary experiences. A meaning-centered classroom is a rich language environment, filled with books, readings, writing ideas, discussions, journals, and student writings. Effective teachers love to read and write, and they spread this love to their students.

It is for all these reasons that meaning-centered teaching is suited to our time. This is why many teachers—elementary, secondary, college—have crossed over or are crossing over. Yet, these reasons do not convey the whole story. It is necessary to look at the changes of the last 35 years to fully comprehend why English teaching must change. This was the period during which I went from a city school student, to a college student, to an English teacher, to an English educator. In Chapter Two, I describe these massive cultural and literacy changes through my own experiences. It is the story of my own crossing over.

Recommended Readings

Beers, K., & Samuels, B. G. (Eds.). (1998). *Into focus: Understanding and creating middle school readers.* Norwood, MA: Christopher-Gordon Publishers.

A collection of essays dealing with issues and problems with middle school readers. Several strong sections, including excellent focus on response-based reading techniques and ideas.

Britton, J. (1970). *Language and learning.* Coral Gables, FL: University of Miami Press.

This seminal work in psycholinguistics provides a basis of how and why children and adolescents learn and develop language. It is here that Britton explains his theory of how children move from writer-based writing (experience) to reader-based writing (transactional and poetic).

Calkins, L. (1986). *The art of teaching writing.* Portsmouth, NH: Heinemann.

This is a comprehensive view of the writing process from one of the primary forces in teaching the art of writing. The book encompasses writing from kindergarten through middle school.

Cooper, J. D. (1997). *Literacy: Helping children construct meaning* (3rd ed.). Boston: Houghton Mifflin.

This meaning-centered text presents a comprehensive view of language development theory and practice in the elementary school years. This book also presents a complete view of elementary language pedagogy and serves as an elementary companion to the theories and practices of *Crossing Over*.

Dixon, J. (1966). *Growth through English*. Edgerton, England: National Association for the Teaching of English.

This is the report of the Dartmouth Conference. The Dixon book is an important document that shows in what direction English teaching was pointed.

Elbow, P. (1990). *What is English?* New York: The Modem Language Association of America.

Elbow admits this book is a subjective and highly metaphoric view of the 1987 English Coalition Conference. However, this book provides flashes of insight that give a portrait of the confused and complex profession of English teaching.

Fosnot, C. T. (Ed.). (1996). *Constructivism: Theory, perspectives, and practice*. New York: Teachers College Press.

This is a collection of essays defining and explaining constructivist theory. Although the book does not directly concern language arts teaching except for one chapter, this is a solid introduction for a person interested in the roots and nature of constructivism, a theory based on students constructing their own knowledge.

Gere, A. R., Fairbanks, C., Howes, A., Roop, L., & Schaafsma, D. (1992). *Language and reflection: An integrated approach to teaching English*. New York: Macmillan.

These authors provide a comprehensive view of English teaching in secondary schools. This book provides many helpful ideas, particularly for preservice teachers. Chapter I includes a concise history of English teaching.

Goodman, K. (Ed.). (1977). *Miscue analysis: Applications to reading instruction*. Urbana, IL: National Council of Teachers of English.

This collection views reading in relation to personal growth. Goodman defines "miscues" as reading mistakes that are actually helpful in measuring the growth of a young reader. Error Analysis is the related field in composition theory.

Goodman, K. (1986). *What's whole in whole language*. Portsmouth, NH: Heinemann.

This is a very concise and clear work defining whole language in the elementary schools. The shortness and directness of the book makes it very accessible for many readers.

Goodman, Y. (1989). Roots of the whole language movement. *The Elementary School Journal, 90*, 113–127.

Goodman gives the theoretical background for whole language.

Harste, J. C., Short, K. G., & Burke, C. (1988). *Creating classrooms for authors. The reading-writing connection*. Portsmouth, NH: Heinemann.

This is a practical view of teaching the reading-writing process in first through sixth grades. This book gives methods of teaching to create authors out of children.

Hook, J. N. (1979). *A long way together: A personal view of NCTE's first sixty-seven years*. Urbana, IL: National Council of Teachers of English.

This book provides a comprehensive history of not only NCTE, but also of English teaching. Hook gives an interesting analysis of the development of the professional organizations that impact on English teaching.

Kafai, Y., & Resnick, M. (Eds.). (1996). *Constructionism in practice: Designing, thinking, and learning in a digital world.* Mahwah, NJ: Lawrence Erlbaum Associates.

This is another good constructivism resource to learn about the nature of this theory. Essays in this book deal more with constructivism and technology than the Fosnot book.

Lloyd-Jones, R., & Lunsford, A. A. (Eds.). (1989). *The English Coalition conference: Democracy through language.* Urbana, IL: National Council of Teachers of English.

This report describes a new Dartmouth-like conference held in the summer of 1987. Although one has to be careful in a global interpretation of the conference, it appears this coalition prefers contemporary English teaching based on the premises of whole language.

Moffett, J. (1968). *Teaching the universe of discourse.* Boston: Houghton Mifflin.

Moffett presents a classic rationale for a naturalistic English curriculum. Although the term "whole language" is never mentioned, this is one of the foundations of whole-language theory.

Routman, R. (1996). *Literacy at the crossroads: Crucial talk about reading, writing, and other teaching dilemmas.* Portsmouth, NH: Heinemann.

Routman presents a solid picture of the disputes in language arts, particularly the conflicts with whole language and phonics. This book is a good source for understanding why language arts teaching becomes political. Also, Routman gives good, rounded arguments in favor of meaning-centered teaching.

Simmons, J., & Baines, L. (Eds.). (1998). *Language study in middle school, high school, and beyond.* Newark, DE: International Reading Association.

A fine collection of articles about language issues that impact our students now and that will be important in the future. This is a very forward-looking collection of articles.

Smith, F. (1992, February). Learning to read: The never-ending debate. *Phi Delta Kappan, 73*, 432–441.

Smith presents an overview of the state of reading theory. He contrasts the phonics approach with a holistic approach.

Smith, F. (1971). *Understanding reading: A psycholinguistic analysis of reading and learning to read* (3rd ed.). New York: Holt, Rinehart & Winston.

Smith's work is a strong break with the behaviorist view of reading development. Much of what Smith claims contradicts a more sequential view of reading development. This provocative work shows important insight into the psycholinguistic view of reading.

Tchudi, S., & Mitchell, D. (1989). *Explorations in the teaching of English* (3rd ed.). New York: Harper and Row.

Tchudi and Mitchell have prepared a general English education methods text. The first chapter gives a strong, condensed history of English teaching.

Crossing Over: A Personal Narrative

> *Truth telling not only required enough care and persistence to get the facts straight, but also enough self-awareness and self-disclosure to allow readers to see my point of view (another term for bias) and make their own judgments about it. Because I believe that a writer's perspective is more than a collection of facts that can be listed in an introduction and then forgotten (Brown, 1992, A56).*

The Library and the Hot Dog

There once was a community library in Pittsburgh housed in an old castle-like building of soot-darkened brick surrounded by a five-foot wall that was so wide that children used it as a walkway. Across the street from the East Liberty Branch of the Carnegie Library was a small drive-in restaurant, Original Hot Dogs. Forty years later, remembering those wonderful hot dogs, I know they were the best I have ever eaten, as any Pittsburgher over forty will testify. The East Liberty Library was constantly bathed in the smell of these hot dogs. Pavlov could not have created a better environment to ensure the love of books, which I will forever associate with Original Hot Dogs.

Almost every inveterate reader who reminisces about where the habit began, can provide "puppy love" testimonials to those early and young reading experiences. These testimonials tell those who teach English and reading a great deal about what they need to know about instruction. Much of modern reading theory has wisely come around to suggest that teachers create conditions to emulate the processes by which strong, dedicated readers learned to read almost naturally.

My testimonials include wonderful now-forgotten books read on the glider of my front porch on rainy summer days. I remember how moved I was by William Saroyan's *Human Comedy* and *Lassie Come Home*. I also remember devouring any Hardy Boys book I could find. "We are all equipped by a nature," writes Wayne Booth, "that has created us out of story" (Booth, 1988, p. 485). My main stories came from books with a dash of the dreaded comic book considered dangerous to youth during the innocent 1950s. Until I was 9 years old, library books, comic books, radio, some movies, family, friends, and teachers were my main sources of information and entertainment. This was very typical of America in the early 1950s, a time more defined by what was about to occur than what was occurring. This was a world that soon would be forever transformed with my generation, the last to be born into the linear, small-town, stay-put America, where books would be the main sources of the stories that, according to Robert Coles (1989), "are a compelling source of our psychological and ideological make-up" (p. 24).

When I was 9, in 1955, my parents bought a black-and-white television and the rest . . . well, the rest is history. I would not travel on an airplane until 1966. I would not travel more than 200 miles from Pittsburgh until 1970 and would not cross the Mississippi until 1973. I would not see my first color television until the late 1960s, a set in a neighborhood restaurant playing the world series, all in baseball-field green. In contrast, my eldest daughter was born in January 1981 in Ohio and would travel by jet to California that March.

Growing up in the early 1950s, my ideas, belief systems, and world views were conditioned by a relatively narrow, technologically restricted media environment that tried to teach me to fear change and accept the conventional wisdom. Most influences on my life were reassuring, conserving, backward looking. Even early television soothed and reinforced. Marshall McLuhan (1964) was correct when he analyzed that early modern electronic media technology took the first generation viewer into the new century looking backward. *Father Knows Best* and *The Donna Reed Show*, early television family sitcoms, were Norman Rockwell caricatures of the perfect 1950s American family, where Solomon-like moms and dads dispensed unerring wisdom to their almost perfect children; where fathers wore ties at home, dressing down by forsaking the suitcoat for the sweater. Even early television variety shows such as *The Paul Whitman Hour* and, of course, *The Ed Sullivan Show* presented, for the most part, entertainment acts from the 1940s. If a 1950s rock and roller got on TV, it was almost considered subversive, as in the famous and controversial appearance of Elvis on *The Ed Sullivan Show*, televised only from the waist up.

Almost everything in my growing up world was premodern—from the three-story brick house with porch on the city street with sidewalk in front, to the horse-drawn vegetable and fruit "huckster" who would stop at our house. My elementary school, Fulton, had a tan-brick façade and three stories of classrooms with "black" blackboards and wooden school desks with inkwells. At Peabody High School, with its premodern heavy brick exterior and columned front door, I knew it was game day by the smell of fresh oil being applied to the dirt football field to keep the dust from flying. There is no question my world in the 1950s was closer to the nineteenth century than to the twenty-first.

I know now that there were other neighborhoods in the 1950s in America where people did travel in airplanes and cross the Mississippi. I know now that there was an intellectual and rebellious America that questioned, sometimes at great risk, the status quo. There was an America of poverty and racism, even of drug addiction and crime. However, for the most part, modes of information were so narrow that the picture of the world many white middle class people formed was of this Norman Rockwell small town, tranquil America that would soon almost cease to exist anywhere except as the main streets of Disneyland and Disney World and in the village green of Dearborn Village, preserved as a fossil by Ford Motor Company.

Schooling

My reading habit was spawned from encouragement and behavior modeled by family and friends, wonderful libraries, and little competition from television. The importance of parents as reading role models is undeniably a major factor in the creation of readers (Olson, Torrance, & Hildyard, 1985, p. 13). Neither my father nor my mother graduated from college. Yet, they read all the time and all kinds of materials—books, magazines, newspapers. Reading was as natural an activity in my house as conversing, arguing, or playing. We all read and thought nothing of it.

However, had I not already been a reader, school would have ensured that I never would become one. The reading I was forced to do was unappealing, dull, and highly forgettable. I do not remember any of the class books I read in elementary school until eighth grade, when our class did an oral reading of *A Tale of Two Cities*, complete with derision of the poor boy (me) who pronounced "Jacques" wrong. In tenth grade, our class was assigned *Oliver Twist*, which, as far as I could ascertain, no one read. The teacher compensated for this by reviewing the plot of this weighty novel on a daily basis. The endless short stories and poems we read were endlessly quizzed. Class discussions were always the same: "Who did such and such to whom?"

I am sure there was inspired, highly motivated English teaching in high schools in America in the early 1960s. Yet, English teachers trained in the 1950s would not have much to go on based on the methods and materials available and what is known about English education (Tchudi & Mitchell, 1989, pp. 14–21). Most likely, teachers learned about English teaching through the various classrooms they experienced as students and their student teaching experiences. These practical models provided the inheritance of the nineteenth century model of English teaching relying on the triad of grammar, composition, and literature as the cornerstone of the English curriculum (Tchudi & Mitchell, 1989) and the familiar methodology of the Industrial Revolution classroom of the late nineteenth century (Dickens, 1966, pp. 2–6).

Of course, the ideas and practices of John Dewey were well known during the 1950s by educational theorists and had at one time influenced many American classrooms (Bleich, 1988, p. 26). Of course, my high school English teachers could have heard of Louise Rosenblatt or knew her works in which she theorized how readers interpret literature in different ways based partially on the experience of the reader, because her book, *Literature as Exploration*, was published in 1938. Even Jean Piaget (1959) had postulated his stage theory of learning through interaction early enough for my teachers to benefit.

Looking back now, I realize that none of these theorists or theories were evident in the classrooms I experienced. The most obvious influences on my English teachers were their college English teachers who cherished the belief that "the classics" were important to teach, a tautology accepted without debate: "The classics are important to teach because they are the classics" (Scholes, 1985, p. 58). If my English teachers took this belief one step further, then they taught the great pedestal literature because of the "great truths" they embodied.

The high school I attended in the 1960s was a high caliber school, easily one of the best in Pittsburgh. Peabody was a city school with an incredible social and ethnic mix of students seldom found in schools today. This was before the huge growth of suburbs, and it was possible to find, inside the city limits, the rich, the middle class, and the lower middle class living within relatively close proximity. Yet, this wasn't always a happy mix, as students brought their social and ethnic prejudices with them, demonstrated by self-segregated halls before and after school, and often bloody after-school fights.

College-bound students, the most academically able, often came from the most affluent backgrounds. They were well conditioned to know what criteria colleges desired and how to go about achieving these criteria. They sought good grades. Most of the students were interested in math and science, which, they believed, had the best teaching in the school and the clearest goals. However, particularly in English, few students equated achievement with learning; A's with knowledge; 650 on SATs with education. These high achievers knew that doing well in high school kept parents happy and would get them into good colleges, but few of them attached any real importance to what was going on in their classrooms, particularly English, which was so confused and undefined.

As far as I could tell, and even now in retrospect, student growth and development did not count much in my high school. The curriculum, particularly in English class, was a hodgepodge of tradition, grammar drill, and "great books." The best of our teachers managed to make some of it interesting, but for most of the students I knew, it was like the ozone layer, way above them and far removed from the world they lived in. Maybe it would have been okay if, years later, we came back to visit our school, thankful for an education we did not understand at the time, but grew to appreciate. This did not happen. The educational experience was too eclectic, too removed from our lives. It just did not work. And we were easy for the most part, brainwashed by the cultural and social blandness of the 1950s. If you could not pull off this kind of education with us, then there was no way you could take this curriculum and impose it on the kids who would come next. I graduated from high school in January 1964 (one of the last of the mid-termers), two months after the assassination of John F. Kennedy. The culture I knew was about to change. The world would never look the same. We were about to cross over to a different mindset created by seismic social upheavals reported and, to some extent, created by a revolutionary change in the tools of literacy. Television and film would become the dominant populist communication media. Kids would rise up and strike at their elders. Hell was about to break loose everywhere.

The Youth Quake

An eruption was about to explode in America in the 1960s. Youth quakes occur in every generation; it is the nature of youth to rebel, a constant source of story from *Romeo and Juliet* to *The Fight Club*. However, this generation was qualitatively different—it was bigger. The babies born after World War II grew to that noisy adolescent age and more of them made more noise. The noise also was louder because as this generation came of age, so did television. Technology and programming propelled television out of the early, nostalgic years into the exciting, cable-ready, color years that made the medium so hot. This generation, my own, crossed over in the late 1960s from a book-oriented literacy to a multiplicity of literacies dominated by the electronic, image-bearing, oral literacy of television and film. These media were not new. Television goes back to 1923 and film was invented in 1894 (Real, 1989, p. 25). But it was in the late 1960s that they took hold and would never let go. Another important catalyst propelling the youth culture was the Vietnam War, a war received by the public like none in the past, partially because of the role television played in portraying it.

My generation was the crossover generation—the last to be born into the world of the old literacy, where print was dominant and radio and film secondary—but the first to be dazzled by the new literacies, television, film, and even radio, coming of age, delivering messages—our messages. The counterculture of the late 1960s and early 1970s was a birthday party, celebrating the end of beginnings, middles, and ends and welcoming the multifaceted, multipronged media that hit our senses before it made sense. Of course, the media experiments didn't always work, and stories today make sense, but media of today, with their heavy experimentation, ambiguity, and reliance on image, could not exist if people hadn't crossed over from the previous literacies to embrace the additional conventions of the new literacies.

It is impossible that any generation after the crossover could be like the generation of the 1950s. The world forever changed in the 1960s, and I was present at the creation of the world my children take for granted.

Three events stand out as change agents propelling me into this media-saturated world. The first event was a traditional literacy experience, the collective reading of *The Catcher in the Rye*. The messages many young readers drew from it created hostility toward the older generation, and the book became one of the staples of the generation gap. The second transforming event was the television coverage of the Kennedy assassination, pushing TV into a new and powerful position. The third event was the acceptance of new movies where technique equaled and sometimes overshadowed story, creating a visual awareness that required a new literacy for viewers, different from reading and writing.

These three events were early manifestations of massive changes in culture and literacy that would soon follow. These experiences crossed me, and many of my contemporaries, into the world we live in today.

In my high school in the early 1960s, there was a small group of students who was isolated from the mainstream social and academic groups. These students were deeply interested in intellectual and aesthetic issues. They were poets, musicians, and artists. They were teenage remnants of the beat generation of the 1950s and would soon be the propelling force of the counterculture movement of the late 1960s.

These young beatniks were a motley assemblage of teenagers who, unknown to them, would become the leading force in defining American culture. They were all readers and many of them made good grades, but they were very dissatisfied with the high school curriculum, particularly with the subject that they felt should be the most stimulating, the most intellectually satisfying, a free zone of idea testing and discussion, the English class.

Because type gravitated to type, these students found each other, but they were not organized, nor were they of one mind. But a relatively future-oriented event was about to occur. A collective media event would articulate the discontent these students felt but could not intellectualize. And this event would become the first powerful statement of the revolution that was about to occur. Ironically, the first major collective media experience of the new generation was a book that was read one by one, by one and all, and at the same time.

The Catcher in the Rye

The twenty-first century generation of students is saturated with collective experiences that engage the hearts and minds of a large group of people. Collective film, television, and musical experiences, such as a rock concert or a high profile television show, dominate modern life. But back in the 1960s, this kind of mass event was rare. For me, the first modern tribal youth experience was the collective reading of *The Catcher in the Rye*. In many ways, this was an "old culture" event, because after all, it is a book and in the early 1960s that's about all we had. Yet, so many young people read it at the same time and seemed to receive the same message that the phenomenon is similar to an MTV special today. The messages from *The Catcher in the Rye* helped shape the youth culture of the late 1960s and the early 1970s.

As incredible as it may seem now, many of the book's young readers found it, like I did, by word of mouth. There was no media blitz or television coverage. J. D. Salinger did not turn up on the *Today* show. The book was spread through small-town-like gossip.

The Catcher in the Rye may have become known by means of the old world, but the messages received were all new generational. My generation may have grown up in a world reminiscent of the nineteenth century, but we were going to be the crossover generation, defining the new parameters of popular culture in America. The following generations would refer to what we did, and so much of what we did began with the world of Holden Caulfield in *The Catcher in the Rye*, the book that took us by the hand and crossed us over.

My generation extracted a collective text from *The Catcher in the Rye* where Holden Caulfield, the novel's protagonist, overtly acted out what many of us felt we were—round pegs in square holes. It was Holden's attitudes about school that were the most relevant to my generation. For Holden, school was a world of phoniness and superficiality. His fellow students were either victims, like the boy who killed himself rather than to submit to bullies (Salinger, 1951, pp. 220–221), or victimizers like his womanizing roommate, who has Holden write his English composition then criticizes it (pp. 53–54). But it was Holden's teachers who made the strongest impressions on me.

The portrait of Mr. Spencer showed a teacher who may have cared, but was completely ineffectual and stripped of all dignity. Here was Holden Caulfield searching for something meaningful, the essence of his existence, being forced to write themes about ancient Egyptian culture.

One of the supreme lessons I took from the book is that you can't trust anyone over thirty. Another lesson I felt Holden taught me is that you cannot be different in a world that respects and promotes conformity. When I reread *Catcher in the Rye* as an adult, I did not re-experience my enthusiasm for the novel. Holden, to the adult me, is a bit of a rich-kid whiner, and the novel is plagued by elitist and sexist attitudes that are hard to swallow today. My reading of *The Catcher in the Rye* certainly corroborates reader-response theory that claims a reader's background has a great deal of influence on how a novel is interpreted. As a volatile, immature 16-year-old, I perceived a set of messages from the novel that articulated deep feelings that I did not quite understand until Holden explained them to me. I was not alone in this, as *Catcher in the Rye* became a phenomenon for my generation.

Many of us were much too hard on our schools, and there were those of us who lacked sympathy and understanding for the well-meaning, caring adults who chaperoned our education. But we were onto something. J. D. Salinger catalyzed our nascent feelings with this novel and articulated for us what was on the tips of our collective tongue. Our schools were not always a positive part of our real world.

The Catcher in the Rye was by no means the first work with the "superiority of youth" theme, nor was it the last. This theme has been used from *Huckleberry Finn* to the film, *Clueless.* But *The Catcher in the Rye* was an important group-think media event of the 1960s.

Television and the Killing of a President

Not all my peers read *The Catcher in the Rye*, for reading was never something that everyone likes to do. Reading for pleasure, after all, is an acquired taste. However, the lifestyle and values spawned by reading the book probably affected everyone my age.

However, there was a media event of the early 1960s that virtually no one missed—the televised coverage of the assassination of John F. Kennedy. One technological event, no matter how important or dramatic, could not make the sweeping changes that would occur, but this one event propelled the changes forward like nothing else could have done. In essence, the assassination advanced the impact, and, thus, the momentum of television by a decade.

Although many people heard of the assassination via radio or word of mouth, television was in place when people got home, and even in 1963 it was a natural act to head straight for the TV and turn it on. Americans sat in front of their TV for almost a week. Viewers saw raw, live, unedited feed from networks that were basically unprepared technologically for this kind of coverage, but did it anyway. Viewers accepted grainy, almost indecipherable pictures; impromptu, often confused and confusing speeches; unexplained breaks in the action; endless repetition and commentary; and a story with no beginning or end. In short, people were thrust into a style of knowing, a new form of communication, a brand new way of perceiving, a whole new literacy style in one weekend.

Not only did viewers accept this; Americans experienced a collective emotion no one had experienced before. Television became a national church, and viewers in the presence of their families or alone in TV-equipped rooms were emotionally bonded to each other—one nation, mourning separate but together, thrust into the new world, the new literacy. Americans watched the first live murder, Lee Harvey Oswald shot by Jack Ruby; viewers saw the scenes of the assassination; the hospital; Air Force One; delivery of the casket; John-John saluting; the riderless horse; the cortege; the walking world leaders. Americans were all there in a way no newspaper could make possible. And no one could forget the experience.

On that November weekend in 1963, Americans embraced television, took it into their hearts, and began a love affair that will last forever. On that November weekend, Americans permanently crossed over into a world of multiple literacies. Print media could "no longer hold their traditional importance" (Graff, 1986, p. 60). Because of television, Daniel Fader observed that "children must now be regarded by their teachers as a species different in kind from the species that inhabited North American classrooms in the first half of the twentieth century" (Robinson, 1983, p. 11).

Movies

Another example of how literacy changed in the late 1960s and in the 1970s was exhibited by movies. Many of the films of this period were long on atmosphere, music, and visuals. The viewing public had finally learned how to "see" a film, and, as a result, more and more movies were made to attract these viewers. Movies that were very "visual," such as *The Graduate* (1967), *Easy Rider* (1969), *Blowup* (1966), and *Bonnie and Clyde* (1967), attracted large audiences. No film better illustrates this changeover and the reaction to it than *2001: A Space Odyssey* (1968).

Stanley Kubrick, the director, created a work that had no precedent. The film was so fresh, so inventive, that the audience had no frame of reference. This was a major motion picture that relied more heavily on images and sound than plot. The film was made in the wraparound technique of Cinerama, which combined three conventional size screens (each showing a 35 mm film) so that a viewer's peripheral vision was engaged. The sound track was mainly orchestral music played as loud as theaters would have it. There was very little dialogue in the film.

The film was as beautiful to see as a painting and as lovely to listen to as a symphony. Looking back at the film, perhaps it went too far in eliminating discernable plot elements. But this film is the grandfather of all the *Star Wars* films and almost all visual action apocalypse movies like *Independence Day* and *Armageddon*. *2001: A Space Odyssey* proved there was an audience out there who would appreciate a film filled with visual and aural wonders, an audience capable of watching a film far removed from the literary world of plot, dialogue, and character. In so many ways, *2001: A Space Odyssey* was a landmark crossover event.

Becoming an English Teacher

As is true with any other college English majors, I was to discover later, I had become one by default. It was slightly more complicated in that I hoped and believed, as my generation of English majors naively did, that great books could sensitize, explain, delight, and educate in the truest sense.

If high school English was a murky, undefined netherland, college English was clear—it was the study of literature, no doubt at all. Even the ubiquitous First-Year Composition ended with a five-star literary spectacular—the final examination. The final was awesome. I've never seen anything like it since. All of us "fresh people" were required to read a "great book," in my case *Tess of the D'Urbervilles*, and at the time trek to the gymnasium to receive the "question" on the work that we would have two hours to address. This would determine our grade in the course. Like lemmings, engineering majors and business majors, pre-law majors, and future physical education teachers marched to the gym to write the theme that, even to this day, I feel was my best in college. It ended, "If only that poor, damn horse hadn't died."

Even if the teaching wasn't always inspired, the books I read in my English classes were. And some of the teaching was inspired, in the sense that there were teachers who gave fabulous model readings. Although impassioned and intelligent class discussions were rare, our professors on occasion showed us how to interpret a text with idiosyncrasy and brilliance.

Teaching High School English

Like so many of my peer English majors, I never thought about what I would do with my degree. And, like so many of my peer English teachers, I decided to teach. I was fortunate to find a method of certification that would also provide me with a master's degree.

I thought I was going to be a far better teacher than any of those I had in high school. However, I learned quickly how difficult it is to be a good teacher. As a beginning teacher, my failings were enormous. Never mind my lack of experience and skill. Also, I lacked a picture of English teaching, a consistent idea. The only real goal I had was to make books fun, and, of course, I found even that to be difficult. Like many of my high school teachers, I talked too much, listened too little. But I grew, and my teaching did improve over the years.

I was among the first generation of Dartmouth Conference-inspired English teachers in America, and perhaps we were the largest education experiment. We attempted to operationalize the tenet that a learner grows through the study of English, "A difficult apprenticeship in naming the world," as Paulo Freire wrote (Emig, 1983, p. 176), and it was our goal to place English in context, to make it meaningful. For us, that meant expanding what literature was studied in the schools and attempting different methodologies in teaching it. In high school, we studied literature that was studied at the beginning of the century: *A Tale of Two Cities*, *Silas Marner*, *Julius Caesar*. Yet, it was the contemporary *The Catcher in the Rye* that so impacted us. It was our teaching goal to provide this kind of powerful literary experience to our students' meaningful bouts with contemporary books. We were going to create lifelong lovers of books.

The Decline

Relevance and meaningfulness became more important than skills in the late 1960s and early 1970s, and my generation English teacher later came under attack for starting the decline in American education. We were teachers trying to cope with the first generation of students born into a world where literacy had to be redefined (Pattison, 1982, pp. vi–vii). To our students, books were not the only show in town. Whereas past generations of English teachers railed against comic books, we would have been happy if many of our students read comic books, or for that matter, anything (Scholes, 1985, p. 15).

We were the first generation of the expanded literacy crisis, of declining test scores:

- Verbal score on achievement tests declined precipitously between 1963 and 1977, as studies by Harnishfeger and Wiley and by Bishop show the peak score of the Scholastic Aptitude Test in 1963 was 478. The score declined to 444 in 1974, and to 434 in 1975.
- By 1977, the scores on the SAT declined 49 points on a scale of 600.
- Scores on the ACT English Aptitude Test also declined from a mean score of 18.7 in 1966 to a score of 17.6 in 1974.
- The National Assessment of Educational Progress in Writing reported that the writing of 17-year-olds declined markedly in quality between 1970 and 1974 (D'Angelo, 1983, p. 99).

We faced the first generation of students overwhelmed and bombarded by communication systems that were potentially more informative and more pleasurable than reading, and as Umberto Eco suggests, "psychologically appropriate to our time" (Carey, 1988, p. 102).

End of the Sixties

In the period loosely labeled the sixties, there was a belief that the generation of youth was redefining the world. Many young people thought their world was going to be a better, safer, kinder place because of them. Events proved them wrong. The killing of students at Jackson State and Kent State Universities by National Guard members suppressing war protests sobered this country into the realization of what political violence could bring. The killings by the Charles Manson cult showed them that the romantic notions rediscovered in this period could lead to a catastrophic rationalization of evil. This was reinforced by the concert at Altamont, where the Hell's Angels gang, employed by the Rolling Stones rock group for security, killed a drug-crazed concert-goer on camera. The loss in Vietnam and the horrors of Cambodia dampened any remaining enthusiasm that youth power could be a healing, better approach to life. The 1960s were over. But this period left us a legacy, a change in technology and behavior as radical as I have ever heard or seen.

These revolutionary changes had occurred by the early 1970s; the new world would change, modify, and grow in the 1980s, but everything that was going to happen was in place in the early 1970s.

The Legacy—Our Time

Except for a few Bart Simpson or Barney costumes, Halloween 2000, at Vista Grande Elementary School in El Cajon, California, could be Halloween 1955. This day is as much for parents and grandparents as it is for their kids, because Halloween is a link to the older America; one of those nostalgia-driven events that provide continuity, a throwback to the mythic, community-oriented society so many Americans see as the golden past. But one small inch below the surface of the schoolyard scene reveals the free x-ray screening of Halloween candy by the local hospital, for we are in the new millennium, immersed in a culture that will not go back, a culture of violence and change and speed.

When I was a child, my comfort zone was about as far as Dave's Market at the corner. What would have plunged me into deep cultural shock and despair, my children take for granted. Their comfort zone extends around the world, and what they see and do would have been science fiction for me at their age. This is their world.

Super Media

The global village McLuhan (1964) predicted has occurred with McDonald's in Moscow and Kentucky Fried Chicken in Tianamen Square. The same movies, same television programs, same songs, same athletic shoes, same fast food, same cars are as common from coast to coast. The computer communication network is called the *world* wide web for good reason.

Communication among school children is global and centralized. Our youth live in an international cultural city, unbounded by time or distance, where all cultural choices are available. Michael R. Real (1989) has named this the City of Super Media, which he defines as "all media of communication ... not merely one medium such as television or film, or one class of media such as electronic or print, or one scale of media such as mass or specialized information sources" (p. 9). Real sees super media providing us with most of the material to "construct meaning and organize our existence" (p. 9). This modern web of communication is neither good nor bad. Real feels the important factor is to gain mastery of super media, which requires thinking critically about it, as well as appreciating and enjoying it (p. 259).

TV

Perhaps the most powerful and pervasive of all super media is television, which is like a hub from which all other media emanate. The most accessible of all the media and the least taxing, television is like a utility, a communication central-heating system that radiates information and entertainment 24 hours a day. Despite all the channel choices and alternatives such as pay-per-view and video-cassettes, television is a presence like air; and like air, television creates an atmosphere, a communication atmosphere that permeates American homes with the sights, sounds, ideas, and ambiance of New York, Los Angeles, and Washington. The style is East Coast-West Coast, and television elevates style above all else, which in turn dictates values and, thus, behavior. One of the goals of education is somehow to challenge this equation with the view that values should dictate behavior. I doubt if the incredibly seductive images of the media can be neutralized by good teaching, but questions can be planted in the minds of students regarding what human beings should value.

Television requires a know-how, an intelligence, even an education for a viewer to use it properly. "Mass-audience television has not only transformed the way its viewers spend their time," Henry Sussman (1989) writes, "it has also exerted a tangible impact on their habits of thought and their relation to language" (p. 10). Sussman sees the need to accommodate the prevailing historical forces and broaden the study of literacy "in terms that accept television with its cognitive and existential effects, as the source for a 'new' literacy" (p. 209). Television has overwhelmed the cultural life of this country and will continue to do so, with young people most vulnerable to the images and messages of this medium.

Print

Print literacy has undergone massive changes as a result of having to compete with television and as a result of new technology. America has national newspapers; one of the most successful is *USA Today*, which is formatted as a print equivalent of television. The section of *USA Today* that could be classified as the most fact-filled, full of complicated tables and great amounts of information, is the sports section. The rest of the paper provides snappy pieces, heavily illustrated. The paper carries large features about television watching. The paper is fun, lively, and relatively new, but it is not *The New York Times*. What makes the paper truly unique is its timeliness and wide availability. Stands are everywhere in the country, and the paper, which has editions Monday through Friday, has last night's scores in one splashy section and today's weather on its multicolored, extremely readable weather page.

This timeliness is made possible by instantaneous print communication provided by microdishes, communication satellites, and fax machines. The paper has printing plants everywhere. The old adage was that newspapers were written to the lowest common denominator, the sixth-grade reader. *USA Today* changes it targeted audience to the new-age, computer-dependent, jet-travelling, television-watching, neo-reader who has been trained to accept nonlinear, quick-paced, timely news. This reader cares most about, in this order: money, sports, weather, media, headlines. It is not surprising that *USA Today* is so commonly given to airplane travelers, because the paper, rather than anchoring a reader to a location, blankets a reader in the never-ending culture of the USA. The traveler reader finds the weather forecast for his/her destination and figures out what will be on the Marriott's cable-equipped TV when she or he arrives. Like a warm glass of milk or a favorite pillow, for the traveler, comfort is the familiarity of the national culture as reported in *USA Today*, found in the coast-to-coast sameness of the motel, and reassuringly available with the "old friends" programming on the television set. Small-town America is a mental phenomenon now replacing the physical small town of a century ago whose residents were confined by low-power vehicles and low-quality roads.

Even books have been affected by the new reader—a reader well equipped to accept nonlinear and unconventional reading material. Therefore, publishers have produced a spate of self-help books, reference books, trivia books, books of lists. One of the ironies of this new publishing direction is that E.D. Hirsch's book, *Cultural Literacy: What Every American Needs to Know* (1987), which bemoans the loss of a common classic-reference system among Americans, appeals so greatly to the neo-reader because of its lists. The very superficiality Hirsch laments, he fosters with the Trivial Pursuit-playing neo-reader who peruses his lists while the television blares in the background.

Wired

How does an adult learn computers? Ask a kid.

We are saturated with the lore and excitement of computers but they have changed the world and many of our students are as natural with technology as my generation was with paperback novels. The last article I wrote never saw paper. I transmitted it through e-mail, and it was edited and sent back to me through the Internet. However, as I type this on my strawberry iMac, I know that when this is published, most of what is written here about computers will be dated. We are moving quickly, too quickly for comfort, but it sure is interesting.

I am amazed at how soon the Internet and the world wide web became dangerous. Humans are so ingenious at doing harm that in no time technology became a threat—through misinformation and even personal exploitation. Do you let your kids go into any old chat room?

As English teachers we owe some debt to technology. It certainly has made writing easier, by eliminating sloppy handwriting, and creating this amazing editing and rewriting capacity. The impact of the grammar and spell check features of computers is arguable, but I find them helpful. The research capabilities of the web are vast but can be extremely dangerous if students are not guided to understand the difference between authentic information and garbage.

Yet, the world of computers is surprisingly friendly to written literacy as long as the Internet stays with writing as the main medium for communicating. We can debate endlessly the quality of writing or the lack of editing of the writing, but it is writing and requires a certain level of clarity and even accuracy. And like all writing, it is out there to be read, interpreted, and misinterpreted. The harsh Internet lesson is this: you better get it right. Friendships are at stake; jobs are at stake; relationships are at stake; money is at stake; everything could be at stake. And it all hinges on writing.

The greatest problem may be young people who do not have access to computers. Most of these kids watch TV and go to movies, yet they lack the tools and the skills essential for this new century. Of course, these kids are trainable on the lowest levels of technology, like punching the pictures on a McDonald's computer/cash register. But they are not comfortable with the wide array of complicated, but essential tasks that computers perform. One old computer in a classroom will not do it for these kids.

A bank of relatively new computers in an English classroom, which can be used for writing as part of a writing center, is a giant step in helping kids who do not have computer access at home. Even better, if at least two of these computers had Internet access so that the use of the web and Internet could be taught and supervised by an English teacher. English teachers can play a big role in the development of fundamental computer skills for all students, especially those without home computers.

Social Upheavals

In addition to all the technological changes, and maybe partially as the result of them, enormous social upheavals have occurred. The changes in the American family, on a steady path since the 1960s, impacts upon an enormous number of our students, many of whom live with one or no parents. In 1970, 85% of American children lived with both parents. In 1991, that percentage dropped to 72%. A child's chances of living in poverty in a one-parent family are six times as high as they would be in a two-parent family. Today, two-thirds of American women work outside the home.

The sexual revolution continues, albeit transformed by the fear of AIDS. Children of all social groups learn about sex in first grade or earlier. Teenagers have tremendous pressure to perform sexually at a very early age regardless of the consequences. Our culture surrounds youth in images and stories of fantasy sexuality.

Almost every generation in the past 30 years has had to cope with high levels of violence. This generation faces criminal violence at unprecedented levels, much of it committed by the students in our classrooms. Disregard for human life is appalling. In the 1960s, a teenager was twice as likely to die of cancer as to be murdered. Today, the opposite is true. Not only do many of our students commit crimes, many of them are victims. Murder and rape are prevalent, as is child abuse—horrible crimes that affect our students. Our students live in a world where criminality has become sadly commonplace, far, far away from my youthful world of unlocked doors and safe streets.

The New Literates

Most young people are not violent druggies hell-bent on the destruction of civilization as we know it. But even those students who are doing well in school are aware of the destructive culture of many of their peers. Of course, all students love the wonderful variety of media available to them, and as a result of their new world, think differently from their counterparts of bygone eras. Our achievers can make good grades in English classes, but despite their abilities, many of them are more prone to varied modern cultural influences than they are to the classics. Although they may be good readers, they are also filmgoers, television viewers, Internet kibbitzers, and phone talkers. They are connoisseurs of style, jet travelers, and kickboxers. In many ways, their lives are very rich as a result. Good students have always been busy with activities such as cheerleading and student council. But in the past, their minds have existed in a linear world of print media. Not true with today's good students who, as a result of top-notch intelligence and keen curiosity, indulge in the multimedia splendor that is America in the new century.

Unfortunately, our average students are tough to teach, because so many of them see no need to read and write and at best view school as a diploma-mill path to a job. This attitude is increasing as the world and schools move further apart and as written literacy for many students is easily replaced by the oral and visual culture that surrounds them.

So many of these students come from homes where television has replaced reading, whereas in former generations, even the most culturally impoverished homes would have newspapers. Thus, students come with few adult-reader role models—from a culture that is oral and visual. Also, teachers must face a panoply of students who come to school as nonspeakers of English. Many of these students are culturally alienated from the English-language bookishness of schools (Gonzalas, 1990, pp. 16–23).

Students of the Millennium

English and language arts teaching, most effective for meeting these challenges, have the following characteristics:

■ Effective teachers contextualize English and language arts. Kids are not separated from their culture as soon as they walk into school. Rather, students study and perform language that is an integrated and relevant part of their lives. Thus, our students not only learn language, but also through language they learn how to live in the highly manipulative culture they are immersed in. Rather than locking the world out of schools, effective practice brings the world into the classroom as the primary subject matter.

■ English teaching makes sense when it's natural for kids. Our students are constantly engaged in creating meaning from visual and auditory texts. Kids are surrounded by an unprecedented array of media. They are not passive; our students are judging, weighing, interpreting, analyzing, comprehending, and of course, enjoying. The trick for English/language arts teachers is to engage students in these same activities with the texts we use in our classrooms.

■ Effective classrooms are humanistic environments in an often unfriendly and technologically cluttered world. These classrooms foster empathy and compassion, and their teachers listen to and read for the messages students want to convey. Effective classrooms promote student-centered meaning-making. They are places that demonstrate the most humanistically positive features of language use.

■ Effective English/language arts classrooms make written texts as interesting, if not more so, than visual and auditory texts. In effective English/language arts classrooms, books are exciting and so is writing produced by students. These classrooms exalt reading and writing, and thus promote full literacy in a world where written literacy is challenged by new technology.

Reflection

"Literacy is one of the chief means of human liberation," writes Robert Pattison (1982, p. 135). It is, as Paulo Freire (1985) sees it, a method for individuals "to reconstitute their relationship with the wider society" (p. 7).

Effective English/language arts classes exalt the richness of written literacy; they are places in our society where readers and writers are created. These English classes generate an increasing network of citizens who own, control, and enjoy all media rather than citizens who, unwilling to read and write, become increasingly desensitized by a manipulative and exploitive mass media whose main purpose is to enrich a few on the spiritual and physical impoverishment of the many.

Recommended Readings

Adler, M. (1982). *Paideia proposal.* New York: Macmillan.

Adler's book is worth reading to see what a philosophically "essentialist" curriculum would look like. Adler provides a comprehensive plan for secondary schooling based on an essential curriculum for all.

Atwell, N. (1987). *In the middle: Writing, reading, and learning with adolescents.* Portsmouth, NH: Heinemann.

Atwell gives a detailed account of her middle-school writing workshops. This book is an excellent example of a personal narrative that provides a detailed picture of a teacher at work.

Bissex, G. L., & Bullock, R. H. (Eds.). (1987). *Seeing for ourselves: Case-study research by teachers of writing.* Portsmouth, NH: Heinemann.

This book is about writing case studies that apply to English teaching. The book includes six long-term and four short-term studies.

Bloom, A. (1987). *The closing of the American mind.* New York: Simon and Schuster.

This book gives insight into what traditionalists perceive is wrong with education in America. The traditionalists have a great deal of power, and Bloom is very influential.

Booth, W. (1988). *The company we keep: An ethics of fiction.* Berkeley, CA: University of California Press.

This is a sensitive and thoughtful account of how fiction makes an impact on values and moral behavior.

Coles, R. (1989). *The call of stories: Teaching and the moral imagination.* Boston: Houghton Mifflin.

Coles describes his approach to using fiction as a means of imparting wisdom as well as knowledge. This famous psychiatrist sees a novel "within all of us" as part of our moral imagination.

Freire, P. (1985). *The politics of education.* South Hadley, NJ: Bergin and Garvey.

Freire goes into much of his educational, social, and political philosophy. He sees language as a powerful force that cannot be removed from social and political considerations demonstrating, "the word is the world."

McLuhan, M. (1964). *Understanding media.* New York: McGraw-Hill.

McLuhan has been dismissed by some critics, but I still find him to be the greatest of all media analysts. This book was prophetic in its analysis of the impact of media on society.

Real, M. (1989). *Super media: A cultural studies approach.* Newbury Park, CA: Sage Publications.

It is worth reading this book just for Real's definition of "super media." Real interconnects all the forms of communication in a logical manner.

Rose, M. (1989). *Lives on the boundary: The struggles and achievements of America's underprepared.* New York: Free Press.

This is a fine example of personal narrative writing as Rose describes his own journey into full literacy.

Scholes, R. (1985). *Textual power: Literary theory and the teaching of English.* New Haven, CT: Yale University Press.

This book really is about meaning-centered teaching in the college English classroom. Scholes gives a positive and insightful view of how texts should be read in relation to the reader. He is a strong critic of "mechanistic" literary pedagogy.

Workman, B. (1992). *Teaching the sixties: An in-depth, interactive, interdisciplinary approach.* Urbana, IL: National Council of Teachers of English.

The book is a description of a high school American humanities course focused on the 1960s era. This book provides interesting information about this turbulent period.

CLASSROOMS: PORTRAITS OF TEACHING MEANING-CENTERED ENGLISH LANGUAGE ARTS

Introduction to Part Two: A Guide to Using the Stories

You are about to read stories depicting the teaching of English. These stories tell about teachers in several schools teaching a variety of lessons. Included are:

- A reading workshop (7th grade)
- A class discussion on *The Pigman* (10th grade)
- A performance-based lesson of *A Midsummer Night's Dream* (12th grade)
- A portrait of several poetry lessons (10th grade)
- Teaching *The Great Gatsby* and *Huckleberry Finn* (11th grade)
- Teaching *To Kill a Mockingbird* (11th grade)
- A writing workshop (10th grade)
- The new literacies of the classroom (12th grade)
- Evaluation and assessment (10th grade)
- Preparing for state proficiency testing (10th grade)

Although these stories cover a lot of territory, they cannot possibly reflect all the potential classroom situations and methods available to English teachers. Rather, these are meant to serve as baseline illustrations of secondary English teaching. What these stories have in common are teachers who, to paraphrase Frank Smith, have a respect for language that is natural and authentic, not contrived and fragmented, and respect for learners who engage in meaningful and productive activities, not in pointless drills and rote memorization (Smith, 1992, p. 440).

Although these stories are meant to illustrate fine teachers at work, they work in classrooms that are of the "here and now," and these teachers attempt to cope with "real" teacher concerns such as grading and correctness in writing.

A story in Chapter Ten differs slightly in format from the other stories because it concerns preparing students for state proficiency tests. This story is more for what we must do than what we ought to do. It depicts an outstanding teacher dealing with the harsh realities of teaching English in our time.

As baseline illustrations, these stories are meant to be analyzed, critiqued, studied, and expanded. You may want to refer to Chapters One and Two for the guidelines and principles of effective teaching and see where and how they fit into the stories. For instance, how do you know these teachers intend to be meaning-centered teachers? How do these teachers think about or reflect on their classrooms?

Probing the Stories

You may wish to use these questions as a basis for exploring the stories:

- How will these lessons work with a variety of students from different cultural and ethnic backgrounds? From urban, rural, or suburban schools?

- How will these lessons work with English as Second Language students?

- Do these stories depict effective teaching as defined in Chapters One and Two of this text? How?

- What are the goals of each of these teachers?

- What problems do they encounter and how do they cope with the problems?

- What have been your experiences with lessons like the ones described in the stories?

- Do you know teachers who use these approaches? What are their classrooms like?

- Do you feel that these classrooms are overly teacher-centered? Not teacher-centered enough? Just right?

- How will discipline problems play a part in efforts to recreate these stories in real classrooms?

Each story describes how a teacher designs a lesson or lessons. You may find it profitable to analyze these stories, based on a breakdown of their components. They may give you a feel for the components of a complex teaching activity. Or you may wish to create your own stories, based on classrooms you know.

Each of the portraits you are about to read has most of the following elements:

1. Introduction
2. The Teacher (a brief description)
3. The School, the Students
4. Introducing the Lesson
5. The Lesson: A description of the body of the lesson
6. The Teacher's Thoughts (throughout the story)
7. Reflections
8. "Teacher as Researcher" questions and activities
9. Recommended Readings

Try These Lessons

If you get a chance, try out some of these lessons, or at least parts of them. You will probably need to modify these lessons to fit the classrooms you face, and you will need to do them more than once to work out the kinks. You may need to create lesson plans based on the descriptions you read. But with some skill and luck, you could turn these into very successful lessons that reflect meaning-centered, holistic English teaching.

Standards and Performance Benchmarks

Before the stories begin, you will notice a section devoted to *International Reading Association/the National Council of Teachers of English Standards for English Language Arts*. These Standards are meant to be criteria on which English teaching is built in the stories. In fact, at the end of most of the stories, you will find a box to show how the English teaching relates to the Standards. In these boxes, Performance Benchmarks are written to describe how the stories match the Standards. This kind of relationship between Standards and assessment is becoming a way of life in teaching, and

chapter THREE

Teaching the Reading Workshop

Introduction

My Front Porch

I know where I learned to love reading. It was on the front porch of my childhood home. This porch, which protected my family from the rain while allowing for a refreshing breeze, was the center of many summertime pleasures. My parents would sip iced tea and listen to the ball game on the radio, or we would just sit there in conversation with each other and with passing neighbors. Sometimes, we would entertain friends on the porch, laughing and gossiping.

But the major use of the porch, for my entire family, was for reading. I loved to lie on the glider with its maroon vinyl-covered pillows. I would stretch out, my head on a pillow, and with very little effort I would rock back and forth, back and forth. I would read on this glider, particularly on rainy days when I couldn't play baseball or ride my bike. It was on this glider that I read those long-forgotten, mustard-stained library books. It was on this glider that I learned to read. The house and the porch are still there on Wellesley Avenue on the East End of Pittsburgh, occupied by a new family. The glider is long gone. But the reader formed on the porch grew up to write this book.

The School, the Students

I have passed the sign to Dobbins Corner High School many times on the way to the rolling, wooded countryside, but I never really believed there was a school building hidden in the thicket of foliage. The day I finally turned left onto the two-lane blacktop, however, I discovered after less than a mile, on a hilltop clearing, one of the most common sights of American high schools—the football field and its wooden bleachers. The school itself is of typically 1950s design—one story, red brick, flat roof, many large windows. I always love rural schools because you can look out of the window and see meadows, fields, and woods. Teachers tell of cows that amble down to the school and peer inside.

This school's setting, however, is somewhat deceptive. For the most part, these are not farm kids. This community is just close enough to a city to allow commuting, so parents who have jobs but who prefer rural living settle here. The moms and dads of these kids are accountants, secretaries, nurses, medical technicians, lawyers, factory workers, and coal miners. And, of course, like many rural areas, you find kids here from poor, unemployed families, one-parent homes, kids who live with grandparents scratching for a living. These kids look, act, talk, and dress like kids from everywhere else in this country. Computers, television, music, and magazines have seen to that. Although the 572 students in this junior/senior high school are predominately White, about 25% of the students are African American or Hispanic, in almost equal numbers.

Teacher

The Teacher	
Joanne Adler, 31	Nine years teaching experience, all in junior high English
Educational Background:	B.A., English Education, 1983; Certified in English and reading (Grades 7 through 12)
Approach:	"You create readers through the love of reading. I am fortunate to have young-adult novels because they are so good and my students like them so much."
Influences:	Summer workshop in the teaching of writing process; mentor reading teacher at adjacent high school who developed reading workshop approach

Introducing the Lesson

The room, fairly dark, was filled with seventh graders in all sizes and varieties. They sat in their chairs, all of them, quietly bonded by a common activity, echoing back to the reading I did on my front porch. This classroom may not have had the gentle summer breezes or the glider, but these 28 students were just as content as I used to be. They sat there reading young-adult novels they had selected with the help of Joanne and her class library. These students were reading one of seven books the teacher had in multiple copies. Her seven included: *A Day No Pigs Would Die*; *Bridge to Terabithia*; *A Wrinkle in Time*; *The Great Gilly Hopkins*; *The Witch of Blackbird Pond*; *Roll of Thunder, Hear My Cry*; *In the Year of the Boar and Jackie Robinson*. The teacher, Joanne Adler, had been in the school for 9 years and knew her way around the system. By requesting funds from the curriculum director, who was also the assistant superintendent, and by requesting small grants in exchange for student-teacher and field-experience supervision, she has been able, over the years, to build her classroom library. Joanne feels nothing is more important than having a supply of good books, and a perusal of her classroom reveals several copies of titles Joanne feels works especially well with her students. Joanne is very possessive about these books and is very careful in the way she distributes them. This is the way she works it.

The Lesson

For this reading cycle, Joanne decides to promote her seven titles because she feels they fit the reading styles and interests of most of her students. For instance, she has several farm kids in here, including Josh and Fred, who are not avid readers. She feels they will probably do very well with *A Day No Pigs Would Die*, a book that is fairly easy to read but may shock the average nonfarm kid with vivid descriptions of nurturing and slaughtering farm animals. Josh and Fred can take it, Joanne says. So many of her students—Amy, Karina, Jennifer, and Don, for instance—read fantasy fiction that she feels she can hook them on *A Wrinkle in Time*, which Joanne feels is a philosophic cut above what they read now. "With some guidance from me," she says, "maybe we can discuss some of the larger issues, such as self-reliance and confidence, from *A Wrinkle in Time*." Joanne points out John and Kathleen from one-parent homes, and Anne, who lives with her grandmother. "These kids may appreciate *The Great Gilly Hopkins* or they may find it depressing," Joanne says, a bit nervous about using this book. In any case, she senses some real reading matches. "My students will become readers if they encounter books that engage them. Because I have such a variety of students, I need a variety of books, and I am lucky to have them."

Joanne starts this round of book reading by explaining the rules. By now her students are very familiar with what they are to do:

- After Joanne introduces the books, each student must select one of them to read.

- The student must then sign out one of the selections. Joanne keeps a careful list of who has which book, including name of the student, the title of the book, and date out–date in.

- Every student must keep a reading/writing portfolio. This is a plain manila folder each uses to keep all of his or her writing and records of writing and reading progress. When you walk into Joanne's room, you see the blue-gray boxes stacked on open shelves underneath the windows. Usually, the first thing her students do is to go to these boxes and take out their portfolios.

Reading Log		
Keep track of the books you read daily		
DATE	**TITLE OF BOOK**	**PAGES READ**

- The students track what they read in a log similar to this one (see Figure 3.1).
- If her students finish a book before the sessions in this book period are complete, they may read another book for extra credit or they may read whatever they want.
- Her students are permitted to take the books home as long as they consistently bring them back to class. If a student has a record of forgetting books, Joanne is cautious about lending them for out-of-class reading to that student.

After Joanne goes over the rules, she then proceeds to what she considers the most important step in initiating the reading, which is her book introductions. She does this so well that despite the time they take, she has a great time and her kids enjoy it as well.

Her book talks are generally broken into four sections. For instance, with *A Wrinkle in Time:*

[Part one] "When I was growing up my favorite books were *Lassie Come Home* and *A Tree Grows in Brooklyn*, a story about growing up during World War II. Recently, I asked a public librarian what book young people check out the most, and she told me *Harry Potter and the Sorcerer's Stone*. I asked her why and she said probably because it was about kids caught in a world filled with fantasy and amazing happenings, kind of like E.T." *A Wrinkle in Time* is very similar to *Harry Potter*.

[Part two] "Listen to how *A Wrinkle in Time* opens":

> *It was a dark and stormy night. In her attic bedroom, Margaret Murry, wrapped in an old patchwork quilt, sat on the foot of her bed, and watched the trees tossing in the frenzied lashing of the wind. Behind the trees clouds scudded frantically across the sky. Every few moments the moon ripped through them, creating wraith-like shadows that raced along the ground. The house shook. Wrapped in her quilt, Meg shook (L'Engle, 1962, p. 11).*

[Part three] "As with so many great books, this is the story of a search. Meg is searching for her lost father. And it will be a difficult and dangerous search, taking her to a host of planets and galaxies."

[Part four] "After you read this, you will know how to travel through space without a spaceship. This is called Tesseracting (a wrinkle in time) and you will find out the amazing power Meg has.

"The journal questions you may use, if you wish, for this reading are:
What is a wrinkle in time? Why is the book called this?
What is Meg's special power? Do you like Meg? Why or why not?
Did you like the book? Why? Why not?
Do you have any questions about the book?

Usually, all Joanne's introductions contain these four sections. The first section is a personal story about the book that she likes to tell. Then, for the second part, she reads a small passage from the book to spark interest. Her third section conveys a sense of what the book is about to help her students get a feel for the story. In the fourth section, Joanne shapes questions to spark curiosity and for students to use as springboards for their journal writing. Her students do not have to use her questions, but they are there if they want them.

"I feel that these four parts are the most effective way to spark interest and enthusiasm for the books, as well as give a preview of the book without ruining it for my students. My ultimate goals with the book talks are to create interest for the work and to match the right reader with the right book."

Here is another introduction example:

[Part one] "When I was growing up, I had a very special friend, Connie. We shared many experiences, but our favorite activity was a secret club that we founded with just us as members. We called this club SPIT, for Sweet People in Twos. Now Connie is a mother with a boy and a girl, and she is an attorney. We see each other about once a year and talk on the phone all of the time. Our club is no longer a secret, but now a wonderful memory of a close childhood friendship."

[Part two] "This is from *Bridge to Terabithia:*"

> *Jess didn't concern himself with what would "become of it." For the first time in his life, he got up every morning with something to look forward to. Leslie was more than his friend. She was his other, more exciting self—his way to Terabithia and all the world beyond. . .*

> *Terabithia was their secret, which was a good thing, for how could Jess have ever explained it to an outsider? Just walking down the hill toward the woods made something warm and liquid steal through his body. The closer he came to the dry creek bed and the crabapple tree rope, the more he could feel the beating of his heart. He grabbed the end of the rope and swung out toward the other bank with a kind of wild exhilaration and landed gently on his feet, taller and stronger and wiser in that mysterious land (Paterson, 1977, p. 46).*

[Part three] "This is a book about a very special friendship between a young boy and a young girl and it is about this special imaginary secret kingdom they create, Terabithia."

[Part four] "Think about these questions and maybe you will want to use them for your journal writing:
Are your special friendships like this one between Jess and Leslie?
Can you explain?
Do you know if boys and girls are ever friends like this?

Why did Jess and Leslie become friends?
How do you think Jess handled the events at the end of the book?

Joanne worries about overleading the students with her introductions. "Sometimes I feel I am placing my interpretations onto the books, but for many of my students, these introductions spark a lot of enthusiasm. After they read the book, if my students interpret it differently than I did, I am delighted. And there are many, many books that my students read for which I offer no introduction."

Her students have another resource to help them make their book choices. After a student is done reading a book, Joanne has them fill out an index card with the following information:

- Name of book and author
- Description of book
- Reaction to book
- Recommendation for future reading (see Figure 3.2)

Joanne keeps these cards in a drawer in her desk and her students are permitted to look up any book they may be interested in reading. If the cards she receives from students are consistently poor, she removes that book as a reading option.

Thus, based on the book talks, the cards, and informal questions that students ask during the selection process, students make their choices. Joanne attempts to find first-choice books from her personal library, but that is not always possible. By the end of the second day of the selection process, all of her students have a book. Sometimes she allows students to take the book home if she feels that they will bring it back to read in class. Sometimes she asks students to return the book to the shelves before they leave and only read during the designated class time. Decisions of this type never end, and her experience and her instincts provide her the judgment to deal with these situations on a case-by-case basis.

Censorship Problems

Joanne is very aware of the potential problems the books she uses may cause in the community. She knows that a parent may object to any book for a number of reasons. Fortunately, she alerts her principal and her English department chair to the titles she is using. Then for more controversial titles, such as *A Day No Pigs Would Die*, which has strong scenes of a cow birth and a pig slaughter, she fills out a rationale form (which can be found in Jim Davis'

figure ◊ **3.2**

NAME _____

PERIOD _____

Summary/Reaction

When you are finished with a book, you need to complete a summary/reaction card.

On a card write the title of your book (be sure to capitalize and underline your title) at the top. The author's name should be written under the title.

Your first paragraph should be a brief summary of your book (2–4 sentences). What was this book about? Do not give the ending away.

Your second paragraph should be your reasons for recommending this book or your reasons for not recommending the book. Include who you recommend this to. Example: boys, girls, adults, high school students, etc.

Sign your name and write your class period.

Example:
The Outsiders
by S. E. Hinton

Two opposing street gangs have a senseless rumble that causes hatred, trouble, violence, and even death.

I highly recommend this book to guys and girls junior high through high school. The characters are realistic and the excitement and tension keep you reading.

[1979, pp. 192–193] book on censorship). The items on this form include:

- Ways in which the book is especially appropriate for students in this class
- Ways in which the book is especially pertinent to the objectives of the course or unit
- Special problems that might arise in relation to the book
- Ways a teacher might handle these problems
- Some other appropriate books an individual student might read in place of this one.

Finally, Joanne is very careful to match the right book with the right student. Although this method may backfire, she has a sense of which student would find *A Wrinkle in Time* a satanic diatribe. And she will quietly warn certain readers to be prepared for aspects of a book, such as the unloving mother and the subsequent abandonment in *The Great Gilly Hopkins*. Even the *Harry Potter* series has been criticized for its witchcraft and wizardry. So far, Joanne hasn't had any problems, perhaps because of her humanistic, flexible attitude about her reading program, but complaints can crop up on any book at any time. She knows it and tries to be mentally prepared.

The Library

Although Joanne has been able to assemble, by most school standards, a fairly large classroom library, she is missing many titles she wishes she had. Fortunately, she works well with the school librarian, who keeps up with the latest in adolescent fiction and maintains a well-stocked library. Because Joanne is so conscientious about monitoring her students, particularly when they use the library, and conscientious about protecting school books, the librarian cooperates as much as possible. So there are several times a year when Joanne takes her class to the library, presents them with shortened books talks, with the aid of the librarian, and allows them to select a book. Joanne's students are never without a book to read.

Reading in Class

Joanne gives her students 20 minutes of reading time in class about two or three days a week and asks them to read two to five books over a semester.

Her workshop goes on all semester but is put on hold during special units such as a drama lesson or a thematic unit. The reading workshop must also compete with the writing workshop (see Chapter Eight for a description of a writing workshop), and sometimes she merges the two, offering her students choices.

Joanne gives her students a set of rules for her reading workshop (see Figure 3.3).

After every session students are given 10 to 15 minutes to write in their journals about the day's reading and whatever else strikes them as interesting. Joanne helps them with the journal writing by providing scaffolding questions in her book talks and offering some generic questions and activities for their use, such as:

- What happened in today's reading?
- How did the characters behave?

- Who do you like the most so far?
- Write a letter to your favorite or least-favorite character explaining how you could help them.
- What will happen next in the book?

Joanne asks her students to record each journal entry on a book journal in their portfolios (see Figure 3.4).

Joanne will grade the journals only on quantity, but if asked she will read a journal entry and comment on it. Examples of those journal entries and comments by Joanne are included (see Figures 3.5, 3.6, 3.7, 3.8, 3.9).

Joanne reads and gives credit to the journals while her students are reading or writing in class. She also circulates, ensuring that students are obeying the rules, but most of the time she sets an example by reading herself. "My students will not consider reading in class credible unless I do it myself."

---

figure ◗ 3.3

READING WORKSHOP

Every day our class will be divided into three parts:

- First 10 minutes—A mini-lesson
- Next 20 minutes—Reading workshop
- Last 10 minutes—Book share time

During reading workshop, the following procedures will be followed:

1. Students must read the entire 20 minutes.
2. Students may not do homework or read any other material.
3. Students must be reading a book. The only time you are permitted to read other materials is when you're finished with your book goal.
4. You may not disturb others.
5. You may sit where you'd like (including on the floor) as long as no feet are on the furniture.
6. There are *NO PASSES*!
7. Be sure to complete all items on your grade checklist as you read.
8. Each day after workshop, I will check reading logs.

BOOK JOURNAL

BOOK TITLE_____

AUTHOR_____

DATE_____ PAGE ON_____ JOURNAL ENTRY #_____

figure ◊ **3.5**

A Wrinkle in Time was weird and made me sad at the same time. For one thing, the names are real funny, like Mrs. Whatsit and for another there are parts that I don't understand, like the writing in a different language on page 40. But I still don't know if I am going to like the book yet. Meg is weird but I know how she feels about her father. When my father moved out last year I thought I was going to die. I still do sometimes, although I've gotten used to living with Mom and Billie. So I might write to Meg and tell her this.

"Dear Meg, Please don't worry too much. You can get used to anything."

Dear Mrs. Adler, What do you think? Will I like the book?

Amy

Dear Amy,

I can't guarantee you will like it, but you're reading it very well so far. I think you will grow to like Meg or know her better as you read on and you will learn more about what happened to Meg's father.

Mrs. Adler

figure ◗ 3.6

> Dear Mrs. Adler,
>   I picked Summer of Fear to read, because I have liked all of the Lois Duncan books that I've read, and a friend said it was good. I also read the back of the book and it sounded like a good book.
>   Bobbi
>
> Dear Bobbi,
>   Good job! You'll like it!
>   Mrs. Adler

figure ◗ 3.7

> Dear Mrs. Adler,
>   I predict one of the kids are going to be shot (probably Glen Kirtland) because he's always talking back to the kidnappers. If I was in Glen's place, I would shut up and not get shot. This book is exciting and keeps you wondering what's going to happen.
>   Brian
>
> Dear Brian,
>   Super job putting yourself in the character's place and good predictions!
>   Mrs. Adler

figure ◆ 3.8

Dear Mrs. Adler,

I have finished reading Taming the Star Runner by S. C. Hinton. I thought it was a pretty good book. There really wasn't as much relation to this book as the other Hinton books except at the end when Travis finds out that Orson and Joe were involved in murdering the twins Billy and Mike. Travis and the horse, Star Runner, are both kind of the same. I felt that the Star Runner wasn't meant to be tamed. Like they both were just meant to live their lives without anyone bothering them, and telling them how they should live. Jeremy

Dear Jeremy,

One of the very best letters I've received on this book — I had a difficult time with this book. I just couldn't get interested. You did a SUPER job comparing it to Hinton's other books. How does the murder make a connection with other Hinton books? You have made an excellent observation and comparison about Travis and the Star Runner! Great job!

Mrs. Adler

figure ◊ **3.9**

Dear Mrs. Adler,

I can't tell you how much I like this book! White Fang is full of hatred for Beauty Smith. Beauty Smith is mean, cruel, and brutal.

White Fang meets Weeden Scott and the like turns to love. White Fang has feelings never aroused before. He loves his new master and everything about him. Weeden Scott loves White Fang and feels for all the bad, cruel things done to him.

This book made me cry. In parts it was so happy. It gave me a feeling of joy to know White Fang would finally be able to experience love.

This book had so many emotional ups & downs that once you started reading you couldn't stop. If I had to recommend one book, it would be this one. I love it!

I just can't get over how White Fang, with all the cruelty, fighting and meanness, could live a life.

If it were me I would have died long ago. I admire White Fang for his love of life and his will to survive.
                                                              Lauren

Dear Lauren,

You don't know how happy I am that you like this! Anyone not knowing what this book is about would think you were writing about a person — do you feel as though White Fang is human as you read?
                                                              Mrs. Adler

Generally, the reading and journal writing go along fine, but occasionally, she will run into the restless student who refuses to read or write that day. Her students are allowed to stretch, get up, do whatever they want as long as they do not disturb anyone else and, of course, they only receive credit for the reading and the writing if they do it. Her biggest challenges are students who finish their books well ahead of schedule. She keeps feeding titles to these students and gives them credit for their voracious reading appetites.

When her students read, a new kind of noise enters the classroom space. You hear the shuffling of feet, kids laughing in the halls, the sound of the mower outside. These kids, most of them engrossed in their reading, show many different styles. There are the kids who place the books on their desktops, and with their heads on their hands, lean over the books; there are the kids who hold their books on their laps and peer straight down; there are the slouchers who stretch out their feet and hold the books at an angle. Joanne has an advantage over her students. She can swivel in her chair while she reads, coming close to the same movement I found so soothing on the glider on my front porch.

Literacy Circles

For discussion, Joanne groups her students based on common books or themes. She explains the rules of this activity this way:

> Since many of you have read the same book, or books with similar stories, you will probably enjoy and learn from discussing it with your neighbors. I would like you to talk about these books with the following questions in mind:
>
> - Did you like the book?
> - Why or why not?
> - Who were your favorite characters? Why?
> - Who were your least favorite characters? Why?
> - What did you learn about yourself from reading this book?
> - Please add any questions you may have.
>
> I recommended that you begin in your groups by doing two things. First, share your journals with each other [Joanne's students know that if they feel their journals are too personal they don't have to, but many share them anyway.] Secondly, talk about what the book is about.
>
> At the end of each group session, I will ask a group member to tell the class what your group had to say about some of these questions.

Joanne will sit in and listen to each group; and occasionally she will even participate. Because Joanne sets a climate in which students are expected to take part in activities, most of her students discuss the books in the group. She will assign specific rules to every group member. Sometimes she will put students in charge of specific questions to keep some of her kids on the topics. Also she will ask students to take notes on the group responses. Sometimes she will not do the group discussions at all, if she feels a particular class cannot work in groups. Sometimes she allows the group sessions to go wherever her students take them. On a good day, here is a typical exchange among her students.

> Bill: "I liked *A Day No Pigs Would Die*, except I thought it was gross."
> Shawn: "Me too. I was really mad when the boy had to kill the pig, and I felt bad when his dad died."
> Sue: "Why did they have to make the book so gross?"
> Katie: "That's the way farms are. We kill chickens on our farm and it isn't pretty and my brothers and my dad have butchered pigs."
> George: "Oh gross!"
> Katie: "You may not like to kill them, but you like to eat them." [Laughter] "My dad works real hard, like the father in the book."
> Fred: "I milk cows before I come to school, and it is hard even with the electric milkers."

Because this school is rural, there are farm kids who can talk about *A Day No Pigs Would Die* from first-hand knowledge. On the other side of the room, meanwhile, the conversation turns angry because of what happens to Leslie in *Bridge to Terabithia*. Those in the group that have read *The Great Gilly Hopkins* try to understand what happened to Gilly Hopkins' mom. The next day, members of the *A Wrinkle in Time* group just don't want to talk to each other about the book, even with Joanne's help.

Human nature will run its course, at times subverting any teaching idea, no matter how good. If there is any lesson Joanne has learned, it is to be patient, flexible, and realistic. Perhaps tomorrow, or next year, she will learn to be the perfect teacher, but, in fact, that is impossible. Teaching, like all complex activities, will never lend itself to perfection, only to near misses, great tries, some successes, and constant reflection.

For instance, when Joanne was asked to reflect upon herself as a teacher, she responded this way:

> "What I do is create enthusiasm for reading and really create better readers by my workshop. It works. Parents tell me all the time how

much their kids love the workshop books and how much they read them at home. These parent and student testimonials have convinced my principal. He is totally supportive. Thanks to Beth (Joanne's high school mentor), my students get one more experience with the workshop method at the high school. When they get to Beth in 10th grade, they are reading workshop vets and reading veterans as well. We create readers, and I am proud of that. I know these methods work, and I believe in them. When given the freedom to read and react to good books, particularly these great new young-adult novels, my students love to read, and some of them become readers for the first time."

Finally, Joanne mused on the importance of finding and using multicultural materials.

"A nice aspect of young-adult fiction is that new books are available all the time. And finally, titles about different ethnic and cultural groups are available in increasing numbers. Although my students are predominately white, they are growing up in a world with a lot of different people. They need to get used to and accept some differences. One of the best ways of getting prepared is by reading books about ethnic, cultural, and racial groups." [See Recommended Readings for a list of multicultural books.]

Open Book Forums

At the end of the four weeks, Joanne places the seats in a circle and asks her students to talk about the books they read. Students may wish to read next a book recommended in this open discussion.

Joanne: "Tell us more about the book you read and why."
Jaci: "I thought *In the Year of the Boar and Jackie Robinson* was cute."
Emile: "Cute, cute."
Joanne: "Come on, Emile, give her a chance."
Jaci: "No, I did. My grandmother tells us stories of what it was like coming to this country from China. It was just like the book, except it wasn't so funny to my grandma."
Jessica: "I read the same book and I thought about the stories my grandparents told us, except they came from Russia. My grandmother learned to read from the words on silent pictures."
Ryan: "Wow, your grandmother must be old."
Jessica: "She died five years ago at the age of 93."

Joanne: "Do you recommend *In the Year of the Boar and Jackie Robinson*?"

Jessica: "Yes."

Joanne: "Why?"

Jaci: "Because it was funny and teaches how a family learned to live in this country."

Leroy: "Mrs. Adler, can I go to the bathroom?"

Joanne: "Take the hall pass."

Ryan: "I tried to read it and thought it was stupid."

Joanne: "What do you mean, Ryan?"

Ryan: "I don't know. It was stupid. I mean, no one lives like that or talks like that."

Joanne: "Okay, how about this. *In the Year of the Boar and Jackie Robinson* is a good book for those interested in what it was like to come to America in the 1950s. Okay?"

Jaci: "It is also a good book to learn a little about Chinese customs."

Emile: "I have a book I read. *Hatchet.* I liked it a lot. It was about this boy who crashed in the woods with only a hatchet and had to survive. It was awesome."

Joanne: "Who else read *Hatchet?* Would you recommend it?"

Bart: "Absolutely. It teaches you how to survive in the woods alone. Except the moose scene was gross."

Allisyn: "I recommend *The Witch of Blackbird Pond* by Elizabeth Speares. I thought it was a really good book that teaches how bad it is to pick on someone because they are different. Even though the main character is white, she is treated the way black people are treated. Just because they are different."

Georgia: "I agree. It was a real good book, and it taught a lot about life in the . . . in the . . . What period?"

Joanne: "The colonial period."

Kara: "I recommend another book, *House of Dies Drear*, which is about being black in America, and it is a good mystery. My grandfather used to tell me stories about the Underground Railroad where slaves were rescued. This is a good book."

Joanne: "Thanks, Kara."

This discussion continues for the rest of the class period. It is informal, friendly, and fairly unstructured. Many books are recommended and some are panned, but students get to air their ideas and opinions.

"It is a good, venting, summary activity for each section of the reading workshop," Joanne says.

Reflection: Some Final Thoughts on Joanne Adler's Reading Class

Joanne is constantly attempting to balance freedom with structure in her classes. "My ultimate goal is to provide the proper structure that will allow students the freedom they need to become both readers and writers through whole and meaningful reading and writing experiences." All of her rules, class questions, and procedures are aimed at providing the scaffolding and bridges her students need to read and write in an open way. She is a secondary teacher who creates the conditions that allow students to engage in meaning-centered language activities that are powerful personal experiences. The books she recommends embody a range of reading that she feels suits the multitude of interests and reading abilities in her class.

On the other hand, Joanne also allows her students to make their own selections from a myriad of titles in the library. Her goal is to create a classroom atmosphere similar to that of my front porch. She wants it to be an environment as natural and pleasant as possible because, for many of her students, this is the only quiet reading spot they have. At home, after work or chores, or encounters with friends, it is television time. Therefore, she feels a school must do for many of her students what homes used to do more often—provide an environment where they can practice reading, and thus, become readers.

But beyond reading, Joanne asks her students to write informally about what they read and to discuss it, either in groups or with her. She encourages reading as a springboard for other language activities because she sees all the language arts as a web and the classroom as a place where students are trained in the creative arts of reading, writing, speaking, and listening. In a sculpting class, an instructor may place his hands on a student's to help her mold the clay. Metaphorically, that is what Joanne does. As best she can, she nurtures and helps students in their creation of language.

Teacher as Researcher

Questions

- Did you read young-adult novels when you were in high school? If so, which ones made an impact on you? Which young-adult novels would you use in your classroom and how would you use them?
- How would you match kids and books? Would you structure a unit using adolescent literature differently from Joanne? If yes, how?
- What are some of the problems you encounter when students work in groups? How do you solve these problems?
- Do you like Joanne's journal questions? Why or why not?

- Would you provide your students with any questions for journal writing? Why?
- What do you think of Joanne's book talks? Explain.
- Do you feel Joanne gets her workshop just right or under-structures or overstructures it? Explain.
- Would Joanne's class be any different in an urban setting? Explain your answer.

Activities

- React to the story. Give your impressions and thoughts.
- Create other activities for a reading workshop to help students become motivated readers.
- Create a personal list of favorite young-adult novels you would use in your classroom.

Gerda Wiessmann Klein's *All But My Life* is the true story of Nazi slave-labor camps. Despite the theme of the book, it is optimistic and life affirming. American teenagers who read the book may discover their own problems in the face of Klein's struggle for life and dignity. Read the book and develop a way of placing it in a secondary curriculum. Think about using this book as part of a unit on injustice. Name other books you would use in this unit. Create meaning-centered activities for this unit.

IRA/NCTE Standards for English Language Arts with Performance Benchmarks for Chapter 3

Standard One

Students read a wide range of print and nonprint texts to build an understanding of texts, of themselves, and of the cultures of the United States and the world; to acquire new information; to respond to the needs and demands of society and the workplace, and for personal fulfillment. Among these texts are fiction and non-fiction, classic, and contemporary works.

Performance Benchmark to Standard One

Students read a wide range of print in class workshops.

Standard Three

Students apply a wide range of strategies to comprehend, in-terpret, evaluate, and appreciate texts. They draw on their prior experience, their interactions with other readers and writers, their knowledge of word meaning and of other texts, their word identification strategies, and their understanding of textual features (e.g., sound-letter correspondence, sentence structure, context graphics).

Performance Benchmark to Standard Three

Students are given workshop tools to build bridges to the texts. These tools include methods for helping students start a text and continue the reading through completion.

Students use a variety of technological and informational resources (e.g., libraries, databases, computer networks, video) to gather and synthesize information and to create and communicate knowledge.

Standard Nine

Students develop an understanding of and respect for diversity in language use, patterns, and dialects across cultures, ethnic groups, geographic regions, and social roles.

Performance Benchmark for Standard Nine

Students read and discuss books with characters from diverse backgrounds.

Recommended Readings

Finding Young-Adult Novels—Where to Look

Browse libraries and bookstores

Look for reviews in *ALAN Review*; *English Journal*; *Journal of Reading*; *Language Arts*; *Publishers Weekly*.

Annotated Book Lists Published by the National Council of Teachers of English

Your reading: A booklist for junior high and middle school students. Urbana, IL.

Books for you: A booklist for senior high students. Urbana, IL.

Books about Young-Adult Novels

Donelson, K. L., & Nilsen, A. P. (2001). *Literature for today's young adults.* New York: Addison Wesley Longman.

Donelson and Nilsen provide a comprehensive view of young-adult literature. This is a helpful companion to anyone interested in this literary area.

Gallo, D. R. (Comp./Ed.). (1990). *Speaking for ourselves: Autobiographical sketches by notable authors of books for young adults.* Urbana, IL: National Council of Teachers of English.

The title describes this book. These sketches provide insight into authors and their works.

Hipple, T. (Ed.). (1997). *Writers for young adults.* New York: Charles Scribner and Sons.

This series includes comprehensive biographies of many young-adult authors.

Kaywell, J. F. (Ed.). (2000) *Adolescent literature as a complement to the classics, Volume 4.* Norwood, MA: Christopher-Gordon.

This book creates a strong bridge between new young-adult literature and classic literature. Often these bridges are thematic. This is a very strong approach to the old and the new.

Lukens, R., & Cline, R. (1995). *Critical handbook of literature for young adults.* New York: Addison Wesley Longman.

This book describes how to make decisions about what young-adult literature to use in classrooms.

Monseau, V., & Salvner, G. (Eds.). (2000). *Reading their world: The young adult novel in the classroom* (2nd ed.). Portsmouth, NH: Heinemann.

This second edition is a collection of useful essays on incorporating young-adult literature into the high school classroom. This book is helpful particularly for teachers who want ideas on how to use young-adult literature.

Stover, L. (1996). *Young adult literature: The heart of the middle school curriculum.* Portsmouth, NH: Heinemann.

A transdisciplinary view of how young-adult literature can be used in the middle school. This is an excellent resource for middle school teachers.

Censorship Problems

DelFattore, J. (1992). *What Johnny shouldn't read: Textbook censorship in America.* New Haven, CT: Yale University Press.

DelFattore provides a sad account of the increasing problem all kinds of school texts now face. This is the story of a nation more fearful than ever of ideas and diversity.

Hit list: Frequently challenged books for young adults. (1996). Washington, DC: American Library Association.

This is not only a list of challenged books, but also a compendium of strategies and responses for beleaguered teachers and librarians.

Simmons, J. A. (1994). *Censorship: A threat to reading, learning, thinking.* Newark, DE: International Reading Association.

This book deals with the impact censorship has on the classroom. Simmons offers practical suggestions on how to protect yourself from censorship.

A Selected List of Multicultural Young-Adult Books

African-American Literature

Angelou, M. (1974). *Gather together in my name.* New York: Random House.

Bonham, F. (1965). *Durango street.* New York: Dutton.

Curtis, C. P. (1999). *Bud, not Buddy.* New York: Delacorte.

Curtis, C. P. (1995). *The Watsons go to Birmingham—1963.* New York: Delacorte.

Draper, S. M. (1994). *Tears of a tiger.* New York: Simon & Schuster/Atheneum.

Feelings, T. (1995). *The middle passage: White ships/black cargo.* New York: Dial Books.

Fitzhugh, L. (1974). *Nobody's family is going to change.* New York: Farrar, Strauss and Giroux.

Fox, P. (1973). *The slave dancer.* New York: Bradbury Press.

Gordon, S. (1987). *Waiting for the rain.* New York: Bantam.

Guy, R. (1979). *The disappearance.* New York: Delacorte Press.

Hamilton, V. (1990). *Cousins.* New York: Philomel Books.

Johnson, A. (1993). *Toning the sweep.* New York: Orchard Books.

Laure, J., & Laute, E. (1980). *South Africa: Coming of age under apartheid.* New York: Farrar, Strauss and Giroux.

Lester, J. (1968). *To be a slave.* New York: Dial Press.

McKissack, P., & McKissack, F. (1996). *Rebels against slavery: American slave revolts.* New York: Scholastic.

Moore, E. (1990). *Whose side are you on?* New York: Farrar, Strauss, and Giroux.

Myers, W. D. (1990). *Crystal.* New York: Dell.

O'Dell, S. (1960). *My name is not Angelica.* Boston: Houghton Mifflin.

Sebestyen, O. (1979). *Words by heart.* Boston: Little, Brown.

Taylor, M. (1990). *Mississippi bridge.* New York: Dial Books for Young Readers.

Wagner, J. (1969). *J. T.* New York: Van Nostrand Reinhold Co.

Williams Garcia, R. (1988). *Blue tights.* New York: Lodestar Books.

Woodson, J. (1991). *Dear one.* New York: Delacorte Press.

Asian-American Literature

Bell, W. (1990). *Forbidden city: A novel of modern China.* New York: Bantam Books.

Betancourt, J. (1991). *More than meets the eye.* New York: Bantam Books.

Ho, M. (1991). *The clay marble.* New York: Farrar, Strauss and Giroux.

Houston, J. W., & Houston, J. D. (1974). *Farewell to Manzanar.* New York: Bantam Books.

Levine, E. (1995). *A fence away from freedom: Japanese Americans and World War II.* New York: G. P. Putnam's.

Lewis, E. F. (1960). *Young Fu of the upper Yangtze.* New York: Holt, Rinehart and Winston.

Miklowitz, G. D. (1986). *The war between the classes.* New York: Dell.

Nelson, T. (1989). *And one for all.* New York: Orchard Books.

Neuberger, A. E. (1997). *The girl-son.* Minneapolis: Carolrhoda.

Strom, Y. (1996). *Quilted landscapes: Conversations with young immigrants.* New York: Simon & Schuster Books for Young Readers.

Tunnell, M. O., & Chilcoat, G. W. (1996). *The children of topaz: The story of Japanese-American internment camp: Based on a classroom diary.* New York: Holiday House.

Vander Els, B. (1991). *The bombers' moon.* New York: Farrar, Strauss and Giroux.

Yee, P. (1994). *Breakaway.* Toronto, Ontario: Douglas & McIntyre/Groundwood.

Yep, L. (1977). *Child of the owl.* New York: Harper & Row.

Native American Literature

Bealer, A. (1996). *Only the names remain: The Cherokees and the trail of tears.* Boston: Little, Brown.

Begay, S. (1995). *Navajo: Visions and voices across the mesa.* New York: Scholastic. (Poetry)

Benchley, N. (1972). *Only earth and sky last forever.* New York: Harper & Row.

Bierhorst, J. (1971). *In the trail of the wind: American Indian poems and ritual orations.* New York: Farrar, Strauss and Giroux.

Erdrich, L. (1984). *Love medicine.* New York: Holt, Rinehart and Winston.

Fleischman, P. (1990). *Saturnalia.* New York: Harper & Row.

George, J. C. (1994). *Julie.* New York: HarperCollins Publishers.

Hale, J. C. (1991). *The owl's song.* New York: Bantam Books.

Hobbs, W. (1989). *Bearstone.* New York: Atheneum.

Hudson, J. (1989). *Sweetgrass.* New York: Philomel Books.

Kazimiroff, T. L. (1982). *The last Algonquin.* New York: Walker.

Kroeber, T. (1964). *Ishi: Last of the tribe.* Berkeley, CA: Parnassus Press.

Lesley, C. (1990). *River song.* New York: Dell.

Lynch, C. (1995). *Slot machine.* New York: HarperCollins Publishers.

O'Dell, S. (1960). *Island of the blue dolphins.* Boston: Houghton Mifflin.

Rappaport, D. (1997). *The flight of Red Bird: The life of Zitkala-Sa.* Dial Books.

San Souci, R. D. (1981). *Song of Sedna.* Garden City, NY: Doubleday.

Sneve, V. Dancing Hawk. (selector). (1989). *Dancing teepees: Poems of American Indian youth.* Illustrated by Stephen Gammell. New York: Holiday House.

Latin American/Hispanic Literature

Carlson, L. M. (Ed.). (1994). *Cool salsa: Bilingual poems on growing up Latino in the United States.* New York: H. Holt & Co.

Castaneda, O. S. (1991). *Among the volcanoes.* New York: Dell.

Cisneros, S. (1991). *The House on Mango Street.* New York: Vintuse Books.

Cofer, J. O. (1995). *An island like you: Stories of the barrio.* New York: Orchard Books.

Merino, J. M. (1991). *The gold of dreams.* New York: Farrar, Strauss and Giroux.

Mohr, N. (1990). *Felita.* New York: Bantam Books.

Nye, N. S. (Ed.). (1995). *The tree is older than you are: A bilingual gathering of poems and stories from Mexico with paintings by Mexican artists.* New York: Simon & Schuster Books for Young Readers.

Soto, G. (1991). *A summer life.* New York: Dell.

Sullivan, C. (Ed.). (1994). *Here is my kingdom: Hispanic-American literature and art for young people.* New York: H. N. Abrams.

Trevino, E. B. (1991). *El guero: A true adventure story.* New York: Farrar, Strauss and Giroux.

Jewish-American Literature

Barrie, B. (1990). *Lone star.* New York: Delacorte.

Hautzig, E. (1968). *The endless steppe: A girl in exile.* New York: Scholastic Book Services.

Levitin, S. (1970). *Journey to America.* New York: Atheneum.

Meltzer, M. (1976). *Never to forget: The Jews of the Holocaust.* New York: Harper & Row.

Rogasky, B. (1988). *Smoke and ashes: The story of the Holocaust.* New York: Holiday House.

Yolen, J. (1991). *The devil's arithmetic.* New York: Trumpet Club.

Young Adult Titles

Fantasy

Adams, R. (1974). *Watership down.* New York: Macmillan.

Brooke, W. J. (1994). *Teller of tales.* Illustrated by Eric Beddows. New York: Harper Collins Publishers.

Cassedy, S. (1983). *Behind the attic wall.* New York: T. Y. Crowell.

Clarke, P. (1963). *The return of the twelves.* Illustrated by Bernarda Bryson. New York: Coward-McCann.

Hunter, M. (1975). *A stranger came ashore.* New York: Harper & Row.

Levine, G. C. (1997). *Ella enchanted.* New York: Harper Collins Publishers.

Lisle, J. T. (1993). *Forest.* New York: Orchard Books.

Mayne, W. (1967). *Earthfasts.* New York: Dutton.

Rowling, J. K. (1999). *Harry Potter and the chamber of secrets.* Illustrated by Mary GrandPre. New York: Scholastic/Arthur A. Levine.

Rowling, J. K. (1999). *Harry Potter and the prisoner of Azkaban.* New York: Scholastic/Arthur A. Levine.

Rowling, J. K. (2000). *Harry Potter and the Goblet of Fire.* New York: Scholastic/Arthur A. Levine.

Mystery/Supernatural

Alexander, L. (1975). *The wizard in the tree.* Kubinyi, illus. New York: Dutton.

Bellairs, J. (1983). *The curse of the blue figurine.* New York: Dial Books for Young Readers.

Bond, N. (1988). *Another shore.* New York: Margaret K. McElderry Books.

Charbonneau, E. (1988). *The ghosts of stony clove.* New York: Orchard Books.

Garfield, L. (1988). *The empty sleeve.* New York: Delacorte Press.

Hamilton, V. (1998). *Justice and her brothers.* New York: Scholastic.

Mahy, M. (1983). *The haunting.* New York: Atheneum.

Nixon, J. L. (1989). *Whispers from the dead.* New York: Delacorte Press.

Norton, A. (1974). *Lavender-green magic.* Illustrated by J. G. Brown. New York: Crowell.

Smith, S. (1993). *Wren's quest.* San Diego: J. Yolen Books.

Wright. B. R. (1983). *The dollhouse murders.* New York: Holiday House.

Historical Fiction

Hesse, K. (1997). *Out of the dust.* New York: Scholastic Press.

Kim, H. (1996). *The long season of rain.* New York: Henry Holt.

Koller, J. (1991). *Nothing to fear.* San Diego: Harcourt Brace Jovanovich.

Lyon, G. E. (1990). *Borrowed children.* New York: Bantam Books.

Myers, A. (1996). *Fire in the hills.* New York: Walker & Co.

Sacks, M. (1989). *Beyond safe boundaries.* New York: Lodestar Books.

Sailsbury, G. (1994). *Under the blood-red sun.* New York: Delacorte Press.

Skurzynski, G. (1992). *Good-bye Billy Radish.* New York: Bradbury.

Slepian, J. (1990). *Risk n' roses.* New York: Philomel Books.

Snyder, Z. K. (1994). *Cat running.* New York: Delacorte Press.

Realistic Fiction

Bauer, J. (1992). *Squashed.* New York: Delacorte Press.

Bauer, M. D. (Ed.). (1994). *Am I blue? Coming out from the silence.* New York: HarperCollins Publishers.

Brooks, M. (1994). *Traveling on into the light: And other stories.* New York: Orchard Books.

Clements, B. (1990). *Tom loves Anna loves Tom.* New York: Farrar, Strauss & Giroux.

Cormier, R. (1983). *The bumblebee flies anyway.* New York: Pantheon Books.

Johnston, J. (1993). *Hero of lesser causes.* Boston: Joy Street Books.

Kerr, M. E. (1994). *Deliver us from Evie.* New York: HarperCollins Publishers.

Myers, W. D. (1996). *Slam!* New York: Scholastic.

Philbrick, R. (1993). *Freak the mighty.* New York: Blue Sky Press.

Wilson. N. H. (1994). *The reason for Janey.* New York: Macmillan.

Wolff, V. E. (1993). *Make lemonade.* New York: Holt.

Good New Books

Bober, N. S. (1995). *Abigail Adams: Witness to a revolution.* New York: Atheneum.

Brooke, M. (1999). *The concrete wave: The history of skateboarding.* Toronto: Warwick Publishing.

Car, O. S. (1999). *Ender 's shadow.* New York: Tor.

Haddix, M. P. (1998). *Among the hidden.* New York: Simon & Schuster Books for Young Readers.

Holt, D., & Mooney, B. (1999). *Spiders in the hairdo: Modern urban legends* (collected and retold by D. Holt & B. Mooney). Little Rock, AR: August House.

Holt, K. W. (1999). *When Zachary Beaver came to town.* New York: Henry Holt.

Jordan, S. (1999). *The raging quiet.* New York: Simon & Schuster.

Kalergis, M. M. (1998). *Seen and heard: Teenagers talk about their lives.* New York: Stewart, Tabori & Chang.

McNeal, L., & McNeal, T. (1999). *Crooked.* New York: Knopf.

Menzel, P., & D'Aluisio, F. (1998). *Man eating bugs: The art and science of eating bugs.* Berkeley, CA: Ten Speed Press.

Meyer, C. (1999). *Mary, bloody Mary.* New York: Harcourt Brace.

Myers, W. D. (1999). *Monster.* New York: Harper Collins Publishers.

Namioka, L. (1999). *Ties that bind, ties that break.* New York: Delacorte Press.

Porter, C. (1999). *Imani all mine.* Boston: Houghton Mifflin.

Reynolds, D. W. (1999). *Star Wars episode I: Incredible cross sections.* New York: DK Publishing.

Scalora, S. (1999). *The fairies: Photographic evidence of the existence of another world.* New York: HarperCollins, 1999.

Sleator, W. (1999). *Rewind.* New York: Dutton Children's Books.

Sones, S. (1999). *Stop pretending: What happened when my big sister went crazy.* New York: HarperCollins.

Zindel, P. (1999). *Rats.* New York: Hyperion.

Short Story Collections

Alcock, V. (1987). *Ghostly companions: A feast of chilling tales.* New York: Delacorte Press.

Asher, S. (Ed.). (1996). *But that's another story: Famous authors introduce popular genres.* New York: Walker & Co.

Brooks, M. (1990). *Paradise café and other stories.* New York: Little, Brown.

Carlson, L. M., & Ventura, C. (Eds.). (1994). *American eyes: New Asian American short stories for young adults.* New York: Henry Holt.

Fleischman, P. (1997). *Seedfolks.* New York: HarperCollins Publishers.

Kimenez, F. (1999). *The circuit: Stories from the life of a migrant child.* Boston: Houghton Mifflin Company.

Soto, G. (1990). *Baseball in April, and other stories.* San Diego: Harcourt Brace Jovanovich.

Thomas, J. C. (Ed.). (1990). *A gathering of flowers: Stories about being young in America.* New York: Harper & Row.

Thomas, R. (1997). *Doing time: Notes from the undergrad.* New York: Simon & Schuster Books for Young Readers.

Zolotow, C. (Ed.). (1986). *Early sorrow: Ten stories of youth.* New York: Harper & Row.

True Stories

Brandenburg, J. (1995). *To the top of the world: Adventures with arctic wolves.* J. B. Guernsey, ed. New York: Walker and Co.

Bitton-Jackson, L. (1997). *I have lived a thousand years: Growing up in the Holocaust.* New York: Simon & Schuster Books for Young Readers.

Filipovic, Z. (1995). *Zlata's diary: A child's life in Sarajevo.* New York: Penguin Books.

Klausner, J. (1993). *Sequoyah's gift: A portrait of the Cherokee leader.* New York: HarperCollins Publishers.

Kraft, B. H. (1995). *Mother Jones: One woman's fight for labor.* New York: Clarion Books.

Levine, E. (1995). *Anna Pavlova: Genius of the dance.* New York: Scholastic.

Lyons, M. E. (1996). *Letters from a slave girl: The story of Harriet Jacobs.* New York: Aladdin Paperbacks.

Meltzer, M. (1992). *The amazing potato: A story in which the Incas, conquistadors, Marie Antoinette, Thomas Jefferson, wars, famines, immigrants, and french fries all play a part.* New York: HarperCollins Publishers.

Ventura, P. (1984). *Great painters.* G. Culverwell, trans. New York: Putnam.

Welton, J. (1994). *Drawing: A young artist's guide.* London: Dorling Kindersley.

Wilson, L. L. (1997). *The Salem witch trials.* Minneapolis: Lerner Publishing.

Traditional Literature

Asimov, I. (1969). *Words from the myths.* Illustrated by W. Barss. New York: New American Library.

Dixon, A. (reteller). (1994). *The sleeping lady.* Illustrated by E. Johns. Anchorage: Alaska Northwest Books.

Farmer, P. (1979). *Beginnings: Creation myths of the world.* Illustrated by A. Frasconi. New York: Atheneum.

Galloway, P. (1995). *Truly grim tales.* New York: Delacorte Press.

Hastings, S. (1981). *Sir Gawain and the green knight.* Illustrated by J. Wijngaard. New York: Lothrop, Lee & Shephard Books.

McKinley, R. (1978). *Beauty: A retelling of the story of beauty and the beast.* New York: Harper & Row.

Napoli, D. J. (1996). *Zel.* New York: Dutton Children's Books.

Pyle, H. (1984). *The story of King Arthur and his knights.* New York: Scribner.

San Souci, R. D. (1993). *Cut from the same cloth: American women of myth, legend, and tall tales.* Illustrated by B. Pinkney. New York: Philomel Books.

Sutcliff, R. (1996). *The wanderings of Odysseus: The story of the odyssey.* Illustrated by A. Lee. New York: Delacorte Press.

A Selected List of Young Adult Books

Aiken, J. (1981). *Black hearts in Battersea.* Garden City, NY: Doubleday.

Ames, M. (1981). *Ann to the infinite power.* New York: Scribner.

Avi. (1984). *The fighting ground.* New York: HarperCollins.

Bach, A. (1982). *Waiting for Johnny Miracle.* New York: Bantam Books.

Blos, J. (1979). *A gathering of days.* New York: Scribner.

Blume, J. (1982). *Tiger eyes.* New York: Dell.

Brancato, R. (1978). *Blinded by the light.* New York: Knopf.

Bridgers, S. E. (1987). *Permanent connections.* New York: Harper and Row.

Childress, A. (1974). *A hero ain't nothin' but a sandwich.* New York: Avon.

Cleaver, V., & Cleaver, B. (1979). *A little destiny.* New York: Lothrop, Lee and Shephard Books.

Cormier, R. (1975). *The chocolate war.* New York: Dell Publishing.

Craven, M. (1973). *I heard the owl call my name.* New York: Dell Publishing.

Crutcher, C. (1989). *Chinese handcuffs.* New York: Greenwillow Books.

Danziger, P. (1974). *The cat ate my gymsuit.* New York: Dell Publishing.

Donovan, J. (1971). *Wild in the world.* New York: Harper and Row.

Duncan, L. (1978). *Killing Mr. Griffin.* Boston: Little, Brown.

Fast, H. (1983). *April morning.* New York: Bantam Books.

Fox, P. (1984). *One-eyed cat.* Scarsdale, NY: Bradbury Press.

Greene, B. (1973). *Summer of my German soldier.* New York: Dial Press.

Hamilton, V. (1982). *Sweet whispers, brother rush.* New York: Philomel Books.

Hinton, S. E. (1980). *Tex.* New York: Delacorte Press.

Holland, I. (1983). *After the first love.* New York: Fawcett.

Hunt, I. (1966). *Up a road slowly.* Chicago: Follett Publishing.

Kerr, M. E. (1986). *Night kites.* New York: Harper and Row.

Klein, G. (1957). *All but my life.* New York: Hilland Wang.

L'Engle, M. (1962). *A wrinkle in time.* New York: Ariel Books.

Lipsyte, R. (1967). *The contender.* New York: Harper and Row.

Mazer, N. F. (1987). *After the rain.* New York: William Morrow.

McNair, J. (1989). *Commander coatrack returns.* Boston: Houghton Mifflin.

Neufeld, J. (1969). *Lisa, bright and dark.* New York: S. G. Phillips.

O'Dell, S. (1967). *The black pearl.* Boston: Houghton Mifflin.

Paterson, K. (1980). *Jacob have I loved.* New York: Crowell.

Paulsen, G. (1980). *Hatchet.* New York: Bradbury Press.

Peck, R. (1989). *Representing super doll.* New York: Dell.

Peck, R. N. (1972). *A day no pigs would die.* New York: Dell.

Platt, K. (1983). *The ape inside me.* New York: Bantam Books.

Rawlings, M. K. (1938). *The yearling.* New York: Scribner's Sons.

Richter, C. (1977). *Light in the forest.* New York: Knopf.

Rylant, C. (1986). *A fine white dust.* Scarsdale, NY: Bradbury Press.

Sachar, L. (1998). *Holes.* New York: Farrar, Strauss & Giroux.

Scoppettone, S. (1978). *Happy endings are all alike.* New York: HarperCollins.

Sebestyen, O. (1989). *Girl in the box.* New York: Bantam Books.

Shoup, B. (1997). *Stranded in harmony.* New York: Hyperion Books for Children.

Sleaton, W. (1984). *Interstellar pig.* New York: Dutton.

Speare, E. (1958). *The witch of blackbird pond.* Boston: Houghton Mifflin.

Taylor, M. D. (1976). *Roll of thunder, hear my cry.* New York: Bantam Books.

Taylor, T. (1969). *The cay.* New York: Avon Books.

Voigt, C. (1983). *Homecoming.* New York: Fawcett Juniper Books.

Yep, L. (1991). *The star fisher.* New York: Puffin Books.

Zindel, P. (1968). *The pigman.* New York: Bantam Books.

List of Newbery Honor and Medal Books

2000	Chistopher Paul Curtis, *Bud, Not Buddy*
1999	Louis Sachar, *Holes*
1998	Karen Hess, *Out of the Dust*
1997	E. L. Konigsburg, *The View from Saturday*
1996	Karen Cushman, *The Midwife's Apprentice*
1995	Sharon Creech, *Walk Two Moons*
1994	Lois Lowry, *The Giver*
1993	Cynthia Rylant, *Missing May*

1992   Phyllis Reynolds Naylor, *Shiloh*

1991   Jerry Spinelli, *Maniac Magee*

1990   Lois Lowry, *Number the Stars*

1989   Paul Fleischman, *Joyful Noise: Poems for Two Voices*

1988   Russell Freedman, *Lincoln: A Photobiography*

1987   Sid Fleischman, *The Whipping Boy*

1986   Patricia MacLachlan, *Sarah, Plain and Tall*

1985   Robin McKinley, *The Hero and the Crown*

1984   Beverly Cleary, *Dear Mr. Henshaw*

1983   Cynthia Voigt, *Dicey's Song*

1982   Nancy Willard, *A Visit to William Blake's Inn: Poems for Innocent and Experienced Travelers*

1981   Katherine Paterson, *Jacob Have I Loved*

1980   Joan Blos, *A Gathering of Days: A New England Girl's Journal, 1830–32*

1979   Ellen Raskin, *The Westing Game*

1978   Katherine Paterson, *Bridge to Terabithia*

1977   Mildred D. Taylor, *Roll of Thunder, Hear My Cry*

1976   Susan Cooper, *The Grey King*

1975   Virginia Hamilton, *M. C. Higgins, the Great*

1974   Paula Fox, *The Slave Dancer*

1973   Jean Craighead George, *Julie of the Wolves*

1972   Robert C. O'Brien, *Mrs. Frisby and the Rats of NIMH*

1971   Betsy Byars, *The Summer of the Swans*

1970   William H. Armstrong, *Sounder*

1969   Lloyd Alexander, *The High King*

1968   E. L. Konigsburg, *From the Mixed-Up Files of Mrs. Basil E. Frankweiler*

1967   Irene Hunt, *Up a Road Slowly*

1966   Elizabeth Borton de Trevino, *I, Juan de Pareja*

1965   Maia Vojciechowska, *Shadow of a Bull*

1964   Emily C. Neville, *It's Like This, Cat*

1963   Madeleine L'Engle, *A Wrinkle in Time*

1962   Elizabeth George Speare, *The Bronze Bow*

1961   Scott O'Dell, *Island of the Blue Dolphins*

1960   John Krumbold, *Onion John*

1959   Elizabeth George Speare, *The Witch of Blackbird Pond*

1958   Harold V. Keith, *Rifles for Watie*

1957   Virginia Sorensen, *Miracles on Maple Hill*

1956   Jean Lee Latham, *Carry On, Mr. Bowditch*

1955   Meindert DeJong, *The Wheel on the School*

1954   John Krumgold, . . . *And Now Miguel*

1953   Ann Nolan Clark, *Secret of the Andes*

1952   Eleanor Estes, *Ginger Pye*

1951   Elizabeth Yates, *Amos Fortune, Free Man*

1950   Marguerite de Angeli, *The Door in the Wall*

1949   Marguerite Henry, *King of the Wind*

1948   William Pene du Bois, *The Twenty-One Balloons*

1947   Carolyn S. Bailey, *Miss Hickory*

1946   Lois Lenski, *Strawberry Girl*

1945   Robert Lawson, *Rabbit Hill*

1944   Esther Forbes, *Johnny Tremain*

1943   Elizabeth Janet Gray, *Adam of the Road*

1942   Walter D. Edmonds, *The Matchlock Gun*

1941   Armstrong Sperry, *Call it Courage*

1940   James Daugherty, *Daniel Boone*

1939   Elizabeth Enrich, *Thimble Summer*

1938   Kate Seredy, *The White Stag*

1937   Ruth Sawyer, *Roller Skates*

1936   Carol Ryrie Brink, *Caddie Woodlawn*

1935   Monica Shannon, *Dobry*

1934   Cornelia Meigs, *Invincible Louisa: The Story of the Author of Little Women*

1933   Elizabeth Lewis, *Young Fu of the Upper Yangtze*

1932   Laura Adams Armer, *Waterless Mountain*

1931   Elizabeth Coatsworth, *The Cat Who Went to Heaven*

1930   Rachel Field, *Hitty, Her First Hundred Years*

1929   Eric P. Kelly, *The Trumpeter of Krakow: A Tale of the Fifteenth Century*

1928   Dhan Mjkerji, *Gay-Neck, the Story of a Pigeon*

1927   Will James, *Smoky, the Cow Horse*

1926   Arthur Chrisman, *Shen of the Sea*

1925   Charles Finger, *Tales from Silver Lands*

1924   Charles Hawes, *The Dark Frigate*

1923   Hugh Lofting, *The Voyages of Dr. Dolittle*

1922   Hendrik Van Loon, *the Story of Mankind*

The Coretta Scott King Award

2000   Christopher Paul Curtis, *Bud, Not Buddy*

1999   Angela Johnson, *Heaven*

1998   Sharon M. Draper, *Forged by Fire*

1997   Walter Dean Myers, *Slam!*

1996   Virginia Hamilton, *Her Stories*

1995   Patricia and Frederick McKissack, *Christmas in the Big House, Christmas in the Quarters*

1994   Angela Johnson, *Toning the Sweep*

1993   Patricia McKissack, *The Dark-Thirty: Southern Tales of the Supernatural*

1992   Walter Dean Myers, *Now Is Your Time! The African-American Struggle for Freedom*

1991   Mildred D. Taylor, *The Road to Memphis*

1990   Patricia and Frederick McKissack, *A Long Hard Journey: The Story of the Pullman Porter*

1989   Walter Dean Myers, *Fallen Angels*

1988   Mildred D. Taylor, *The Friendship*

1987   Mildred Pitts Walter, *Justin and the Best Biscuits in the World*

1986   Virginia Hamilton, *The People Could Fly: American Black Folktales*

1985   Walter Dean Myers, *Motown and Didi*

1984   Lucille Clifton, *Everett Anderson's Goodbye*

1983   Virginia Hamilton, *Sweet Whispers, Brother Rush*

1982   Mildred D. Taylor, *Let the Circle Be Unbroken*

1981   Sidney Poitier, *This Life*

1980   Walter Dean Myers, *The Young Landlords*

1979   Ossie Davis, *Escape to Freedom: A Play about Young Frederick Douglass*

1978   Eloise Greenfield, *African Dream*

1977   James Haskins, *The Story of Stevie Wonder*

1976   Pearl Bailey, *Duey's Tale*

1975   Dorothy Robinson, *The Legend of Africania*

1974   Sharon Bell Mathis, *Ray Charles*

1973   Jackie Robinson, *I Never Had It Made: The Autobiography of Jackie Robinson*

1972   Elton C. Fax, *Seventeen Black Artists*

Discussing Books

Introduction

Class discussions that go well, really well, are about as satisfying an activity as any I know as a teacher. When discussing *The Pigman*, I have had students talk deeply and honestly about their relationships with the elderly, both relatives and nonrelatives. In *Bridge to Terabithia* discussions, I have witnessed students confess reactions to death experiences similar to what Jess goes through in the book. In my best discussions, students address students, to clarify, analyze, and expand. My best discussions move along effortlessly, so it seems, making the length of class feel like mere minutes.

The School, the Students

Calvin is a city neighborhood, yet it feels like a small town set in 1952. Main Street has a coffee shop, a lawnmower repair place, a public library, and a wonderful old used-book store. Even the prices in the shops seem reasonable, especially compared to those for the same services just two miles away in downtown.

Yet, the high school on the hill looks nothing like an old-fashioned school. The school is a large monolithic, red brick structure, surrounded by parking lots on two sides and old city neighborhoods on the other two. There are no apparent windows anyone looking at the school can see, and, in fact, there are no windows except in the administrative wing where the principal has his office.

The 1,532 students in this school are city kids and come in all sizes and varieties. But it would be wrong to assume that this racial, ethnic, and socioeconomic mix reflects the neighborhood for, in fact, it has always been an enclave of German-Americans who have kept it as a small pocket of convivial, monochromatic ethnicity, surrounded by a very diverse city. The school reflects the city, not the community, because of a busing program that brings students from a variety of city neighborhoods.

Teacher

The Teacher	
Bob Sanderfelt, age 42	Twenty-one years teaching experience, first ten in junior high school In city system he currently works; last eleven years teaching tenth grade at Calvin High School
Educational Background:	B.A., English Education, 1972; Certified in English and Speech (grades 7–12); MA, Secondary Education, 1989
Approach:	"I dislike classroom discussion where questions are literal, teacher-centered. The open-ended literary discussion is an ideal laboratory to stimulate and develop thinking."
Influences:	Master's course on responses to literature; read Rosenblatt and Probst in course; experienced model discussions and developed reader-response discussion techniques for project.

Much of the school's success can be attributed to its outstanding principal, a large man who is respected and liked by both staff and students. At any given time, a visitor can walk into the school and get a sense that kids are in the classroom with their teachers and that the school is working the way it is supposed to.

Introducing the Lesson

Bob's classes have a variety of activities, including a full-fledged workshop (see Chapter Eight). And his students are constantly engaged in discussions—about writing ideas, independent readings, poems, and short stories, movies and television, literacy, and learning English. Bob holds open discussions on class novel readings about three times a semester, and he enjoys these very much, even though it is difficult to select one book for an entire class.

> "I pick very carefully, based on books that I know have the depth and literary quality to sustain a whole class. I know that I will not please all my students and that I am imposing my sense of 'good' on them. But I am not asking my students to like the book. I am asking them to grapple with it, think about it, and learn from each other. So an occasional

in-common reading provides a springboard for lively discussions filled with personal readings and disagreements based on a collective literary experience. When I do a whole class reading, I empower students through the discussion, if not the selection."

Bob Sanderfelt's 27 tenth graders meander in and take their seats, which are arranged in a horseshoe shape with Bob's desk at the open end. Bob is at the door when they come in. After they sit down, many of the students take out their journals and put the finishing touches on an entry they must turn in based on their reading of *The Pigman*. After both in-class and out-of-class reading, they must convince Bob that they read this book, and they need to let Bob know how they felt about it and why. After his extensive introduction of the book, Bob gives them questions to use if they need them to stimulate their writing. Questions run from the very general such as "Do you like the book? Why?" or "Do you dislike the book? Why?" to the more specific, such as "Why do you think Mr. Pignati allows John and Lorraine to fool him?" or "What did John mean at the end by saying, 'We build our own cages'?" Bob's rules for writing journal entries are as follows:

- He would like them to be at least a page and a half.
- They need not be carefully edited; they can be informal. Bob is not going to edit or red-pencil these entries, although they should be readable.
- Students must convince Bob that they read the book and they must react to the book.

Bob will grade these entries quickly, assigning credit or no credit based on his reaction to their reading. On occasion, a student has complained to Bob that she or he has read the book but has not been given credit for it. If Bob feels the student is being truthful, he will change the grade. Every once in a while, if the journal entry is exceptionally strong, Bob will give extra credit to a student, but he does not make a big fuss over this.

"By asking my students to commit themselves in writing, I know that all of my students have had to go beyond the reading and that written statements require a thoughtfulness and reflectiveness that enhance the reading. I realize how difficult it is to make writing statements about books, so I free students from the worry of structure or grammar. All I really want my students to produce is a raw, unedited reaction.

"The reason I ask for the writing is to make sure my students have something to talk about. I know that my students have written their opinions and ideas about the book, and if asked, they will be prepared to enter in my discussion," Bob says.

These students have been well trained for this discussion and know that Bob will listen, will not allow interruptions, and will not tell them that they are wrong. They know that their opinions will be valued. Not all Bob's students contribute and not all discussions go well, but many do. When that happens, the students learn to understand the book under discussion in a very special way.

The Lesson

Discussing *The Pigman*

Bob has prepared for this discussion by thinking through the many possible questions on many possible levels. Here are some examples of questions and topics Bob has available to him:

> Describe John and Lorraine.
> Do you like Mr. Pignati?
> Is he realistic?
> Contrast both sets of parents.
> How do you feel about the teachers in this book?
> What do you think living in New York is like?
> What is John's philosophy of life?
> What does John learn at the end?
> What does Lorraine learn?
> Why does Mr. Pignati like the zoo so much?

"These questions are basically inferential and application, but I don't expect to use these," Bob explains. "I prepare them just in case I need them, and to stimulate my thinking about the book before the discussion begins. It is my experience that the discussion will travel in unexpected directions and my main job will be to direct traffic, keep the discussion going, and on occasion clarify and probe. I believe that through these open-ended discussions, my students gain new understandings of the book, are trained in disciplined thinking, and learn that one of the ultimate purposes of reading is to gain personal insights and empathy."

Bob does not, and probably could not, develop decent behavioral objectives for his lesson. But he has faith in the learning that takes place because of the intelligence and thoughtfulness of so much of the discussion. And the journals and writing assignments give him a concrete knowledge of the learning that occurs. Bob is trained and committed to reader-response techniques. "I believe in the empowering of my students through these techniques."

Bob begins the discussion with a question that he knows his students can answer because they just wrote about it:

Bob: "What did you think of the book? Did you like it?"
Bill: "No, not really. I thought Mr. Pignati was pathetic and I didn't
     understand the end. You know, the part about the baboons."
Tabitha: "I kind of liked it. I liked the way John and Lorraine wrote each
     chapter."
Jocelyn: "I felt bad for Mr. Pignati. Why did he allow John and Lorraine
     to trick him?"
Stacey: "He was lonely and wanted someone to talk to."
Tabitha: "My grandmother lives alone, and she loves it when I come to
     visit. I think it's good to make friends with an older person. It
     makes them feel better."
Dani: "Yeah. It must have made Pignati feel a lot better when the kids
     destroyed his pig collection."
Bill: "That's right. He never gets better. When Bobo, his ape, died, he
     had nothing to live for."
Bob: "Was it better that John and Lorraine made friends with him for a
     little while, or did they contribute to his death?"
[Silence. No response. Bob knew he has broken a serious rule about
     teaching. The conversation was going perfectly fine until he
     interrupted it. Oh, well. He had to crank it up again.]
Bob: "Bill, you said you didn't understand the ending. What happened
     at the end? Would you read starting with 'We had trespassed too,'
     on page 140 until the end."
Bill: "Me?"
Bob: "Yes, please."
Bill: (reading)

*We have trespassed too—been where we didn't belong, and we were being
punished for it. Mr. Pignati had paid with his life. But when he died,
something in us had died as well.*
*There was no one else to blame anymore. No Bores or Old Ladies or
Nortons, or Assassins waiting at the bridge. And there was no place to
hide—no place across any river for a boatman to take us.*
Our life would be what we made of it—nothing more, nothing less.
Baboons.
Baboons.
*They build their own cages, we could almost hear the Pigman whisper, as
he took his children with him (Zindel, 1968, pp. 148–149.)*

Dan: "What does that, 'We build our own cages' mean?"
Stephanie: "You make your own life. If you drink and drive and kill
     someone, it's your own fault."
Roberta: "So you think John killed Mr. Pignati?"

> Georgeann: "John and Lorraine gave Pignati some friendship at a very lonely point in his life. It was better for him to die a litter sooner than not to have that friendship."
>
> Don: "I wonder how Pignati feels about that?"
>
> [Some quiet laughter from the class.]
>
> Bob: "John felt he trespassed. I don't think it was good for these kids to be friends with an elderly man. It just doesn't work."
>
> [Bob has made a statement. He feels this will go over better than a question, and it does provoke a reaction.]
>
> Roberta: "I visit my grandfather all the time. He teaches me a lot and he is a lot of fun. My life is better because of him, and I know I make him happy."
>
> Johnnie: "Yeah, I agree. Our class, three years ago, visited a retirement home and brought the old people books that we wrote about ourselves. They loved it and so did we."
>
> Georgeann: "John and Lorraine didn't kill the Pigman. They had nothing to do with it. He died because he was sick and because Bobo died."

At this point, the discussion begins to bog down. Bob brings it to a rapid conclusion, pleased with the results, although as with any class, it was far from perfect.

After class, Bob told me that about six students seemed bored and listless and probably did not read the book. About six or seven read the book but chose not to participate in the discussion. "I could have called on these students for their opinion, but chose not to do that, a judgment call. In some discussions, I do ask questions of students who have not volunteered. I go on instincts and experience, basing my decision to do this more on the body language and eye contact of my students than on any other factors.

"Yet, the last time I judged from the body language of a student that she wanted to participate but was too shy to volunteer, Tina looked at me and said, "I just do not feel well enough to say anything." Bob laughs at his own miscalculation; he knows that is just the way it happens in teaching. On other days, however, the nonvolunteers give simple and pleasant responses. You never know.

Discussing *Roll of Thunder, Hear My Cry*

It was obviously just a coincidence that Bob scheduled his open discussion on *Roll of Thunder, Hear My Cry* for the day after Cincinnati burst into violence. His racially mixed class walked in tense and somber. The news was bad and it had affected them. He had no idea how the discussion would go, considering the events, but decided to proceed as planned. Bob hardly said anything except to offer a weak opening gambit: "What do you think?" His class instinctively knew he was asking about *Roll of Thunder, Hear My Cry* and issues related to the book.

Andrew: "I think a lot of black people are very angry about their treatment in this country."

[Pause. Silence.]

Tom: "We like each other in this class."

Andrea: Come on, let's face who we are. White kids and black kids sit at separate tables at lunch; white kids and black kids meet in their own halls before and after school. There's a lot of problems here."

[More pauses. Silence.]

Larry: "Aren't things getting better? I mean, isn't life easier now for black people than it used to be?"

Bob: "Mildred Taylor wrote *Roll of Thunder, Hear My Cry* based on stories her father told her about life for black families in the Mississippi of the 1930s. How was life back then compared to now?"

Lorretta: "It sure was bad back then. The school the Logans had to go to was awful with those discarded books."

Georgann: "Our books are pretty old, too. And in some of my classes, we don't have enough books to give to everyone, so we can't take them home."

Maria: "But in our school it's bad for everyone. In the schools in Mississippi back in the thirties, it was worse for black kids. The white kids got those books when they were new."

Bob: "Would Cassie's life be any different if she lived here and went to this school today?"

Ramona: "Yeah, she wouldn't have to be afraid of white people."

Susan: "She wasn't afraid of white people. Look what Cassie did to Lillian Jean."

Loretta: "Yeah, but she had to do it sneaky; nobody would know."

Ramona: "If life is so much better now for black people, why did this riot thing happen?"

Eric: "In *Roll of Thunder*, whites and blacks are treated differently. Nowadays, whites and blacks are treated the same."

Bob: "Okay, now one at a time, Phil."

Phil: "The police treat blacks a lot differently than whites."

Bob: "So we haven't made much progress in race relations since *Roll of Thunder, Hear My Cry*? How can you say that? Look at the separate school the Logans attended. Look how Cassie had to apologize to Lillian Jean. Look at how the Logans had to fear the Wallaces."

Andrea: "So now we go to school together. But black people are still not equal to white people here."

Jill: "I don't know. My grandma would tell me stories that were like *Roll of Thunder, Hear My Cry*. You know, about night riders like in the book. Now my dad is an attorney and that couldn't have happened in Cassie's time. Some things have gotten better."

Jon: "There are good whites and bad whites, even back then. Wallaces were bad. Mr. Jamison was okay."

Bob: "So where do we stand? Do you like the book?"

Jill: "I don't think it's so good to read about all that depressing stuff. Times are different and this book only causes trouble between people."

Ramona: "I liked the book. We all need to know about this kind of thing. I wish the lives of black people had gotten better."

Jon: "How do you feel about the book, Mr. Sanderfelt?"

Bob: "I like it or I wouldn't have picked it for this class. I didn't plan on having Cincinnati explode the day before we discussed this book."

Andrea: "I'm glad we had this discussion today. It was on everybody's mind."

Bob: "I hope your generation of grown-ups does a better job of living together than my generation has managed to do. Thanks class, that was an excellent discussion. Talking to each other like this, I believe, is a step in the right direction."

On Short Stories

Bob remembers a time when short stories dominated the English classroom. In some ways, the new young-adult novels have supplemented the more traditional short story. Bob is happy to say goodbye to some of the overtaught stories, such as *The Most Dangerous Game*, *The Lady and the Tiger*, and *The Lottery*. However, when Bob does use short stories, he applies the same techniques he uses with *The Pigman*—journal writing and open-ended discussion. Usually there is not as much to write or talk about with most of the conventional plot-driven short stories Bob finds in anthologies, and he prefers to use the shorter, easier young-adult novels in their place.

Reflections on Discussing Books

How Reader-Response Discussions Work

No formula or book could possibly explain all the nuances and dynamics of classroom discussions. Leading them is a true art that can be learned through practice and careful reflection. However, Bob knows that before a class can have an open-ended discussion, certain conditions must exist. He follows the conditions outlined by Robert Probst in *Response and Analysis: Teaching Literature in Junior and Senior High School* (1988):

Receptivity: Allow for open responses. Bob does not lead his class to his conclusions. He honestly believes in reader-response principles, that his kids have something worthwhile to say. His students know that their opinions count and therefore are willing to give them.

Tentativeness: Students are allowed to guess, to speculate. Bob's students know they will not be attacked because they say something that is hard to justify. Everyone is allowed his/her opinion in Bob's class.

Rigor: Students are asked to back up much of what they say with evidence from the books they are reading. Often, in Bob's class, students will ask other students where they got the idea they expressed. Texts are not ignored in Bob's class. They are the baseline for the ideas and the discussion, and when the discussion goes well, Bob's students fairly demand textual evidence for much of what is claimed.

Cooperation: Students must show a willingness to listen to each other, to be fair minded, and to cooperate. These conditions are not impossible to achieve in American classrooms but they are sometimes difficult to find. Bob trains his students to cooperate with each other. It is a slow, building process that Bob starts at the beginning of the year and takes a while to achieve. In classes where students never seem to cooperate, Bob cannot lead discussions, ever.

Suitable literature: Bob matches the right books with his students. In this case, Bob felt *The Pigman* provided the right mix of readability, themes, characters, and ideas. He knew he wasn't going to captivate all his students with any one selection, but he was hoping if he selected well, he would come close. In this case, he felt he lost about six students that he knew about and perhaps a few more that he was not aware of. But most of the class seemed to care enough about this book to respond to the discussion in some fashion. And Bob felt most of the class gained a considerable amount from it.

What did Bob's students get from the discussion? Bob feels that reader-response discussions of books are like riding bicycles—both activities involve many discrete and complex skills you do not think about while you are doing them. But Bob does believe his students achieve the following:

Intense insight into a book. The discussions help students interpret a book, particularly in relation to their own lives. Bob feels this is one of the most important reasons for reading literature, and his students become trained through discussions to relate to literary works.

Disciplined discourse. Bob sees his students trained to think in a logical and reasonable way. Community response often requires that a student modify his/her response because of the arguments of others. Or students may be asked to provide more evidence to reinforce what they have said. In both cases, disciplined thought is nurtured and trained.

Empathy. These discussions ask students to relate to characters and situations found in literature. Many students tell personal, deeply-felt stories that are thematically relevant to the book under discussion. These conditions often force students into a compassion and sensitivity that is one of the *raisons d'etre* of literary experiences and literary discussion.

A love of reading. When these discussions go well, students come away with a renewed interest in reading and books. Good reader-response discussions are characterized by an enthusiasm for books that carries over into the next readings.

Teacher as Researcher

Questions

- In classroom discussions, what kinds of questions provoke the most student response? What kinds of questions provide the least? Do students respond to students, or is all the talk teacher to students? Students to teacher? Do students get interrupted by other students or the teachers? Or are all statements completed before other questions or statements are made?
- Is it possible to hold a discussion based on several books read by the class? If yes, how?
- Was *The Pigman* discussion realistic? Explain.
- How does a teacher maintain class control during a discussion?
- Are there ever any reasons to ask literal questions about a literary work—questions such as, "What happened?" and "To whom?" Explain your answer.
- Bob hates quizzes on literary works. Do you? Explain your answer.
- Is Bob's writing assignment too unstructured to work? Explain your answer.
- What other ideas do you have for Bob in his *Roll of Thunder, Hear My Cry* discussion?
- Is it okay with you that Bob, in his writing assignment, over-looks grammar, punctuation, spelling, and even structure? Yes? No? Why?
- Can you add or subtract from Bob's list of what he feels students gain from a literacy discussion? If yes, do it.

Activities

- React to the story. Give your impressions and thoughts.
- Select a novel you would like to teach and make up a list of discussion questions. Analyze these questions. Are they literal, inferential, or application? Do you already know the

answer to these questions or are they open ended? Do you think these questions will provoke connections between the novel and your students?

Example

Literal questions—Questions asking for specific details that can be found in the book.

What did Mr. Pignati collect?
What department store did Mr. Pignati take the kids to?
From *The Pigman*

Inferential questions—Questions requiring speculation about why something happened in the book.

Why did Stacey dig the hole to wreck the school bus?
Why was Mama fired from her teaching job?
From *Roll of Thunder, Hear My Cry*

Application questions—Questions requiring the application of life experiences and personal judgments to analyze and probe the book.

Do John and Lorraine relate to Mr. Pignati the way you relate to people who are older?
From *The Pigman*

Did you like Cassie in *Roll of Thunder, Hear My Cry?*

Make up a set of "etiquette" rules for the classroom discussions. How would you enforce these rules?

IRA/NCTE Standards for English Language Arts with Performance Benchmarks for Chapter 4

Standard Three

Students apply a wide range of strategies to comprehend, interpret, evaluate, and appreciate texts. They draw on their prior experience, their interactions with other readers and writers, their knowledge of word meaning and of other texts, their word identification strategies, and their understanding of textual features (e.g., sound-letter correspondence, sentence structure, context graphics).

Performance Benchmark Standard Three

Students apply a wide range of strategies to comprehend, interpret, evaluate, and appreciate texts through carefully crafted reader-response discussions.

Standard Four

Students adjust their use of spoken, written, and visual language (e.g., conventions, style, vocabulary) to communicate effectively with a variety of audiences and for different purposes.

Performance Benchmark Standard Four

Students adjust their use of spoken language to communicate effectively through reader-response discussions.

Recommended Readings

Bleich, D. (1975). *Readings and feelings: An introduction to subjective criticism.* Urbana, IL: National Council of Teachers of English.

Bleich presents a theory similar to Rosenblatt's, but his reader-based theory is more subjective. This book is worth reading to get a feeling for a different reader-based theory.

Claggett, F., & Reid, L. (1996). *Recasting the text: Inquiry-based activities for comprehending and composing.* Portsmouth, NH: Heinemann.

This is an interesting approach to both reading and writing as students actively engage in reading by recasting texts in various forms.

Clifford, J. (Ed.). (1991). *The experience of reading: Louise Rosenblatt and Reader-Response Theory.* Portsmouth, NH: Heinemann.

The book is a collection of essays based on Rosenblatt's theories and provides a modern extension of reader-response.

Farrell, E. J., & Squires, J. R. (Eds.). (1990). *Transactions with literature: A fifty year perspective.* Urbana, IL: National Council of Teachers of English.

This collection of essays was assembled to honor the 50th anniversary of Rosenblatt's *Literature as Exploration.* This book gives a modern spin to reader-response theory.

Langer, J. A. (Ed.). (1992). *Literature instruction: A focus on student response.* Urbana, Il: National Council of Teachers of English.

The book is a collection of essays on the state of literary instruction from elementary school through college. Although the essays are comprehensive, the primary focus is on response-based teaching.

Probst, R. (1988). *Response and analysis: Teaching literature in junior and senior high school.* Portsmouth, NH: Heinemann.

Probst takes what Rosenblatt started and operationalizes it. This useful book shows how reader-response theory can be applied to classrooms. Probst's book is a classic in its own right.

Purves, A. C., Rogers, T., & Soter, A. O. (1990). *How porcupines make love II: Teaching a response-centered literature curriculum.* New York: Longman.

This book offers a wide range of approaches for applying the reader-response ideas of Louise Rosenblatt and others.

Rabinowitz, P. J., & Smith, M. W. (1998). *Authorizing readers: Resistance and respect in the teaching of literature.* Urbana, IL: National Council of Teachers of English.

Although this book seems at odds with reader-response theory, as the authors wisely claim, it really doesn't have to be. The intent here is to provide readers with the necessary understanding of the context of the book, particularly the authorial context. This contextualization seems very important for historically embedded narratives such as *Huckleberry Finn* and *To Kill a Mockingbird*. It seems to be impossible to read *To Kill a Mockingbird* with understanding without knowledge of conditions of apartheid in American in the 1930s.

Rosenblatt, L. M. (1938). *Literature as exploration.* New York: The Modern Language Association.

This is the classic work in which Rosenblatt lays out her philosophy of reading. This book, over 50 years old now, helped change the landscape of literary critical theory.

Rosenblatt, L. (1978). *The reader, the text, the poem: The transactional theory of the literary work.* Carbondale, IL: Southern Illinois University Press.

Rosenblatt basically defines reader-response in this classic work. The book gives a well-rounded picture of reader-response theory.

Zirinsky, D., & Rau, S. (2001). *Classroom of teenaged readers: A nurturing reading process in senior high school.* New York: Addison Wesley Longman.

This book describes a student-centered approach to developing lifelong reading for teenagers.

Teaching Drama

Introduction

> I called it an in-school field trip, taking my ninth graders to the cavernous and empty school auditorium. I was a new teacher, and I had just about lost all hope of doing anything worthwhile with Julius Caesar. I tried everything I could think of from class readings, to text explications, to history lectures. Whatever I did with the play fell flat on my docile students. This was it—my last effort. My students were given a chance to put on the play, performing scenes for each other on a large stage in an empty auditorium.
>
> After much reticence, my students started getting into it. They were enjoying themselves, I noticed, hesitant to get too excited. Furthermore, they seemed to understand what they were doing. With some help from me, the words of Shakespeare were making sense to them. It turned out to be a great day for me, one of the first successes I had as a new teacher. I had found the power of teaching drama through performance.

The School, the Students

Friendship High School is set in the middle of a pleasant middle-class neighborhood. The building is so out of place in this community of small homes that I was taken aback by my first view of the massive red brick structure. Friendship is a large school, with 2,142 students who are very diverse economically and ethnically. This school sends more students to college than any of the other city schools in town. Yet, Friendship High has to educate a large group of students who will not go on to higher education. The racial and ethnic composition is about 40% white, 40% African American, 15% Hispanic, and 5% Asian. Friendship High is in every way a school in an urban area that reflects diversity.

Teacher

The Teacher	
Anne Jackson, age 36	Eight years of teaching experience, all in Friendship High School, where she currently teaches
Educational Background:	B.A., English Humanities, 1980; Master of Arts in Teaching (certification), 1982; certified in English
Approach:	"Shakespeare can be made meaningful if a teacher makes the play accessible and keeps the dramatic base as the center of the classroom activity."
Influences:	Courses in English and English Education during master's program. Consistent attendance at English teachers conferences.

Introducing the Lesson

Anne Jackson's classroom is as undistinguished as any other at the school. Thirty-five desks for students arranged in a large circle dominate the empty room. It may be hard for a visitor to imagine that what is about to happen in her classroom will be magical.

It began years ago, in her first classrooms, when she attempted to teach Shakespeare to ninth graders. She loved teaching *Romeo and Juliet*. She used the paperback that contained both *Romeo and Juliet* and *West Side Story*, and she had the fine Zeffirelli film as a resource. For Anne, the best moments of this activity occurred when her students read the play aloud at their seats. Most English teachers can testify to the success of oral play reading. When all else fails, this is an activity that works.

Throughout the years, Anne had taught various plays, including many of the traditional-school Shakespearean selections such as *Macbeth* and *Julius Caesar*, and she had taught them in a fairly traditional manner—out-of-class readings, comprehension discussions, and quizzes. But in her heart, she always felt that performance-based teaching of Shakespeare was the clue to bringing the work to life, making the plays meaningful to students.

And then Anne attended a National Council of Teachers of English conference in Pittsburgh where a theater troupe performed a one-act Pinter play and held a discussion about the teaching of drama. "Why don't English teachers treat plays as they were intended, by creating classroom performances?"

an actor mused. "I thought this was very accurate," she says, "and from that moment, I was determined to develop a classroom-based performance of a Shakespearean play."

Anne has been doing this for years now, and past plays she has done include *The Tempest* and *As You Like It*. Now her students work with *A Midsummer Night's Dream*. Anne assembles a classroom set of the plays from various sources including the local Goodwill store, where she manages to purchase several tattered paperback copies for a quarter each. Somehow, she gathers enough copies for all of her students. The editions are different, the page numbers do not match, the notes range from helpful to none, but the words are the same. Anne feels purists who insist on the finest editions would have a tough time making it in a public school.

The Lesson

Beginning the Play

Anne's 12th-grade class starts filling the chairs in the circle. Twenty-eight of these young people filter in, not quite knowing what to expect. From a tape deck in the corner of the room comes the soft sounds of what students consider classical music. When the bell rings, Anne asks them to listen quietly for a bit and promises that soon they will recognize the music. In a short time, the familiar strains of Mendelssohn's *Wedding March*, one of the most recognizable melodies in the world, fills the classroom. Anne turns down the volume and begins.

> What you just listened to was Felix Mendelssohn's *Incidental Music to A Midsummer Night's Dream*, which is based on a play by William Shakespeare. Did you notice the mood of the music? Lighthearted, happy, magical. This is very much in the spirit of the play.
>
> Notice the music ends with the famous wedding march. Well, this play builds to a wedding, a wedding night anyway. Actually a wedding party. The wedding itself is done off stage before the last scene.
>
> You, as a class, are going to change to an acting company, and your task for the next four weeks is to prepare and put on, for each other, selected scenes from William Shakespeare's *A Midsummer Night's Dream*.
>
> [At this point, the students gasp collectively.]
>
> Your most important job is to create the atmosphere of this play as Mendelssohn's music indicates. This play is a party, a Mardi Gras, a carnival. This play has MAGIC! And it has lovers who are in love with the wrong people. And wedding receptions with entertainment. And much music.

[Anne pauses for a moment, looks around at the somewhat stunned faces.]

Our final step is to understand the simplest level of this play, the plot. It is important that we know what happens before we ever begin reading the play.

Anne then hands out a simple plot outline that she has prepared as a springboard for her embellishing storytelling (Figure 5.1).

While Anne and her students go over this outline together, Anne tells the story of the play in much greater detail and with obvious enthusiasm. She is a master at motivation. Her eye contact and intonation are remarkable. Almost every student in class comes under her spell when she speaks. But Anne's most outstanding ability is to make a meaningful story for her students from *A Midsummer Night's Dream*. She tells them about a stiff and unyielding father who forces his daughter, Hermia, to flee with her lover rather than marry the man her father favors. Anne tells her students about the strange occurrences in the woods, the magic of Oberon, and the baseness of the actors rehearsing the wedding play. Anne finishes by discussing the wedding parties she has seen and then asks her students about weddings they have attended.

Tina: "When my mom got remarried we had a tiny reception back at the house. It hardly felt like a wedding."

Rosalie: "I went to San Jose last summer to see my cousin get married. We had a blast. We danced until 2 a.m. After the reception we went to the hotel where we partied until dawn."

Ralph: "I had a friend whose sister got cold feet at the last minute. So there was no wedding, but it was too late to call off the party, so they held it anyway."

Anne: "Wow. Let me tell you about the wedding party they have at the end of *A Midsummer Night's Dream*."

She describes the wild play within the play. She ends with a reading of the epilogue of the play, explaining as she goes along.

Anne believes the introduction of this project is crucial. It is here that she attempts to build enthusiasm for the play and a basic understanding of the story. Often Anne will use students to come to the front of the classroom and represent a character. This helps bring the story to life. Yet, this is a very hard part of teaching for Anne because her enthusiasm for the play runs counter to the feelings of many of her students, who are wary of the whole idea. Although they like and trust Anne, they know she does some strange classroom activities. However, they also know how much last year's seniors loved this project so they are willing to give her a chance.

A MIDSUMMER NIGHT'S DREAM
by William Shakespeare

PRINCIPAL CHARACTERS:

Theseus, Duke of Athens
Hippolyta, Queen of the Amazons
Lysander, in love with Hermia
Demetrius, in love with Hermia
Hermia, in love with Lysander
Helena, in love with Demetrius
Oberon, king of the fairies
Titania, queen of the fairies
Puck, fairy page to Oberon
Starveling, Snout, Bottom, Quince, Flute

1. Act I
   A. Theseus and Hippolyta plan their wedding.
   B. Hermia must marry Demetrius although she loves Lysander.
   C. Helena is in love with Demetrius, although he loves Hermia.
   D. Hermia and Lysander plan to flee Athens and marry.
   E. Demetrius and Helena plan to follow Lysander and Hermia into the woods.
   F. The Rural Mechanics plan their play for the royal wedding.

2. Act II
   A. Titania and Oberon fight over custody of small Indian boy.
   B. Puck unknowingly anoints the wrong Athenian's eyes with a love potion; Lysander falls in love with Helena.
   C. Titania's eyes are anointed with love potion.

3. Act III
   A. The Rural Mechanics rehearse their play; Puck changes Bottom's head to an ass's head; Titania falls in love with Bottom.
   B. Demetrius' eyes are anointed and he falls in love with Helena. Thus, both Lysander and Demetrius love Helena instead of Hermia.

figure ◦ **5.1**	**(Continued)**

---

4. Act IV
   A. The love charms are removed (except for Demetrius) and the couples are properly paired.
   B. The lovers think that all that has happened has been a dream.

5. Act V
   A. The three couples are married; Theseus and Hippolyta, and Hermia and Lysander, and Helena and Demetrius.
   B. The Athenian Workingmen perform their play, *Pyramus and Thisby*.

On the other hand, Anne knows that although this probably will be a very successful activity, it is a difficult process that will frustrate some of her students. She wonders how much longer she will have the energy to pull this off.

Making the Assignments

The introduction takes two class periods. The next day the real work begins. Anne explains the specifics of the project to her class:

> "You will act out selected scenes from *A Midsummer Night's Dream*. Each of you will be asked to select three parts you may wish to play. You will select these parts after we have done a class reading of the scenes we will be acting out.
>
> "I will attempt to give you your choice of character. I will group you according to scene. Therefore, we may have one Hermia in act I and another in act II."

Writing Assignments

Then Anne describes the writing she will ask her students to do for this project.

- Journal writing: Keep actress/actor journals that include ideas about your characters, problems with acting, problems with language, solutions to language problems, costume ideas, set and scenery concepts, ideas for other performers, general thoughts and feelings. The journal will be graded on quantity only and can be done during class time. At least 10 journal pages are required.

■ One-page description of responsibilities: Include what you did for the group, how you prepared for your part.

Classroom Reading

Anne does not have her class act out the entire play. Rather, she has selected key scenes based on their range of characters, clarity, interest level, and plot advancement. In *A Midsummer Night's Dream*, she selected the following scenes:

■ Act I, scene i establishes the plot for the entire play and is a nice contrast to the later scenes in the woods. Anne feels this scene set in the court is stiff and full of courtly intrigue; it lacks the magic and wonderment of the rest of the play, but does provide an opportunity for her students to perform a "political intrigue" scene. However, some very hard speeches in this scene require pruning and careful and selective rewriting. Often Anne uses the performers from this scene to play the small parts in act V.

■ Act I, scene ii is perfect as is. This scene has the Athenian laborers discussing the play they plan to perform for the wedding party. This scene allows for a lot of mugging and silliness on the part of the student performers, and it could take place in a tavern, which her students love. Because this is a short scene, this cast often plays the same characters in act V.

■ Act II, scenes i and ii are confusing but fun. The four lovers get totally mixed up because of magic that goes awry. Everybody is in love with the wrong person, and the Shakespearean love cursing is clever and actable. Puck provides a slightly bizarre twist to the scenes. The relationships among the characters provide a great deal of spirit young performers can relate to.

■ Act II, scene i is the famous scene in which Bottom gets a donkey's head. There is much actable magic in this scene, and the Athenian laborers are great for student performers.

■ Act III, scene ii is important to do because it straightens out much of the plot.

■ Act V, scene i, which is all of act V, ends the production.

This last act is a complicated one, and maybe some of the writing needs pruning, but it is a fulfillment of this entire project. This is the act with the play within the play that the Athenian laborers perform (*Pyramis and Thisby*, a slapstick version of *Romeo and Juliet*). The play, performed for the wedding party, is a comedic tour de force. No amount of student overacting can kill this, and it is a hilarious conclusion to A *Midsummer Night's Dream*. Of course, Oberon, Titania, and Puck get the last words, ending the play on a magical note with some absolutely beautiful Shakespearean poetry. This act requires careful staging and close supervision because it is complicated, but it is a great way to close the student production.

Anne may take out a scene or two if she feels it is too much for the class to handle, but she carefully selected the scenes that, for her, provide the real heart of the play. Also, she allows some of her very shy students to have large costume and scenery responsibilities and perform minor characters.

Anne and all her students read these scenes as a class. During the reading she stops to clarify the meanings of the lines, which, on occasion, are impossible. But in general, the play is very readable for her students, who pay fairly close attention to this initial reading because they know they soon must select characters to portray. Here Anne and her students make some initial decisions about what lines to cut. For instance, despite the beauty of the poetry, the class is in agreement about pruning much of the beginning of act II, scene i because of the difficulty and length of the lines.

Rehearsing the Play

The classroom reading takes about three class periods to complete. When the reading is over, Anne asks her students to give her, in writing, the names of three characters that they would like to perform. While they are making their choices, she circulates among them, calming their fears, helping them make their choices, promising small parts to her students who are petrified about acting in public. Many of her students are very enthusiastic about this project and want the largest parts possible. Some do not care and are willing to accept whatever Anne decides.

Her casting decisions are very important because her students are going to work in groups, based on scenes. Each group will require at least one strong and cooperative student to keep the work together. Anne knows that she will be a major part of some of these groups, but she also knows she can depend on other groups to be self-sufficient. Also, Anne knows that the difficult language and fear of performing will cause frustration, and she will have a strong involvement in helping many of her students overcome these handicaps. Because the first scene is the most difficult, she has placed some of her strongest students here.

After she has made her decisions, Anne announces the cast and gives the following rules and regulations and rehearsal schedule:

- Cast members must act responsibly and prepare adequately.

- Language cuts and changes may be made when necessary but must be approved by the teacher.

- Performers must attempt to memorize their parts, but scripts may be transferred onto note cards and may be held as memory aids during the performance.

■ Each group may decide on costumes and sets, which must be approved by the teacher.

The rehearsal schedule is as follows:

■ Read the scene through.

■ Discuss the scene and agree on an acting concept; decide where most of the language problems may occur; get some tentative ideas for costumes and scenery.

■ Read through and make any necessary language changes. See me first.

■ Act out the scene with the language changes.

■ Block and act out. Remember to face front when you are speaking and to not block other performers.

■ Rehearse. Finalize costumes and scenery.

■ Rehearse.

■ Dress rehearsal. Have lines memorized or know them very well.

■ Performance.

Anne keeps these nine rehearsal steps on the board and has the groups sign off as they complete each of them.

When she is done explaining the rules, she lets her students begin. Now her students own her class. The success of this project will depend on them. Giving up control of a class is a hard step for a teacher, and Anne gets a little nervous at this point every year.

On the first day of rehearsal, she stays out of the groups but watches closely as they read the play. She is allowing her students time to adapt to each other, and she is sensing any difficulty that may be arising. This year, she notices the difficulty those in act I, scene i are having reading the lines. Anne will become a part of this group tomorrow and help them prune and revise so they can control this act. She also notices less-than-enthusiastic looks from those in act I, scene ii (also the play-within-the-play cast in act V, scene i), where she placed some of her problems. She will deal with that group tomorrow as well.

Group Work

The length of group rehearsal time varies each year. It is a teacher's trick to adjust the amount of rehearsal time to a level where her students feel the pressure. Although the scenes vary in length and complexity, most of the rehearsal time is well spent. It is better, in Anne's opinion, to have too little time to prepare rather than have too much. Nothing creates more havoc in a classroom than kids in groups with nothing to do.

Anne sits in on act I, scene i for the first part of the second group day. This act contains a lot of long speeches. She counsels patience and goes over the speeches line for line, with this group collectively interpreting as they go along. Theseus, the Duke of Athens, is having the most trouble and the group decides to reduce a long speech to

> For you, fair Hermia . . . fit your fancies to your father's will
> Or else the law of Athens yields you up . . .
> To death, or to a vow of single life . . .
> Come.

Anne explains to this group she feels the tone is somber and deceitful. When in the court, people are stiff and unyielding. This scene is like a visit to a principal's office, Anne suggests, and it sets up a stark contrast to the magic that is ahead. Anne is desperately trying to create a mental image, a bridge between the experiences of her students and this scene that will allow for a performance based on life experience.

Anne leaves the group after helping Suzanne, who plays Helena, with the long passage that closes the scene. Helena wants to do this passage relatively unchanged, and she is willing to struggle with lines such as

> Love looks not with the eyes, but with the mind;
> And, therefore, is winged Cupid painted blind.

"You know, Suzanne," Anne offers, "love is blind. Lovers are irrational. They don't see the flaws of the objects of their love."

"Oh, yeah, I get it," Suzanne replies. "I think."

Anne and Suzanne continue to go over this speech, and Anne is confident that the student will do it and do it well.

Meanwhile, those in act I, scene ii are having a great time mugging it up in the tavern, but Anne is worried about Bob's penchant for subverting the class. She keeps her eye on him, just in case, but he seems to be enjoying his role as Snug, the joiner who will play the lion in *Pyramis and Thisby*.

Anne's act II, scene i students are having a great time. Demetrius is enjoying hurling insults and spurning the doting Helena.

> I love thee not, therefore pursue me not.
> Hence get thee gone, and follow me no more.
> I am sick when I do look on thee.
> I'll run from thee and hide me in the brakes,
> And leave thee to the mercy of wild beasts.

Anne watches in quiet amusement as this group rehearses.

So this is what Anne does during the group work. For Anne, this is the most difficult part of the activity. This is tough. Some of her students are frustrated and fearful; many of them lack confidence and have problems with the language. Anne serves as a general consultant to her students. She does all of the following during the group work:

- She helps clarify the lines and helps with the language problems.
- She provides staging and costuming suggestions, if asked.
- She creates mental bridges connecting scenes to the experiences of her students.
- She provides enthusiasm and support.
- She maintains classroom control.
- Every once in a while, she plays a bit part in a production.

This is a high-level example of collaborative learning and student-centered teaching, but Anne isn't thinking in these terms at this point. Anne sees this as potential chaos, anarchy, and extreme educational and curricular stupidity on the part of a teacher, namely her. Anne is not a happy educator at this point in the production. Also, Anne could use a student teacher to help out. In any case, Anne feels like screaming.

The Performance

Eventually her students begin to put it together. A scene takes shape; costumes appear. Anne can actually hear laughter in the classroom, and best of all, she hears Shakespeare. It is time to squeeze her students.

"Okay class, you have rehearsed for three class periods. You have two more rehearsal periods. Performances start on Monday." She hears some groans, but they seem half-hearted. The groups are teams and they are ready. Anne no longer needs to be with them. Now her students are teaching themselves Shakespeare! While each group signs off on the rehearsal schedule she has on the board, Anne reads the journals her students wrote during rehearsal breaks. The entries are getting more positive and focused. Entries have moved from "This makes no sense," "I don't understand this," to "Steve is a great Puck. He's going to do it on roller skates." Anne begins to relax. But...

But there are the performances. On the last day of rehearsal, Anne checks in with each group and makes sure everything is in working order. Some of her students have memorized the lines; some will read off of notecards. There are prompters for the memorizers. Anne limits the audience to her class and a few friends who have study halls. Although she does not invite parents to the performance, she videotapes it and offers to provide copies to students who want them.

It takes four class periods to do the entire cycle. In many ways, the first group has the hardest job. Anne believes it is the hardest scene to learn, and it is the hardest to perform because it is not funny. Anne selects comedies because mistakes can be laughed at without ruining the performances. Comedy, she believes, is more forgiving. But the first scene of act I is serious. Her students put a modern spin on it by dressing up in skirts, suits, and ties. They perform it admirably, reading most of their difficult lines from cards but appearing to understand what they are saying and acting with a certain amateur conviction. Helena has memorized her lines, and when she blurts out, "How happy some o'er other some can be! Through Athens I am thought as fair as she," the class feels her conviction. The scene ends to applause, and Anne is gratified to get past the hardest part of the performance.

The next scene is a comedic high point, with the Athenian workingmen dressed as bums. It is easy for most high schoolers to pull off, as they mimic drinking tequila and sucking on lemon and salt in a neighborhood tavern. Needless to say, this scene ends in riotous applause, which makes a nice segue to Puck's foul-ups and Demetrius' insults in the next scenes.

In act III, scene i students rap some of the song lines and do a nice job turning Bottom's head into that of an ass. Act III, scene ii is done with hillbilly accents that work fairly well with the Elizabethan poetry. Many of the lines are pruned away, particularly those of Puck and Oberon. And this group steals a part of act IV, where Oberon says: "Sound, music! Come, my queen, take hands with me; And rock the ground whereon these sleepers be." At that point, the ensemble breaks into a boisterous limbo to the resounding applause of the audience.

The play within the play in act V is hilarious. This group made only minor rewrites, but they had quite an impact on the performance. For instance, Pyramus changed "Not Shafalus to Procrus was so true," to "Not Cruise to Kidman was so true." And in his death scene, "o spite" became "o spit" and "dainty duck" became "daffy duck." It is a fitting conclusion to this project and a relaxed Puck delivers a prologue to a very satisfied audience:

> If we shadows have offended,
> Think but this, and all is mended,
> That you have but slumber'd here
> While these visions did appear.

The Debriefing

Anne will give each student a grade based on the quality of his or her contribution to the performance. It is not difficult to earn an A in this project if the student worked hard and enthusiastically. Those students who did well in the play but did not contribute as much as others receive a B. On occasion, a student will go through the motions and perform a minor part in the play grudgingly and that student may receive a C. In very rare instances, where a student harms the production, sets back a scene, contributes next to nothing, Anne may feel a D or even an F is deserved, but this seldom happens.

Anne's students are required to turn in short summaries of what they contributed to the production of the play. Anne uses these summaries as aids for grading, but also finds them interesting and a worthwhile writing assignment for her students. Here are examples from these student summaries (Figures 5.2, 5.3, 5.4).

After completing a long and successful project, the students appear at a loss. The goal of the last several weeks has been accomplished, and a small letdown settles in. But to Anne, the project is not quite over. She has some surprises in store, beginning with a ceremony she calls "The Tootsie Awards," named after the movie starring Dustin Hoffman disguised as a soap-opera matron. She figures this is appropriate considering how much Shakespearean comedies depend on misleading identities. It also allows Anne to reward each of her students with a Tootsie Roll Pop and to end the project with all-around good feelings.

But it is the very last activity that is the most rewarding to Anne. She shows selected scenes from a videotaped professional production of *A Midsummer Night's Dream*. These are the scenes that her students just performed, and they mouth the lines with the actors. The students watch the tape with an incredible intensity, and they have strong opinions about the taped production. It is remarkable how well the students know this play. Anne knows that had they studied Shakespeare in a more conventional mode, her students would not be intently watching and relating so well to this video. Anne knows that this was an extraordinary project that created not merely an understanding or knowledge of this difficult play, but a sense of ownership. As she watches her students watch the play, Anne feels the specialness of the activity. She relaxes and savors the finest day of her year.

Reflections on Teaching A Midsummer Night's Dream

There is no question that this is a difficult and risky project. But the rewards are immense. Although Anne believes she could fail with this, it has never happened. Anne knows that any student-centered activity has the potential to fail because students have so much power over the activity. But the alternative is bleak—teacher-centered learning, an oxymoron in Anne's mind.

"I create a structure at the beginning of this project which serves as a bridge for my students to get them over their initial fear and confusion with a complex work like *A Midsummer Night's Dream*," Anne says. "The beginning of this project is very controlled, but my students will soon be released to interpret

figure ◊ **5.2**

Where do I begin? How about a week and a half ago, when we started this adventure. As we read the book aloud in class, I slowly began to sweat at the thought of acting it out. I never thought in a thousand years that I would be able to do this. Once we were assigned our parts and we were put into our groups, I felt a bit more comfortable. Kim, Joyce, Amy, Bill, and Jim are all very nice people.

We ran through the lines a couple of times the way Shakespeare wrote them. That didn't last very long. Kim has a wonderful sense of humor. She was the one who thought of the lines, "Whip me, beat me, make me feel cheap... Spurn me, strike me, make me write bad checks." Once we put those lines into the dialogue -- the creative juices just kept flowing. I had a very hard time pronouncing the lines, "You draw me, you hardhearted adamant," and I wanted to drop the line. My tongue kept getting tied up. So we changed the lines to, "You draw me, you hardhearted maget." This put me a figure ◊ **5.2** | (Continued)

little more at ease, with the humor involved.

I really enjoyed getting involved. Every time we added something new, the more I got excited. Bill and Joyce's scene was excellent. Bill made the suggestion he would do his lines as a rapper -- we all loved it. The music, I think, really made the scene for both Joyce and Bill. As a group, we brainstormed ideas so well. All of our suggestions were somehow/somewhat implemented.

Kim had a great deal of old Halloween costumes and we were all game to put on any costume to make our scene the best. When I started to pull out my gum, the whole group went crazy -- they loved it.

Kim, Joyce, Bill, Jim, and Amy made working and creating so much fun. All of us were really getting into it. I practiced my lines and tried to make them funny as I said them. I thought it would be funny to stress the same word Kim did with the lines, "For I am _sick_ when I do look on thee." And I am

figure ◊ 5.2   (Continued)

sick when I look not on you."
Another reaction to the lines, how
funny. I also enjoyed saying the lines,
"In my opinion, you are all the
world," and "When all the world is
here to look on me?" Those were again
fun lines to say.

What started out as fear, ended up
being great fun. I loved our group,
they made all the difference. I think
it could have been a whole other
scene with other people. I really enjoyed reading, rehearsing, and putting
on the play, a Midsummer Night's
Dream.

I was very pleased at the outcome
of the final version. All of our lines
went according to plan, and made
our scenes very successful. I was
shocked at myself, on how comfortable
I felt being in front of the class.
For 15 minutes, it just felt natural,
fun and comfortable to be someone
else. What fun! There is no doubt
in my mind -- I won an academy
award yesterday (ha-ha).

figure	◊ 5.3

Our first day working together we just read over our parts and discussed things we didn't understand. We also tried to come up with different ways of presenting our parts (the rude mechanic guys). We thought about being bikers, but no one had the props to go along with that. Then I mentioned being just a bunch of rednecks in a hillbilly bar, but no one seemed interested in that. Eventually we settled on being surfer dudes. This way we didn't need a lot of props and most of us had an idea of how surfer dudes talked.

Our next step was to change the language. Boy, did we have fun doing that! Unfortunately, not everyone in that group was there, but we still came up with a lot of good ideas. After we changed all of our lines, Sheila and I went over to the computer center and typed up our lines for Act I Scene ii, so no one would get confused about his/her lines. We met again I think, on Thursday where we did some, but figure ◊ **5.3** | **(Continued)**

> not much, blocking. We then worked on changing the lines in Act V so they would fit our portrayal of the characters. Again Sheila and I hopped on over to the computer center and typed it up.
>
> Monday we started to do more blocking. Talk about chaotic! It was crazy, but it was fun. Every time I thought it couldn't get better, it did! Like when Bill did his lion part, who would have thought? It was great!

the play any way they wish. But had I said at the beginning, 'Put the play on. You are on your own,' my students would have floundered. Most need the initial teacher direction into the student-centered part."

"Students are empowered to create their own interpretations. My structure at the beginning is to make the empowerment possible. As they state in their writings to me, my students have an ownership of this work by the end of this project," Anne says proudly.

Here is what she feels her students gain from this project.

- Information on how to read a difficult work well and closely. The students read, saw, discussed, and analyzed *A Midsummer Night's Dream*, or parts thereof, 7 to 16 times.

- Confidence in their ability to handle difficult material. Anne's students have an enlarged view of their learning capacities. Now they know they have the ability to read and understand other difficult material. And, of course, almost any contemporary play will be easy after this experience.

- A very specific understanding of *A Midsummer Night's Dream*. These students could pass a conventional quiz or test on this play, and in previous

Performance Benchmark for Standard Two

Students learn, read, perform, and respond to *A Midsummer Night's Dream*.

Standard Three

Students apply a wide range of strategies to comprehend, interpret, evaluate, and appreciate texts. They draw on their prior experience, their interactions with other readers and writers, their knowledge of word meaning and of other texts, their word identification strategies, and their understanding of textual features (e.g., sound-letter correspondence, sentence structure, context graphics).

Performance Benchmark for Standard Three

Students are given strategies to understand the language of Shakespeare. These strategies include prior experience, interactions with other readers, knowledge of word meaning.

Standard Four

Students adjust their use of spoken, written, and visual language (e.g., conventions, style, vocabulary) to communicate effectively with a variety of audiences and for different purposes.

Performance Benchmark for Standard Four

Students orally interpret *A Midsummer Night's Dream* to make sense for a modern young audience. Students do this with very little change in the language, but by using props, voice inflections, costuming, and minor edits.

Recommended Readings

Shakespeare has written many plays that will work in a secondary school classroom. I recommend any of the following for a performance-based lesson:

A Midsummer Night's Dream
The Comedy of Errors
Romeo and Juliet
As You Like It
The Tempest
Much Ado about Nothing
Twelfth Night

The following books are useful aids for the teaching of Shakespeare:

Cullum, A. (1968). *Shake hands with Shakespeare*. New York: Scholastic.

This book contains scripts of eight Shakespearean plays, edited for performances in elementary schools. The scripts are all original Shakespeare, cut only for comprehension purposes. This excellent collection is out of print and difficult to find, but definitely worth a hunt for anyone interested in simplified scripts of *Hamlet, Macbeth, Romeo and Juliet, A Midsummer Night's Dream, Julius Caesar, The Comedy of Errors, The Taming of the Shrew*, and *The Tempest*.

Egan, L. H., & L. O. Egan. (1998). *Teaching shakespeare, yes you can: Fun and easy activities for teaching any play*. New York: Scholastic.

This book is a compendium of activities to engage students in Shakespeare. These activities are meant to clarify as well as motivate.

Gibson, R. (1988). *Teaching Shakespeare: Cambridge School Shakespeare Series*. Cambridge, England: Cambridge University Press.

A Shakespeare teaching guide by one of the foremost Shakespeare teachers.

Isaac, M. L. (2000). *Heirs to Shakespeare: Reinventing the bard in young adult literature*. Portsmouth, NH: Heinemann.

This book shows how young-adult literature incorporates Shakespeare and how Shakespeare can relate to a modern young audience.

Kelly, P. P., & Self, W. (Eds.). (1989, Spring). Drama in the English classroom. *Virginia English Bulletin*. Blacksburg, VA: Virginia Association of Teachers of English.

This journal contains a collection of essays, many of them helpful articles about the teaching of Shakespeare. It is available from NCTE.

O'Brien, P. (1993). *Shakespeare set free: Teaching Romeo and Juliet: Macbeth: A Midsummer Night's Dream*. New York: Washington Square Press.

O'Brien, P., Roberts, J. A., Tolaydo, M., & Rosenman, J. (Eds.). (1994). *Shakespeare set free: Teaching Hamlet, Henry IV, Part I*. New York: Washington Square Press.

O'Brien, P., Roberts, J. A., & Tolaydo, M. (Eds.) (1995) *Teaching Twelfth Night and Othello*. New York: Washington Square Press.

This series is a wonderful guide to teaching Shakespeare in a classroom. Much of the ideas are for classroom-based performances of Shakespeare.

Robinson, R. (1988). *Unlocking Shakespeare's language: Help for the teacher and student*. Urbana, IL: The National Council of Teachers of English.

This book is a useful guide that helps teachers work with the difficult language problems involved with the teaching of Shakespeare.

Rygiel, M. A. (1992). *Shakespeare among school children*. Urbana, IL: The National Council of Teachers of English.

This book is an eclectic but helpful guide to teaching Shakespeare in secondary schools.

Salomone, R. E. (Ed.). (1985). *Teaching Shakespeare. II. Focus*. Southeastern Ohio Council of Teachers of English.

This is a collection of nineteen articles solely devoted to the teaching of Shakespeare. It is available from NCTE.

The following books are useful aids for drama teaching:

Gallo, D. R. (Ed.). (1990). *Center stage: One-act plays for teenage readers and actors.* New York: Harper and Row.

This is a collection of short and thematically appropriate one-act plays for young adults. This is a fine source for a reader's theater.

O'Neill, C., & Lambert, A. (1982). *Drama structures: A practical handbook for teachers.* London: Hutchinson.

This book provides a practical thematic approach to teaching and incorporating drama into the classroom.

You will find a unit plan for a similar project in Chapter Fourteen: Three Sample Unit Plans.

Teaching Poetry

Introduction

It was your typical beautiful autumn day in Southern California. I was only a few miles from the beach, but I could have been in any town because I was closeted in a tiny library carrel writing this book. I kept trying to concentrate on the section I was writing but my mind kept wandering. My thoughts kept returning to my brother-in-law, who would die within the week from pancreatic cancer. What I needed to do then was to write this goodbye poem:

To Dave

I closed my eyes
And saw the Ocean
From the Inside
Grey and Murky
Up and Down
One and the Same
Until
The Bubbles stopped
And then
I left my body
For where I was afraid to go
Alone
Until they brought me Dave
Twinkling of Blue Eyes
With White Beard
and Sunbeam Smile
And Together
Wordless
We Ascended.

Hal Foster

I have had other moments when I needed to write poems, so I have a small and very personal collection. Each poem I have written has been a way of cutting through the conventions of language use and allowing myself the freedom to express emotions, to get to the essence of language. I am convinced that the poems I have written have made me a better prose writer by expanding my ability to use language in a powerful and direct way.

The School, the Students

Tom McKenna loves to teach poetry to his 10th graders. His high school classroom lacks what most people would consider poetic qualities. This is an old classroom inside an old city school. Tom's blackboards are just that—blackboards, chipped and stained with years of use. The wood trim is old and could use a coat of varnish. The lighting is fluorescent and the desks are the modern, multicolored molded type. Tom accepts his environment as unconditionally as he accepts oxygen. It is his work space, nothing more, nothing less.

East End High School is in a desolate, run-down section of the city. The school is about 50% minority, primarily African American and Hispanic, and 50% white. The black students, as a whole, come from a more prosperous part of the community and have a more stable home life than many of their white counterparts.

His 10th-grade students are oblivious to their surroundings. These are schoolrooms—unadorned and generic. As 10th graders go, they come in all sizes, 14 girls and 12 boys in this class—city kids, basically, from working class homes. Ten years of experience has taught Tom how to eliminate all serious discipline problems, and his students take their assigned seats organized in the traditional rows found in most classrooms.

Teacher

The Teacher	
Tom McKenna, age 49	Twenty-five years in the classroom, first at a junior high school, and for the last 10 years at East End High School
Educational Background:	B.A., 1965, English Education; Master of Arts in English, 1976; 30 plus hours beyond master's
Approach:	"My goal is to create readers and writers of poetry—kids who see poetic statements as part of their lives."

Influences:	Student teachers who piqued his interested in "creative teaching methods" and a poetry workshop conducted by Stephen Dunning.

Introducing the Lesson

On the surface, Tom McKenna appears to be a very conventional teacher. He always wears ties, and he has a certain aloofness about him. But Tom is adventurous, and he has a strong philosophy of English teaching that is consistent with meaning-centered theory. In his classrooms, Tom's students create meaning through reading, writing, speaking, seeing, and listening.

Although Tom responds to poetry and, on occasion, writes it, he does not consider himself a poet, as some English teachers do. But he loves to teach poetry for the challenge of helping students appreciate the genre, which he more often than not succeeds in doing. He also believes that reading and writing poetry help his students become more sensitive readers and writers of prose.

Much of Tom's poetry teaching is informal. He does this to keep poetry rich and alive and to make sure it is not overtaught. "I keep meanings and feelings at the center of my poetry teaching," Tom explains. Tom is always copying sets of poems that he passes around when he has a few minutes left at the end of the period. Usually these poems are simple and direct. For instance, with about 20 minutes left one class period, Tom passed around copies of "Dreams" by Langston Hughes.

> Hold fast to dreams
> For if dreams die
> Life is a broken-winged bird
> That cannot fly.
> Hold fast to dreams
> For when dreams go
> Life is a barren field
> Frozen with snow.

Tom tells his students a bit about the poem's author. "He was an African-American poet, born in 1902, who grew up in Cleveland, Ohio. He died in 1967. He was a great writer who wrote stories, novels, and poems about the black experience. He wrote during a period called the Harlem Renaissance, a time noted for excellent black authors."

Then Tom reads the poem aloud and has it read three more times by students he calls on.

Tom: "What do you think?"

Lafreda: "Everyone has to have hope."

Dawn: "I plan to become a lawyer. I know I have to study hard, but it
keeps me going."

[Silence.]

Tom: "What do the last three lines mean to you:

'For when dreams go
Life is a barren field
Frozen with snow' "?

Billie: "If you don't have a dream or a plan, life isn't worth living."

Tony: "If this guy was black, he knows how much harder it is to hold on
to a dream. It's not easy to get ahead if you're black."

Tom: "Maybe this is why this poem was written. Because it is so much
harder to hold on to your dreams for African Americans."

Veronica: "For all minorities it's hard. It's hard for Hispanics also, but
my mom works real hard for us and I plan to hold onto my
dreams. It's not impossible."

Tom knew the poem was clear and direct enough that it required little explanation. Too much explanation, he believes, dampens the experience. For instance, Tom could ask:

Tom: "What does the poem mean?"

Student: "It means you've got to have dreams."

Tom: "Good."

Tom believes the only thing achieved by restating a simple poem is to make the message less poetic.

Tom also could point out the metaphors or ask about them.

Tom: "A metaphor is a direct comparison without using 'as' or 'like.' For
instance, if I said the sky is a blue ocean, that would be a
metaphor. Can you point out the metaphors in the poem?"

Student: "Life is a broken-winged bird."

Tom: "Good. What does this mean?"

Student: "It means without dreams, a person has no hope."

But Tom seldom does this. "Why bother? The students get the picture," he says. "By constantly harping on these beautiful images, it diminishes the impact." A poem, Tom feels, is not meant to be sliced and diced but to be understood and felt.

The Lesson

Tom doesn't always approach poetry quite as casually as he did "Dreams." Sometimes, he likes to do what he calls a "model reading" of a poem. Tom feels that this gives his students a baseline for how to read a poem, which, he points out, should often be done aloud. Tom does such readings several times a semester, using poems of varying difficulty and themes. Because his high school is a big basketball power in the city, one of the poems he uses for his model reading is "Foul Shot."

> Recently, I was watching a tennis match. Boris Becker was playing in the finals and was having a tough time but was winning the match. It was one of those five-set matches that go on forever and seems to test athletes. Becker got to match point, the winning point. It was Becker's serve, and he was obviously very tired. He picks up the ball and looks at it. Bounces it a few times and serves. When the dust cleared, it was obvious that Becker won the match on a perfect serve, what is referred to in tennis as a service ace. Somewhere inside him, when it counted the most, he summoned the strength and concentration to make the perfect serve. Where does a professional athlete get that kind of skill?
>
> For instance, in any important basketball game there will be a number of fouls and, of course, sometimes the outcome of the game depends upon the player making the shot from the foul line. Often, the opposing team will call a timeout and let the foul shooter think about the pressure. When the time comes for the shot, the fans who are sitting behind the basket will be screaming and waving, attempting to distract the shooter. Yet, if it's Michael Jordan or Patrick Ewing, nothing can stop them—they have enough concentration and skill to make the shot.

Then Tom reads the poem aloud, carefully pausing at each line for emphasis. His students have copies so they can follow along.

With two 60s stuck on the scoreboard
And two seconds hanging on the clock,
The solemn boy in the center of eyes,
Squeezed by silence,
Seeks out the line with his feet,
Soothes his hands along his uniform,
Gently drums the ball against the floor,
Then measures the waiting net
Raises the ball on his right hand,
Balances it with his left,
Calms it with fingertips,
Breathes,
Crouches,
Waits,
And then through a stretching of stillness,
Nudges it upward.
The ball

Slides up and out,
Lands,
Leans,
Wobbles,
Wavers,
Hesitates,
Exasperates,
Plays it coy
Until every face begs with unsounding screams
And then,

And then,

And then,

Right before ROAR-UP,
Dives down and through.

The poem works, of course. His students like it, some a lot, some a little, but they all have a friendly experience with an immediately gratifying poem.

Tom also asks his students to share poems with their classmates. Tom has a lot of poetry anthologies, including his source for the two poems cited here, *Reflections on a Gift of Watermelon Pickle.* This anthology, compiled by Stephen Dunning, is the best collection of young-adult poems Tom has ever seen. He also uses poetry sections of old anthologies and college poetry texts, and borrows collections of poetry from the library.

"I allow my students to browse through these sources and select one poem from them that they will share with the entire class," he says. "Students also are allowed to bring in poems that they find on their own or that they write. Of course, I have to approve of the selection. I am concerned about poems of dubious taste and language that could be trouble. Kids are kids. But I usually allow most song lyrics and poems I would consider more appropriate for greeting cards than the classroom. My goal is not to inflict my taste on my students but to allow everyone in the class, including me, to model read a poem and share it."

After a student selects a poem to read, Tom gets class sets made and holds onto them. During those 10 minutes or so left at the end of a writing or reading workshop, he passes out copies of the poem and calls on the responsible student to read it. Tom will ask the student to comment on the poem and tell why she or he selected it. Then Tom allows his other students to comment. Tom is very careful not to embarrass a student if she or he mispronounces a word. Sometimes Tom gently corrects the student during the reading; sometimes he waits and mentions it in private afterward.

His students select a wide range of poets. He sees poems by Edgar Allan Poe, Countee Cullen, and Robert Frost, as well as by Madonna. Children's poems are popular, especially those by Shel Silverstein. Between the poems

Tom reads to his students and the poems they bring in, his class is filled with poetic language. Tom's enthusiasm for poetry is infectious, and many of his kids would like to share three or four poems with the class, which "I try to fit in if I can." On occasion, a student prefers that another student read his or her poem, which Tom permits. Tom almost always asks that the poems be read aloud more than once. And he always asks for an introduction. If the poem is not immediately clear to Tom or to his students, Tom may ask for clarification by having his students interpret it line by line.

Stacey is one of Tom's better readers, and she has selected a poem Tom greatly admires, "Thumbprint" by Eve Merriam.

"We are all unique," Stacey remarks in her introduction. "That is why I like this poem so much. Fingerprints are unique to all of us. Eve Merriam expresses in her poem how everyone is an individual all over and in every way." Then Stacey reads the poem.

Thumbprint

In the heel of my thumb
are whorls, whirls, wheels
in a unique design:
mine alone.
What a treasure to own!
My own flesh, my own feelings.
No other, however grand or base,
can ever contain the same.
My signature,
thumbing the pages of my time.
My universe key,
my singularity.
impress, implant,
I am myself,
of all my atom parts I am the sum.
And out of my blood and my brain
I make my own interior weather,
my own sun and rain.
imprint my mark upon the world,
whatever I shall become.

After the first reading, Tom asks Stacey to read the poem again. And then Tom asks his students what is meant by the lines

And out of my blood and my brain
I make my own interior weather,
my own sun and rain.

Ed says that to him, it means everyone creates his own moods and feelings. Tom accepts this and asks for any other responses. Sue says that she likes the poem a lot and Tom asks her to read it for one final time.

The Writing of Poetry

When Tom has his students write poetry, he offers four different approaches.

- He accepts poems on any subject at anytime.
- He has his students imitate the poems they read.
- He borrows ideas from Stephen Dunning, particularly with the writing of "found" poems and "concrete" poems.
- He borrows ideas from Kenneth Koch about teaching students to write poetry.

Any Poem, Any Time

Tom's students write journals, of course. They often are asked to react to the class poems in their journals, but Tom recommends that they also try to write a poem as an entry, a poem about something important to them. Throughout the semester, Tom's class reads and discusses all kinds of subject matter that lead to poetic statements from his students.

On the Outside
(A poem based on a discussion of the S. E. Hinton novel *The Outsider*)

I see myself
on the Outside of the Room
No Entry
No Entry
In Neon-Red Light-Bruising My Eyes
I hear the laughter
On the Inside of the Room
Harsh and shrill
Harsh and shrill
Striking me like nails on a Blackboard
I am lonely and want in
To no avail.

Charlene

This is fairly typical of the kind of attempts Tom's students make. They know they are free from the convention of rhyme, but they have learned the importance of the rhythms of the lines and stanzas. They have learned this through discussions of the poems they read. Sometimes the journal poems are for his eyes only, and sometimes he recommends that they be shared. He asks that Charlene share this with the entire class, which she does.

Imitating Poems

Tom uses models of poems to stimulate student writing. He does this whenever he finds a poem he feels can be easily copied by his students. This idea comes from Stephen Dunning, who calls it *copy change*.

For instance, Tom reads his students "On Reading Poems to a Senior Class at South High" by D. C. Berry.

Before
I opened my mouth
I noticed them sitting there
as orderly as frozen fish
in a package.
Slowly, water began to fill the room
though I did not notice it
till it reached
my ears

and then I heard the sounds
of fish in an aquarium

and I knew that though I had
tried to drown them
with my words
that they had only opened up
like gills for them
and let me in.

Together we swam around the room
like thirty tails whacking words
till the bell rang
puncturing
a hole in the door

where we all leaked out

They went to another class
I suppose and I home

where Queen Elizabeth
my cat met me and licked my fins
till they were hands again.

After the reading, Tom asked his students to write a poem using the beginning of "On Reading Poems to a Senior Class at South High":

Before
I opened my mouth
I noticed them sitting here
as orderly as . . .

Tom gives an example: "as orderly as chewing gum in a wrapper"; he continues: "Slowly sounds of foil removed from gum fills the room and then I heard chewing." He also does a similar activity with a poem called "June Twenty-First" by Bruce Guernsey.

June Twenty-First

My mother's cigarette flares and fades,
the steady pulse of a firefly,
on the patio under the chestnut.
The next door neighbors are over.
My father, still slender, is telling a joke:
laughter jiggles in everyone's drinks.

On his hour's reprieve from sleep,
my little brother dances
in the sprinkler's circle of water.

At fourteen, I'm too old
to run naked with my brother,
too young to laugh with my father.

I stand there with my hands in my pockets.
The sun refuses to set,
bright as a penny in a loafer.

Tom asks his students to write poems that are shaped around a day or a memory—either good or bad—that is similar. That's all he asks for this imitation. However, Tom brainstorms with the class for ideas. Together they discuss those small days: picnics, car rides, dinner conversations, rainy days at home, small excursions, TV watching. Tom begins an imitation poem for his students.

April 27th

My mother's radio ebbs and crackles
the steady pulse of a ballgame
on the porch under the moonlight.

Tom tells his students they do not have to copy the original as faithfully as he did unless they want to. This is more difficult than the formula writing Tom sometimes asks for, so the level of frustration is higher than usual, but Tom is patient and nonjudgmental as he works the room, aiding his budding poets. His students know and trust him and try to write simple, direct statements from their hearts.

A January Day (based on the poem, "June Twenty-First")

My brother's sled bobs and weaves
careening down down
the hill
stopping
on the path under the tree.

The neighbors and friends
laughing and shivering in hot cider cups.

My little brother dances
with cold near the fire's circle of warmth.

At fourteen, I'm too old to sled with my brother
too young to sip cider with the boys from the college.

I stand there with my hands in my pockets
The snow falling lightly
white as the fur of my kitten.

Darla

Kenneth Koch's Ideas

Although the poet Kenneth Koch deals mainly with teaching children in his book *Wishes, Lies, and Dreams* (1970), Tom adapts several of Koch's group poetry writing ideas to his high school classroom. For instance, on occasion Tom has his students write a class poem using adapted Koch rules:

"Everyone write two lines. The first line begins with 'I wish.' In one line include a fun activity and a color. In the other line include a school activity and a mood. Here are examples:

I wish I was skiing on the white powder slopes.
In school writing poetry makes me think."

Every student reads her or his lines aloud to create a class poem.

Tom does a similar activity with Koch's "I used to/But now" idea. For instance:

> "I used to love the songs of summer
> But now winter ballads give me hope.
>
> I used to water-ski without the skis and on one foot
> But now I am the spotter in the boat.
>
> I used to wear red and sideburns and have a beard.
> But now I cut my hair twice a month and wear only autumn browns.

Tom does the same thing with "I seem to be/But really am."

> I seem to be a restless sort
> But really am peaceful and serene.
>
> I seem to be a know-it-all
> But really am I-wish-I-knew-more.
>
> I seem to be up on the air.
> I really am inside the earth.
>
> I seem to be a short giraffe.
> I really am a tall sparrow.

Stephen Dunning's Ideas

One of Tom's best sources is Stephen Dunning's poetry books. Tom treasures his well-used copy of *For Poets* (1975), where he found many of the ideas he adapts to his classroom. For instance, Tom helps his students find and write "found" poems. These are simple poems made from words or phrases that are found anywhere. The trick with "found" poems is to arrange the lines in a way that changes, for instance, a newspaper article into a poem. These poems are easy to create and are often entertaining. "Found" poems can be a refreshing way for students to view language. Tom pulls up the movie screen and his students see the following on the board:

News Item: Mondo Bizarro—The Story

Satan himself—described as having fiery red eyes, long pointy fingernails and very bad breath—has been captured by four Spanish monks, who imprisoned the Evil One in a metal tool shed within the walled enclosure of their mountain monastery.

Mondo Bizarro—The Poem

Satan himself—
described as having
fiery red eyes
long pointy fingernails
and
VERY BAD BREATH
has been captured
by four
by four
by four
by four
Spanish monks, monks, monks, monks
who imprisoned
The Evil One
in a
Metal Tool shed

within the walled
enclosure
of their mountain
monastery.

Then Tom has his students reread the poem. He tells them what "found" poems are and explains that they will get 20 minutes to find a poem, either in teams or alone. After that, some of the poems will be placed on the board.

Tom passes around newspapers and magazines and his students go at it. The class is noisy, filled with laughter, but Tom does not mind. After 20 minutes Tom circulates, reviewing the poetry his students have created by rearranging the lines of recipes, magazine articles, and newspaper briefs. His students bring a freshness, a new language-life to the most common, everyday reports. It is a small lesson in composing but a nice one. Tom has students place many of their found poems on the board, and the class readings spill over to the next day.

Tex-mex

LOVERS
of Mexican Foods
had two ways
to purchase
Tortillas
American tastebuds
have gone wild for
Mexican

Tex-mex
and Southwestern cuisines
Bill

Half the Calories
but
still
All of the taste
Dorothy

Tom also uses the concrete poem idea from *For Poets*. On this day when Tom's students walk into class they find a copy of "Merry-Go-Round" on their seats. "Concrete poems either look like the object the poem is describing or look like something the poem is about. Here's a concrete poem," Tom tells them. "It was written by one of my students three years ago. Read it please, Alison." (Figure 6.1)

---

figure ◑ **6.1**

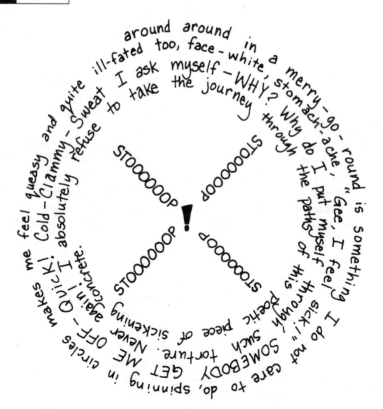

figure ◊ **6.2**

"Do you think you can write one of these?" Tom asks. "Let me try first." Tom asks his students to help him think of a subject, and after much searching for an object he can both write about and draw, he settles on a shoe (Figure 6.2).

Tom's students groan at this effort and pledge to do better. For the next 20 minutes, they write concrete poems about telephones, baseballs, footballs, cats, houses, skyscrapers, and ice cream cones. Three students write single-word poems (Figure 6.3).

Pattern Poems

Tom shares with his students poems that use formal rhyme and rhythm schemes. He explains the rhyme scheme of a Shakespearean sonnet: abab cdc efef gg. He also shows how 17 syllables in three lines is a form of disciplined

figure ◊ **6.3**

drip

double   1 st

poetry often found in Japanese nature haiku. On occasion, Tom asks his students to write poems with specific rhythms. But Tom's pattern poems offer his students a bit more freedom than sonnets or haiku. He offers his students a pattern game that he found in *For Poets*.

"I would like you to write nine words on three subjects. Help me come up with one-word topics like 'television.'" The brainstormed list his students produce includes:

cars   food
clothes   telephone
movies   television
friends   school
vacations

After the list is complete, Tom offers an example of nine words about cars: "I love to hear the engine rev winter mornings."

His students groan at his insipid poem, once again proving to them that they can do better than their teacher. Then they attack this project. Most of them are successful, except for Tonya, who demands 11 words for her telephone poem.

Telephone: "Calling long distance to my next-door friend after we fight." After his class has completed this part of the project, Tom tells them to do this:

"Now place these nine words into a pattern, such as

3
3
3

"For instance:

I love to
Hear the engine
Rev winter mornings.

"Or you could have a pattern of:

1
3
3
2

"For instance:

I
Love to hear
The Engine Rev
Winter Mornings."

"Make your poems in the pattern you feel is most effective."
Tom walks around the class, helping where needed. Basically, he isn't needed much. He just does a bit of watching as his students write their poems. When they are done, he has a sampling of the poems placed on the board.

Telephone:

I have	2
Telephone Neck	2
Right Leaning	2
Receiver Ready	2
Dial	1

Ed

Television:

Bart Simpson's Dad	3
Used to Live	3
With my Mom	3

Penelope

Friends:

Kicking Leaves	2
In Autumn Brown	3
With My Best Friend	4

Gene

Friends:

Kara, Katie, Mary	3
Faye, Robin, Barry	3
Amie, Jane, Larry	3

Kelly

Vacation:

Hello Boys and Girls	4
My Name is Mickey	4
Mouse	1

Roberto

School:

Lineup	1
Single	1

File	1
Do	1
Not	1
Talk	1
Or	1
Pass	1
Or	1

Loretta

Tom's students enjoy this little exercise in rhythm, stanza, and imagination and are very proud of their creations.

Reflections on Teaching Poetry

Tom's teaching program is only partially devoted to poetry activities, but they are important to him. He sees much value in poetry teaching, not the least of which is that his students enjoy both the reading and the writing. Any language activities that students enjoy is okay with Tom and a credit to him as well because poetry is often one of the most abused and hated forms of literature teaching in English classes.

Tom makes his poetry teaching enjoyable by following some of the simple principles Stephen Dunning (1975) developed years ago.

- Have enthusiasm for the poems you teach.
  Tom really likes the poems he shares with his students. He finds them in all kinds of places including poems brought to him by students in previous classes. Tom teaches "classic poetry" along with more accessible "young-adult" poems, and he files them all. He does not feel obligated to teach poems just because they are in an anthology. He ignores the poems that he cannot teach because he feels they will not work for his students.

- Keep experience of the poetry at the center of the teaching.
  Tom interprets this to mean that he and his students read, understand, and relate to the poem. Tom knows that his students come in with very negative attitudes about poetry, and he sees his job as the creation of enthusiastic readers. "If I can get my kids to like poetry," he says, "then it will be much easier for college professors to teach all the technical stuff." Tom is being slightly defensive here, but his point is a good one. He will provide baseline definitions of terms so that his students have a poetry vocabulary. For instance, he will discuss simile, metaphor, rhyme, meter, and stanza, and he will use examples of them. But the "technical stuff" is not at the heart of his poetry teaching. He feels he cannot create readers by shoving terms down his students' throats. Instead, he creates readers by

using the principles of creating meaningful reading experiences for his students. He gets criticized by some colleagues for not teaching enough of the "mechanics," the underlying principles of the art, but Tom is firm in his belief system that sees poetry as a real-life experience. He won't budge.

- Do not overexplain poetry. This usually happens when you go overboard with the "technical stuff."
  Although Tom understands that good and worthwhile poems may be very hard, he prefers, when possible, to underexplain them. He feels that replacing a poetic statement with a prosaic class explication is one of the dullest forms of teaching. This principle leads Tom to select simple, easy-to-understand poems. Tom reads them with the class but does not ask his students to do a great deal of clarifying. Maybe Tom creates problems here. Perhaps he avoids more difficult poems that would be big hits with his students. Perhaps he leaves his students with too little explanation for certain poems. But Tom feels these mistakes are less serious in the creation of enthusiastic readers than others he could make.

- Allow students to select the poetry they will read, study, and discuss.
  Allowing students to select a poem and model a reading gives them a sense of ownership. Tom's model readings often include poetry that he feels is a slight stretch for his students. He explains the reading using personal contact points as a means of clarification. Tom believes this is a good way of demonstrating how a poem and a person meet. He does not trick his students with questions that force them to guess the teacher's interpretation. Instead, he offers his students a forum to model readings of poems that they find meaningful.

- Teach poetry on occasion, not always as separate units.
  Tom loves to practice this principle when there are only 10 minutes left in the period. This casualness allows room to experiment. If his students do not relate well to the poem, Tom has blown 10 minutes, not 3 weeks. Also, this informality gives Tom the space not to shove all his poetic interests down the throats of his students. He feels no need to sell a poem, only to share it. This goes for his students as well, allowing them to cloak strong feelings behind a tentativeness and a rescue by the brevity of the interval before the period ends.

- Ask students to write poetry.
  Tom is always searching for ways to help his students create poems, although he is never satisfied with his methods. Either, Tom feels he is providing too much structure or not enough, but somehow his students produce poetic statements in which they take pride. Tom sees his search for the perfect poetry writing format as a never-ending battle, and he is probably right.

The principles Tom follows provide intact poetry experiences. He is an effective teacher, and his guiding spirit leads him to meaning-centered activities. As a result, Tom believes that his students understand and appreciate poetry in a deep and personal way. Tom is satisfied. And he trusts his students enough to share with them the best superficial poem about iced tea he has ever read.

Sun tea
Iced and chilled
Translucent, mirror of grass
Brewed for hours, caressed by sun
Too beautiful to drink.

Hal Foster

Teacher as Researcher

Questions

- What experiences did you have with poetry in junior or senior high school?
- How do you feel about poetry?
- Would you feel comfortable sharing poetry you have written with your students?
- How would you approach a student who says, "I hate poetry."
- What kind of approaches would you use to get student poets to share their poetry?
- How is teaching classic poetry different from teaching poetry like "Foul Shot"? How can both kinds help your students write better poetry?
- Can you make a list of poems you would love to teach in secondary school? If yes, which poems and why?

Activities

- React to the story. Give your impressions and thoughts.
- Try to write a few poems based on Tom's formulas.
- Create poetry-teaching activities around imitating popular song and rap lyrics.
- Use television-show theme songs to create poetry writing activities.
- Create classroom activities around license-plate slogans or bumper-sticker messages to express succinctly a feeling or idea.

IRA/NCTE Standards for English Language Arts with Performance Benchmarks for Chapter 6

Standard One

Students read a wide range of print and nonprint texts to build an understanding of texts, of themselves, and of the culture of the United States and the world; to acquire new information; to respond to the needs of society and the workplace; and for personal fulfillment. Among these texts are fiction and nonfiction.

Performance Benchmark for Standard One

Students read and respond to poems selected by the teacher and also by themselves.

Standard Two

Students read a wide range of literature from many periods in many genres to build an understanding of the many dimensions (e.g., philosophical, ethical, aesthetic) of human experience.

Performance Benchmark for Standard Two

Students read poems selected from many sources by the teacher and by themselves and are asked to respond in discussion and in journals to the poems and to the responses of peers.

Standard Three

Students apply a wide range of strategies to comprehend, interpret, evaluate, and appreciate texts. They draw on their prior experience, their interactions with other readers and writers, their knowledge of word meaning and of other texts, their word identification strategies, and their understanding of textual features (e.g., sound-letter correspondence, sentence structure, context graphics).

Performance Benchmark for Standard Three

Students apply a wide range of strategies to interpret, and enhanced by class participation, evaluate and appreciate poetry. These strategies are aided by thoughtful open-ended reader-response questions offered by the teacher and peers.

Standard Four

Students adjust their use of spoken, written, and visual language (e.g., conventions, styles, vocabulary) to communicate effectively with a variety of audiences and for different purposes.

Performance Benchmark for Standard Four

Students, given a system, write poems with a variety of styles and purposes.

Standard Five

Students employ a wide range of strategies as they write and use different writing process elements appropriately to communicate with different audiences for a variety of purposes.

Performance Benchmarks for Standard Five

Students employ many writing strategies based on various formats to write poems of different styles and different purposes. Students use written, spoken, and visual language to share poems written for many different purposes.

Recommended Readings

Dunning, S., Carrigan, A., & Clay, R. (1970). *Poetry: Voices, languages, forms.* New York: Scholastic Book Services.

This workbook provides a nice collection of poetry for young people, with simple but imaginative exercises aimed at helping readers interpret the poems.

Dunning, S., Lueders, E., & Smith, H. (Eds.). (1966). *Reflections on a gift of watermelon pickle . . . and other modern verses.* Glenview, IL: Scott, Foresman.

This is still one of the finest collections of modern poetry for adolescents ever assembled. This short anthology is a classic.

Dunning, S., & Stafford, W. (1993). *Getting the knack.* Urbana, IL: National Council of Teachers of English.

This book is filled with detailed suggestions of how to create poetry. The ideas in this book are clever and echo the writing processes of two fine poets.

Grossman, F. (1991). *Listening to the bells: Learning to read poetry by writing poetry.* Portsmouth, NH: Heinemann.

This book was conceived as a middle-school poetry text designed to help students read and write basically introspective poetry.

Janeczko, P. B. (Ed.). (1983). *Poetspeak. In their work, about their work.* Scarsdale, NY: Bradbury Press.

This is a nice eclectic collection of modern poetry. Each section contains comments from the poets about their poems and the writing of poetry.

Johnson, D. M. (1990). *Word weaving: A creative approach to teaching and writing poetry.* Urbana, IL: National Council of Teachers of English.

This book gives many examples of poems and ideas for writing poetry in the classroom.

Koch, K. (1974). *Rose, where did you get that red? Teaching great poetry to children.* New York: Vintage.

This book contains ten poetry writing lessons for children based on classic poems like William Blake's "The Tyger."

Koch, K. (1970). *Wishes, lies, and dreams: Teaching children to write poetry.* New York: Harper and Row.

Koch provides imaginative ways of stimulating poetry writing from children. His ideas are easily adaptable to middle school.

Tsujimoto, J. I. (1988). *Teaching poetry writing to adolescents.* Urbana, IL: National Council of Teachers of English.

In the first section of the book, the author shares his ideas about teaching poetry. The second section gives specific classroom examples of poetry writing activities and student poems.

chapter SEVEN

Teaching the Novel

Introduction

Classic American Novels in the Classroom

I am always searching for the methods and techniques that will enable me to present literature to my students in a meaningful way. For instance, I wonder, it is possible to build bridges connecting classic literature? Is it possible to do this with what I consider to be the trickiest of all literature teaching—using a "classic" adult novel with a group of teenagers?

The School, the Students

Roosevelt High School is the quintessential suburban school, surrounded by large, comfortable homes. The student population, all 1,724, come from the immediate area. Most are reasonably economically secure, although there is very little great wealth in the school district. The students are mostly white, with a 20% minority enrollment.

The Teacher	
Ron Schmidt, age 29	Five years in teaching, all at Roosevelt High School
Educational Background:	B.A., English Education; certified in English and Speech
Approach:	"I believe there is a place for the classic novels in a secondary English curriculum. But I want to create an impact for my students. That is the challenge—to avoid overfragmentation and to make the novel a meaningful experience."

Influences:	A mentor teacher in the Roosevelt High School English Department and an undergraduate methods class. Also, a student teaching experience that was in the spirit of meaning-centered instruction.

Teaching *The Great Gatsby*

Ron Schmidt has probably read and studied *The Great Gatsby* more than any other novel. He first read the book on his own when he was in 11th grade. He then encountered it in an American Literature course in college. Soon after he graduated, he taught the book in an 11th-grade class, and now he uses it every year. The book has changed dramatically for Ron over the years. When he encountered the book in college, he felt he knew it and possessed it. He loved the book, the beauty of the writing, the romantic quality of Gatsby, the insightfulness of Nick.

However, now the novel troubles and confuses Ron. Perhaps part of the reason Ron perceives *The Great Gatsby* differently is because Ron perceives his students differently. Now, Ron is much more aware of his students as young readers, and he has a concern with their ability to identify with a book and understand it on a deep, personal level. Ron feels the mature themes in Gatsby— marriage, adultery, greatness—plus the ambiguity of having to know the book through the character Nick, make it a real stretch for his 16-year-old students. Also, Ron's classes have changed. Now they are much more ethnically diverse, which has made Ron more aware of what he considers the ethnic and racial insensitivity of the novel.

Despite these problems, Ron chooses to teach the book. He approaches this teaching unit as a collective class reading. Ron does not pretend to give the right reading to this novel. Although he explains to his students that this is considered a classic American novel, he allows his students to view the book as fatally flawed if they wish. Ron hopes that his students learn from this how to make personal transactions with a complicated, ambiguous novel that is potentially flawed by an archaic and cruel value system. Ron divides the teaching of this novel into two basic parts. In the first part, he helps his students with the reading difficulties many teenagers encounter with *The Great Gatsby*. In the second part, Ron structures the transactions between the students and text.

Introducing the Lesson

Ron uses two themes to introduce his 11th graders to *The Great Gatsby*. Sometimes he uses "The Roaring Twenties" as his way into the book. This semester, he uses the other theme:

> A few Sundays ago, I was flipping some dials on my television when
> I came across a marathon. I was intrigued because the runners
> were passing what appeared to be a bombed-out vision of a
> cityscape-boarded stores, empty streets, expressway abutments. I always
> thought that marathons were run in sections that cities took pride in.
> This was a very strange landscape for a televised marathon.
>   Suddenly, the lead runners turned a corner and were in a park. The
> camera tracked them from the front until the marathoners turned into a
> grassy knoll. There, the camera angle changed and it all became clear
> to me.
>   The end of the race was Liberty Park in New Jersey, and when the
> camera angle moved to show the finish line, the skyline of New York
> City became visible—this beautiful Gotham City dominated by the
> World Trade Center, the sun glinting off the steel, glass, copper, cement
> and marble buildings. Like the magical spaceship in *Star Wars*, or like
> the world's largest and most beautiful jewel, the city radiated beneath
> the sun across the harbor. I knew now why they set this marathon
> here.

Ron asks his students if they have ever been to New York City. "What's it like?" he asks.

> Rhonda: "I have an uncle who lives in Queens. He takes us into
>   Manhattan when we visit. Wow! It is so big and exciting. There
>   are all kinds of people."
> Jason: "When I was in New York I saw *Phantom of the Opera*. The
>   tickets cost like $100. Everything is so expensive there. I
>   remember seeing people sleeping on the sidewalks and
>   everybody ignored them."
> Marta: "My parents lived in New York when they first came to this
>   country. They thought it was very crowded and a little scary. But
>   there were a lot of people that spoke Czech, and it was easy for
>   them to get used to America. When they came here they found a
>   smaller community from Europe. It was harder for them that
>   way."

At this point, Ron discusses the "New York Thing"—having big dreams, making it big. New York is the place where anything can happen and anyone can live, including Jay Gatsby.

Here, Ron holds up a copy of *The Great Gatsby* and explains to his students that they will be reading this book, which is set in New York. He also tells them that the story takes place in the 1920s, known as the Roaring Twenties or the Jazz Age. "What do you know about the 1920s?" Ron asks.

> Amanda: "Wasn't it the time before the big depression and didn't people go wild?"
>
> Ron: "Yeah, good."
>
> Sharon: "Didn't people drink a lot? Was this the time drinking was illegal?"
>
> Ron: "Yes, it was called Prohibition."
>
> Billie: "Yeah, *The Untouchables*, Eliot Ness."
>
> Ron: "Right. Even though drinking was illegal, many people broke the law and drank and partied."
>
> Amanda: "Short skirts and the Charleston."
>
> Ron: "Right. Morals loosened and the rich held extravagant and gaudy parties. It all ended in 1929 with the stock market crash when many people lost their life savings and investments."

The Lesson

The Characters

"I have to help these kids crack this book. For most of them, it is too difficult to say 'just go and read it,'" Ron observes. "So at the beginning of my *Great Gatsby* unit, I help them figure out the characters. My goal is to get them started understanding it and to motivate them. But when the reading is over, the book is theirs to interpret and appreciate in any reasonable way they wish."

Effective teaching means that a teacher's goal must be to provide a scaffold, a bridge, that will allow for a student-centered, empowered reading. This is what Ron does.

Ron feels it is necessary to preview the characters in *The Great Gatsby* for his students. Naturally, he begins with Nick Carraway. Because Nick introduces himself at the beginning of the book, Ron asks his students to read aloud the first four pages. Ron tells his students that Nick will tell the whole story, so "how much you believe will depend upon how much you believe Nick." Ron provides his students with a generic character worksheet, which will require a creative interpretation of the text. Ron asks his students to include this in their journals (see Figure 7.1).

Ron tells his students that he would like them to fill in this sheet for Nick. He asks his students also to prepare a character analysis for one other character they will meet. He divides his class into four sections: one section does Tom; one does Daisy; one, Jordan; and another Myrtle.

Answer as many of the following as best you can. If the answers are not provided by the text, make up your answers based on what you know about the
character (try to do this well, but have fun with it).

Color hair

Color eyes

Favorite clothes (likes to wear)

Skin tone

Shoes

Jewelry

Car

Hobbies

Favorite foods

Favorite films

Favorite books

Political party

Favorite leisure-time activities

Job

Likes the following characteristics in friends:

Sports interests

Pet peeves

Least likely to . . .

Favorite school subjects

Overall opinion of character

Make up your own questions

Ron asks that they be prepared to discuss their character assessments on
Friday, two days from now. Ron will grade these quickly, based on students'
overall understanding of their characters. He tells his students to read Chapters
1 through 4 by Friday, when they will have to write, in class, a paragraph or two
describing the chapters and a paragraph or two describing their reactions to
them. Ron will grade these pass/no pass, based on his sense of whether the
students have read the assignment.

Ron has to do one last activity to prepare for the reading of *The Great Gatsby*.
He has his students read pages 4–10 from the book aloud. As they read it, Ron

and his students discuss the events in the book. Ron does this as an induction into this book.

As a result of Ron's introduction, his students get a sense of the book's theme; they have been introduced to the setting, to Nick, and to the style of the language. Ron knows that the collective class reading has at least started familiarizing his students with the plot of the novel, and he has given them a tool to help them crack the characters.

What about motivation? Ron hopes his New York and Roaring Twenties discussion will get his students curious about the book and that the collective reading will further spur their interest. However, the nature of this book will make it tough for many of his students to continue reading. Ron's big challenge is to keep his students engaged with the book until they finish it.

The Writing Assignment

Ron's students begin this period by preparing the following writing assignment:

- Describe some of the events that happened in the first four chapters. You may write this in paragraphs or just make lists. Make a list of questions and statements about the first four chapters.

- Write a brief paragraph describing how you feel about Chapters 1 through 4. Do you like the book so far? Are you confused by it? Do you have any questions?

- This is a journal assignment and will be graded pass/no pass based on completion of the assignment and a sense from the writing that you read the book. If you have read the book and I have given you no credit, discuss the book with me and I'll change your grade.

Ron allows 20 minutes for the writing. His students are generally comfortable with this assignment, although about four or five are obviously struggling, either not writing or writing in fits and starts. Ron does not intervene, although he will answer questions and deal with pleas for help.

After the writing, Ron asks his students to take out their character assessments. Then Ron divides his students into groups of three in which each student has a different profile. For example, each group has a Nick and two of the following: Tom, Daisy, Jordan, or Myrtle.

Ron gives his students about 15 minutes to share their assessments, five minutes for each character, and then asks his students to share them with the entire class.

Ron: "Okay, who is Nick?"

[Many students raise their hands; Ron calls on Tim first.]

Tim: "Blue eyes, sandy hair." [The class laughs.]

Ron: "Okay, what else?"

Samantha: "Real conservative looking, buttoned-down all the way, pinstripe suits."

Lisa: "Yep, put on him tortoise-shelled glasses, give him *The Wall Street Journal* and a briefcase and you've got him."

Ron: "Good. What else?"

Bob: "He slicks back his hair into a tail, and wears a diamond earring." [Everyone laughs.]

Sue: "No way. Maybe Tom, but Nick is a banker all the way."

Ron: "Okay. Nice job with Nick. Do you trust him? He says he is one of the few honest people he has ever known. Do you agree?"

Lisa: "It's hard to say. He describes everything in such detail that I tend to believe him."

Tom: "I wouldn't believe anyone who tells me he's so honest." [Snickers in the class.]

Jill: "As much as I hate to admit it, I kind of agree with Tom. [More snickers.] Nick makes himself appear to be too good to be true."

Ron leads the class in the same kind of discussion about Tom and Daisy, but goes into less detail about Myrtle and Jordan. Ron now feels certain his students have a mental image of the characters that will help them understand the book.

"Of course, we have ignored the main character, Jay Gatsby," he tells the class. "Finish the book for Monday and we will discuss Gatsby. Why does Fitzgerald call him 'The Great Gatsby'? What is this book about? The American Dream, love, ambition? What do you feel about the book?

"When you walk into class on Monday, I will ask you to write me a note explaining the book and your reaction to it, the same assignment you wrote for today."

Over the weekend, Ron reads his students' journal assignments. He skims them quickly and feels only about four students did not read at least three of the chapters. The rest of the class showed varying enthusiasm and understanding of the book. Tom wrote that the book was slow and confusing, but he liked Nick. Lisa thought the parties would be fun, although there was too much drinking and she hated Tom and thought Daisy was an airhead. George was completely confused and did not know what was happening in the book or why.

Ron questions five students' critical responses and passed the others. He responds to about a half-dozen questions, including, "Why did Tom break Myrtle's nose?" Ron's answer: "My guess is that Tom is a brutal, mean guy and Myrtle was taunting him about his wife, Daisy. Don't you think Tom uses women? What do you think?"

Another question: "Why does Gatsby have all these parties for people he doesn't care about or know?"

> Ron: "I guess because these make Gatsby into a kind of myth—a larger-than-life hero. He is trying to impress Daisy. Do you think it will work? Will Daisy buy it? John Hinckley shot President Reagan to try to impress the actress Jodie Foster. Is this the same sort of thing?"

The Discussion

Ron begins the class with 20 minutes of journal writing on the book and then opens the discussion with his question: "Did you like the book?"

The class response is like the whoosh of air escaping when a new can of coffee is opened. They are ready to talk about it. They came a long way to get to this point.

> Tom: "It was hard to understand. It went by and it was like I hadn't read anything.
> Lisa: "Why didn't anybody come to Gatsby's funeral?"
> Sue: "Because he had no friends; he was such a liar."
> Amanda: "What happened at the end? Who killed Myrtle?"
> Tom: "I think Daisy was driving, but Gatsby took the rap for her."
> Ron: "Can someone find that in the book?"
> Bette: "Here it is on page 144":

> > *Gatsby says"Well, I tried to swing the wheel?" He*
> > *broke off, and suddenly I guessed at the truth.*
> > *"Was Daisy driving?"*
> > *"Yes," he said after a moment, "but of course I'll say I was."*

> Sue: "What did Gatsby see in Daisy; she was so helpless, so shallow? Look at what she says about her child on page 14:

> > *'I'm glad it's a girl. And I hope she'll be a fool—that's the*
> > *best thing a girl can be in this world, a beautiful little fool.'*
> > Yuck!"

> Ed: "What did Daisy see in Gatsby? All he was interested in was money and fame."
> Billie: "What did Nick see in Gatsby? Didn't Nick make a remark about Gatsby being better than everybody? Here it is. What Nick said

to Gatsby was,"

"They're a rotten crowd," I shouted across the lawn.
"You're worth the whole damn bunch put together."

Billie: "And then Nick goes on to say,"

"I've always been glad I said that. It was the only
compliment I ever gave him, because I disapproved of him
from beginning to end."

Andy: "This is so weird. What does all of this mean?"
[The rest of the class echoes Andy.]
Ron: "Well, it's what you make of it. I, too, am confused about it, and I
have known this book for a long time. I want you to help me. Tell
me about it. Why is Gatsby great?"
Jill: "Because he had a dream."
Ron: "Which was what?"
Ed: "Daisy, I guess."
Ron: "So what?"
Lisa: "Well, he was the only one in the book, including Nick, who had a
goal, had an ideal. Unfortunately for Gatsby, it was all too real,
and all too less than ideal. His ideal was the shallow, sad, confused
Daisy."
Samantha: "Yeah, and Daisy was a married woman. Shouldn't have
Gatsby known better? I mean, what was so great about
Gatsby?"
Amanda: "Even Gatsby was hollow. He lied about everything. He was
so materialistic. He didn't respect marriage."
Ed: "Kind of like this country."
Class: "What?"
Ed: "Read the last page. Doesn't all that stuff about the continent and
all being behind him, and that 'orgiastic future that year by year
recedes before us,' doesn't all that stuff kind of indicate that the
American dream is over?"
Ron: "So you're saying that you think *The Great Gatsby* is saying the
whole system is corrupt?"
Wendy: "I don't know. Nick is part of the system and he portrays himself
in a favorable light. It's more like Fitzgerald seems confused and
uncertain about his characters and his ideas."
Ron: "What about the racist stuff. You know. Let me read it to you."

> *As we crossed Blackwell's Island, a limousine passed us,*
> *driven by a white chauffeur, in which sat three modish*
> *negroes, two bucks and a girl. I laughed aloud as the yolks of*
> *their eyeballs rolled toward us in haughty rivalry.*

Ron: "And on the same page

> *A small, fat-nosed Jew raised his large head and*
> *regarded me with two fine growths of hair which luxuriated*
> *in either nostril. After a moment I discovered his tiny eyes in*
> *the half-darkness...*
> *"Who is he anyhow, an actor?"...*
> *"Meyer Wolfsheim? No, he's a gambler." Gatsby*
> *hesitated, then added coolly, "He's the man who fixed the World*
> *Series back in 1919."*

Ron: "These passages are not Tom, the racist pig, speaking about the
rise of the Colored Empires. These passages come from the
mouth of Nick. It seems to me readers have to either perceive
Nick as a racist, see these passages as not racist at all, or perceive
Fitzgerald as having elitist and racist sensibilities."

Edna: "That's the problem with this old literature. Why does anybody
think it is so good anyway? It always has stuff like this in it. I'm
offended."

Laura: "Me, too. They were all racists back then. Why should the author
of this book be an exception?"

Ed: "This is a difficult book to figure out. You are left with more
questions than answers."

Lisa: "The characters in the book were sloppy, careless people who only
believed in money and themselves. *The Great Gatsby* stands as a
warning against a valueless world."

Ron: "This world comes to an end with the Depression and World War
II. Perhaps *The Great Gatsby* stands as a monument to an
imperfect time which it doesn't only depict, but it also reflects."

Amy: "Kind of like our time now."

Ron: "What do you mean?"

Amy: "Don't you think our values are declining? Look at crime, drugs,
teenage pregnancies."

Tom: "Okay, okay."

Ron: "'*So we beat on, boats against the currents, borne back ceaselessly*
into the past.' We just keep trying to make things better despite
all the obstacles. Thanks class; good reading. That's it for
today."

Teaching *Huckleberry Finn*

The *Huckleberry Finn* Problem

Along with *The Great Gatsby*, *The Adventures of Huckleberry Finn* is one of the most frequently taught books in American schools. Like *The Great Gatsby*, Ron has had a long and changing relationship with *Huck Finn*. "How can I claim there is one truthful interpretation of a book, which I am to teach to all my students, after what I have been through with *Huck Finn?*" Ron states. "When I first taught the book, I saw Huck as the center of the book. I felt Huck was this thoughtful kid who, through a transcendent moral sensibility, rescued Jim. But my students, over time, have made me rethink this book and look at it from Jim's point of view. Now I see a grown man treated, at best, like a child by another child, Huck. And then I see a black male adult treated without respect and with scorn by two white boys, Huck and Tom. *Huck Finn* is a lot of different books for a lot of different people."

Ron teaches *Huck Finn* using the same basic methods he uses for *The Great Gatsby*. During this unit he holds open-ended discussions that often touch on some of the more racially controversial sections of the book. Ron allows his students to interpret the book however they see it, but he makes sure they at least grapple with the racial issues *Huckleberry Finn* raises. Actually, the hardest part of teaching *Huckleberry Finn* is getting students through the last part of the book, which takes place after Huck leaves the river. Many of his students have difficulty maintaining their interest through this section. Of course, for many of his 16-year-olds, *Huck Finn* works like it always has, as the story of a roguish teenager bent on an adventure outside of the restrictions of parents, schools, and other "civilizing" institutions.

The Lesson

Dealing with the Dialect in *Huckleberry Finn*

"In this book a number of dialects are used, to wit: the Missouri Negro dialect; the extremest form of the backwoods Southwestern dialect; the ordinary 'Pike County' dialect; and four modified varieties of this last." (Twain, Explanatory Note, p. i)

Over the years, Ron's students have made him more than aware of the difficulties of reading and understanding the dialects used in *Huck Finn*. Ron spends a great deal of time discussing dialects with them, and he feels most of his students are aware of the richness and colorfulness of dialect. So Ron, in an effort to help his students appreciate and understand the dialects in *Huckleberry Finn*, plays a little game.

"Okay, class, here's the scoop. You're Hollywood script writers assigned to update *Huckleberry Finn*. Make it modern, catchy, something today's teenager would want to see. I am the big Hollywood producer who will decide if we're going to buy your script, so I want to see a sample of updated dialect. Do this: Pick a selection from the book about a half-page in length. This selection should contain a great deal of dialect. Rewrite in "modern speak" for the script. I want to see these samples. I will select from those samples which of you will write the script."

After this, Ron gives his students an example and then divides his class into groups of three. Each group goes at this project with great zeal. Ron travels from group to group, helping where he is wanted.

The next time his students come to class, they put the finishing touches on their rewrites. After Ron has checked to make sure the rewrites are in acceptable taste, each group reads aloud the Twain passage and follows this with its rewrites. The class has a great time with this very humorous activity. Here are some examples:

Twain:

> He took up a little blue and yauer picture of some cows and a boy and says: "What's this?"
> "It's something they give me for learning my lessons good."
> He tore it up and says:
> "I'll give you something better—I'll give you a cowhide."

Bruce, Jodi, and Melissa:

> Well Pops takes out this gorgeous picture of Axl Rose—you know, the one where he is jumping off the stage onto the heads of his fans—and Pops says:
> "Say what?"
> "Well, dad," I say, "I was awarded this portrait for knowing where all the major mountain ranges lie in North America."
> "Well you should have seen Dad eat that picture. How can anyone digest Axl Rose?" And then Pops says:
> "Forget about the Porsche tomorrow. You're going to the dance in the Hyundai."
> "Uurrghh!"

After this very dramatic reading, great applause breaks out with the laughter continuing.

Here's another example:

Twain:

> "Don't it 'sprise you de way dem kings carries on, Huck?"
> "No," I says, "it don't."

"Why don't it, Huck?"

"Well, it don't, because it's in the breed, I reckon they're all alike."

"But Huck, dese kings o' oum is rapscallions dat's jist what dey is; dey's regular rapscallions."

Johnnie, Suzi, and Geoff:

"I say, the Queen went too, too far this time, don't you agree, duckie?"

"Why no, I do not agree."

"My deah, how can you say that?"

"Well, you see, all of the royal family behave poorly... Too much inbreeding you know."

"But, my deah, all those dudes are rad, real rad, for sure."

After this activity, Ron gives all the groups credit for doing well. The activity has helped his students in two ways with *Huckleberry Finn*. First, they got a fine preview of the book by searching, reading, and translating the dialect passages. Second, they got needed practice in reading and translating the difficult dialect pages.

Discussing *Huckleberry Finn*

Here is a sample of the kinds of issues and concerns Ron's students bring out during a discussion of *Huckleberry Finn*.

Billie: "I loved the river part, but when they got on land I thought it was stupid."

Suzi: "Yeah, that Duke and Dauphin business was hard to take."

Melissa: "My favorite part was when Huck helped Jim escape. I thought that was great of Huck. I mean, Huck thought it was the wrong thing to do."

Johnnie: "It must have made Jim feel stupid to have to be rescued by a kid."

Melissa: "But things were like that then, weren't they? I mean, black people were slaves and what could they do?"

Johnnie: "I know I wouldn't let a kid take care of me. Look at what Tom did at the end of the book to Jim. Look at how Tom makes fun of Jim, a grown-up. This book makes me sick."

Ron: "There are people who feel like you do about this book, that it is demeaning to African Americans. Yet others see it as a strong moral statement about Huck. How do the rest of you see it?"

Geoff: "I see Huck as a very straight guy. Huck goes against all the laws and has his own sense of right to save Jim. Listen to this from

page 118: 'Then I thought a minute, and says to myself, hold on; 'spose you'd 'a' done right and give Jim up? Would you feel better than you do now? No way I'd feel bad—I'd feel just the same way I do now.'
So Huck does the right thing, even though he thinks it's the wrong thing."

Suzi: "Huh?"

Johnnie: "I hate the way the word "nigger" is used in this book."

Ron: "I guess there is no real answer to how to read *Huck Finn*. Everyone sees it a little bit differently."

Jodi: "I thought it was just a great adventure story about a kid without parents who ran away, got on a raft, and floated down a river. How neat."

At the conclusion of the discussion, Ron tells his students the following story:

I have a friend who teaches in a rural school district that is overwhelmingly white. She was teaching *Huckleberry Finn* as the curriculum prescribed. In her class of 30 she had two black kids, and their parents complained about the use of the book. They were offended by the word "nigger" and felt 10th graders were not mature enough to deal with the book. My friend was about to stop teaching the book when her principal made her continue. Then my friend tried to provide alternative novels for the students who had problems with the book. That pleased no one. In essence, the school fought these parents tooth and nail and the school won. The book stayed in the curriculum, and you know what happened? One of the black families moved out of the district. I just don't know what to make out of this sad event. All I know is that *The Adventures of Huckleberry Finn* is a continuing problem for teachers and students.

Teaching *To Kill A Mockingbird*

Introduction

Ron knows of nothing more difficult in English teaching than the teaching of one classic novel to an entire class. The novel has to be worth it, big enough to capture the interests and attention of a teenage audience over an extended period of time. If any novel fits this, it is *To Kill a Mockingbird*, a novel Ron recently placed in his curriculum. This is the story of how Ron approaches the complexity of scaffolding or bridging this novel, leading students over this bridge to their ownership of this literary work. With this novel, Ron does this with a technique he learned at a conference. The acronym for this technique is CORE. First, he creates **C**onnections with the novel; then he develops an **O**wnership for his students, which leads to the open-ended **R**esponses all meaning-centered English teaching is about. Finally, Ron provides **E**xtensions upon which his students build a lasting relationship with the big ideas or themes of the book.

Although this is a detailed approach to *To Kill a Mockingbird*, the structure of the unit can be used with any class novel. CORE is a method of creating a bridge for students to read and appreciate complex, difficult literary works. Ron's formal unit plan is presented in Chapter 14, " Three Sample Unit Plans."

Ron Selects *To Kill a Mockingbird*

English teaching begins with a love of reading. So it was for Ron, whose passion for reading is as old as his memory. He cannot remember back to his prereading days. Ron reads a lot of things: books, magazines, newspapers, the works. He reads widely. Ron loves his books from Ernest Hemingway to Toni Morrison. Zora Neal Hurston to Ann Tyler. You would think a reader like this has difficulty selecting an all-time favorite. Amazingly, Ron can point to one novel that for him transcends everything he has read. For Ron one book stands out in the shaping and reinforcing of many of his values. Perhaps it was the time of life when Ron first read this book, when he was in eighth grade. So many of the events and issues in the book were important to Ron at that age. Perhaps another reason for this book's impact on Ron resides in the 14 years between his first reading and his second reading. Ron read the book again because he was planning to teach the book to his 10th graders. He remembered a great deal about his first reading. But he forgot many of the details. When he read it the second time, 12 years later, it was like a Wordsworthian peak experience. It was the stories from the first reading that became some of the central paradigms that guided Ron's actions and beliefs in several realms of his life while growing up. The book: *To Kill a Mockingbird*.

After Ron finished his adult reading of *To Kill a Mockingbird*, he had two strong reactions. The first was "so this is where I encountered so many of my beliefs in story form for the first time." He encountered strong values about fatherhood through one of the great literary fathers of all time, Atticus; stories about how children form their moral universe; how Scout and Jem learned to value justice by witnessing and learning to hate injustice; how reading can be a natural part of life; and how school can distort that at times, when Scout was told she was reading wrong by her first grade teacher. Ron also encountered again his sense of outrage at how good people can perpetuate evil acts. Ron thought that Scout's questioning of the teacher who condemned Nazi persecution of Jews but seemed to support the injustice done to Tom Robinson was one of the great moral chapters in all of literature he had read. Scout couldn't quite reconcile her teacher's reviling German racism while supporting white American racism.

As Ron finished the book, gentle tears welled in his eyes as he experienced the remarkable knowledge of the place where deeply held beliefs were nailed down in childhood. The stories in *To Kill a Mockingbird* brought back the flooding memory of a child learning the lessons taught in a great moral classic.

The second reaction Ron had was of panic. Ron had committed himself to teach the book as he had convinced his curriculum director to order a class set. How could he teach this book? Ron mused. *To Kill a Mockingbird* is completely self-explanatory. It does not need a teacher. Worse, Ron thought, the book reveals itself slowly one section at a time. This book does not declare itself. A first time reader starts it and thinks it is about growing up in a small southern town. About a quarter of the way through, the book becomes the story of an evil, terrible miscarriage of racial justice in the south of the 1930s. However, the book changes again with both these themes coming together in a sad and beautiful ending, explaining the mysteries unsolved at the beginning of the book.

How can I teach this book? If I introduce it as a book about race, this will give away the slow and important segue into the racial theme. If I do not mention race I will have students surprised and maybe jolted by the explicit and ugly events of the middle of the book. What do I do?

Slowly and with much thought Ron finds a way to teach the book. He is now in his third year of teaching *To Kill a Mockingbird* and has found he has added more structure to his plans. As always, teaching *To Kill a Mockingbird* is a site under construction and he continues to learn how to do it. But he is content with what he has done so far. For the most part Ron feels successful even though his teaching is not perfect and he does not capture the hearts and minds of all his students.

Introducing the Lesson—Connections

Ron's Memory Activity—The Use of Foreshadowing

To Kill a Mockingbird is a memory book, so Ron starts with a memory activity based on the opening structure of the book.

A. A Memory Activity
Tell a story from your childhood, preferably about a brother or sister. Begin the story by teasing us with information about the ending, but do not give the entire story away.

Here is my ending:
I told Lizzy, my daughter, to wipe the blood off her face, stop talking, and go to bed.
The End.

B. Ron waits until his students hand into him the ends of their stories. He carefully selects volunteers to tell their stories, but first makes sure the stories are appropriate to hear in a classroom.

Amanda's ending is about the police finally releasing her brother, and her story is about how her brother was in the wrong place at the wrong time, mistaken for a kid who broke a store window.

Cheryl's ending is about placing her favorite stuffed bear on her pillow and crying. Her story was about moving into an apartment with her mom after the divorce.

After selected students tell their stories, Ron tells his:

My family and I were at a wedding party at a party center near our house. Both my daughters were there. About 10 p.m., my oldest wanted to go home so I drove her. When I returned I walked through the doors and encountered a friend of mine carrying Lizzy, my youngest daughter. Blood seemed to be pouring out of her left leg. He carried Lizzy into a room where another friend, a cardiologist, began treating Lizzy's deep cut. Slowly and carefully he applied pressure to the wound while I held Lizzy's head against my chest. She cried softly in my arms. Terry, the cardiologist, stopped the bleeding and bandaged the wound.

It seems that Lizzy was sitting near a glass on the floor when one of her friends came running over, inadvertently stepped on the glass sending shards everywhere, including one into Lizzy's left leg.

"Not bad for a heart doctor," I told him.

He smiled at me and told me to take her to Children's Hospital for stitches.

When we got to the emergency room, the triage nurse reassured me he would get to us fairly quickly, although Lizzy wasn't that badly hurt, not nearly as badly hurt as the guy who had the beer bottle broken over his face in a bar fight. The battered guy looked a lot worse than he was, but the triage nurse had a lot more sympathy for me. So, we got in very quickly.

The best thing about the treatment was that the doctor was a woman and the suture nurse was male, great role models for Lizzy and for all of us. I almost lost it watching Lizzy get stitched up, but by midnight we were out of there. At home, Lizzy kept chattering away describing the night in excruciating detail to her sister until I had enough of it and told her to wipe the blood off her face and go to bed.

C. After this activity, Ron reads aloud the beginning of *To Kill a Mockingbird:*

When he was nearly thirteen, my brother Jem got his arm badly broken at the elbow. When it healed, and Jem's fears of never being able to play football were assuaged, he was seldom self-conscious about his injury. His left arm was somewhat shorter than his right; when he stood or walked, the back of his hand was at right angles to his body, his thumb parallel to his thigh. He couldn't have cared less, so long as he could pass and punt.

When enough years had gone by to enable us to look back on them, we sometimes discussed the events leading to his accident. I maintain that the Ewells started it all, but Jim, who was four years my senior, said it started long before that. He said it began the summer Dill came to us, when Dill gave us the idea of making Boo Radley come out.

Ron explains, "This is exactly what we just did, an example of telling the ending at the beginning. It will take the whole book to find out how Jem broke his arm. This is an example of foreshadowing or fore, meaning to go first. So, this means the shadow of the end comes first, thus fore or first the shadow, foreshadowing the end of the book."

Ron's Journal Writing Introduction—Ownership

A. Journal Writing Assignment

Describe an incident that may have happened to you or someone you know who was treated badly for unfair reasons. Think of someone who was picked on for being a different race, or because of being a girl, or because of a handicap, or because of being different in any way.

How could this incident have been prevented?

Why do these things happen?

For instance, Amanda, why was your brother taken in by the police? I will read the journal entries, mark sections that can be read aloud, and ask permission to have the students read these sections aloud.

Ron walks around to help his students with the journal writing. Philip, as usual, refuses to do any writing, and Eric won't write about himself. Someone you know, Ron counsels Eric. As for Philip, Ron shakes his head, sighs, and gives up.

"No, you can't have the hall pass, Philip," Ron says quietly to his request. Philip goes back to sleep, a bad example for the other kids who tend to ignore this kid. The bell rings and Ron collects the journals.

Here is an example of Brette's journal entry to Ron.

> I am in the marching band and really love it. I play the clarinet and have lots of good friends who do it, too. We are going to Disney World in the spring. The band is one of the neatest activities in the school. When I first joined the band, we had to go to band camp for a week in the summer. I was all excited then and I went all excited. But then something bad happened. The seniors were allowed to initiate us, and they made me wear a shirt that said I liked to eat. I admit I am overweight, but I still look good and most of the time feel good about myself. I was very ashamed when I had to wear that shirt and I was going to drop out of band but my friend, Jeannie, made me stay. I'm glad I did and now I love the band. When I am a senior, I won't do that to anyone. How could it have been prevented? Maybe the teacher could of stopped it or maybe the seniors could not be so cruel. Why do people do things like that? What's surprising is that some of those seniors became my friends.
>
> Mr. Smith, you can read parts of this, but please don't read out loud the part about my weight. Why are we doing this assignment?
>
> Brette

> Dear Brette:
> Thanks for the honest journal entry. I may read the parts I am allowed to. You will see where this is leading when we begin our novel *To Kill a Mockingbird*.
>
> Mr. Smith

The Reading Workshop

After reading sections from journals and having students read sections from the journals, Ron explains that this book is about good people who are trapped into doing very bad things. This book deals with race and how white people in a small southern town do a very evil thing. He continues:

> Some of this book may bother you because the book is told by a woman remembering when she was a child. So the book presents bad things but doesn't say they are bad. And the book uses a very bad, evil term to describe black people. I cannot use this term in class. You will recognize

it when you see it. You may get angry at the book for using this term or you may feel this is realistic. Even the narrator, Scout, uses this term as a little girl. I would rather we did not use the word in class, although we may need to talk about its use in the book.

One last word before we begin reading the book. I believe *To Kill a Mockingbird* is a moral book, one that teaches the right lessons. I would not use a book in my classroom that I felt taught the wrong lessons. I will defend this book. Some readers disagree with me. You may disagree with me and argue for your reading. Let us keep our arguments polite and let us base what we can from the text of the book itself. I am allowing you to read this book, not because I can make you agree with my point of view about it, but because I think you are mature enough to read it. I love this book; you may see it differently.

Ron then gets his students to crack the book by reading the beginning aloud and reading much of it in class. Advice from Melissa, one of his students, echoes in his mind. This honor student suggested that he have his students read much of the book in class. My friends almost never read the book at home, she told him. Read it in class.

This teacher dilemma, as old as English teaching, is so difficult to resolve. How do you get your students to read a book? How many English teachers, Ron ponders, never realize how few students are reading the assignments. The ways of learning a book without reading it are so numerous it would take a book to describe them all.

Many students have difficulty reading any book. Ron knows that if he has a class full of challenged readers, he cannot teach *To Kill a Mockingbird* or *The Great Gat*sby. But if he has a class full of indifferent readers, kids who really do know how to read, he has a shot at creating interest in these books for many of these kids. So he is willing to try, hoping for a good percentage.

Well, Ron continues the campaign by his class reading. He begins the book aloud and knows that he has to get past the first several pages before these kids will buy into it. The Alabama history section at the beginning is a quick teenage killer of this novel. So Ron begins the reading and has his students follow along for the first page. His students will always sit and read along. It's easy, they don't have to do much, and they are used to it. Not the most dynamic lesson, but part of the necessary trench warfare required to get kids into the novel.

Ron allows his students to read aloud parts of this section. However, he makes sure he is reading when he hits some of the not suited for classroom words found in the book. Finally, when he gets to the section where Dill arrives and the students are beginning to discuss Boo Radley, he goes to silent reading. His kids do that well, with the exception of Philip who as usual wants the hall pass. Philip will do nothing Ron asks him no matter what. Philip is the enigma of this class. Ron feels lucky to have only one this term, although there are several other students who will resist this novel. Ron considers the novel unit the low percentage unit in the English teaching repertoire. Ron is skilled enough to get most kids to read during workshop; he gets most of them to write during workshop. But he will lose a large minority of students when he teaches one class novel, particularly a difficult novel like *To Kill a Mockingbird*. *To Kill a Mockingbird* may not seem difficult to a strong adult reader or even a strong teenage reader. But, to his class of unselected regular 10th graders, it is difficult because it is remote. Ron believes, mostly correctly, that if he can get these kids an entrance into this book, they will be able to do it. It's these, the connections, that are difficult to make.

So Ron uses reading workshop time for the reading of *To Kill a Mockingbird*, first after the aloud reading in his class, then for the next two class periods. For a novel such as this, he sets up two kinds of reading experiences. For those students who prefer to read silently, usually the more experienced advanced readers, he has his silent half of the room. For those students who like to hear the novel read, he has set up a section of the room where either he or an appointed student reads the novel aloud to the group.

The Lesson

Setting the Novel

Geography Connection.   Ron waits until his students have read a great deal of the book before he helps set it up for them. He feels this gives them some information upon which to understand his setting. He first does this travel activity setting the place of the book:

Traveling to Maycomb: Ron

- Has maps for everyone. He explains that the fictional town of Maycomb is really Monroeville, Alabama.

- Has his students drive to Monroeville tracing their route with crayon.

- Uses a map on the board to trace the route and uses tour books to discuss the states and cities that students will pass through.

Race in America in the Thirties—Period Connections

At the library:

- Ron has Mrs. Myers, the media specialist, prepare books and reference materials about the 1930s. She also helps students with web sites related to the thirties and *To Kill a Mockingbird*.

figure **7.2**

Discussion Questions
—What were the thirties like in America?
—What were the roads like?
—How long would it take to get to Monroeville?
—What kind of places would you spend the night in?
—Where would you eat?
—If you are African American, what would you have to worry about
  when you traveled in the South?
—What does apartheid mean (look it up)?
—How does this apply to the American South?

Extended questions
—What was the South like in America?
—What were homes like?
—What were roads like?
—What were cars like?
—What were the methods of communication?
—What did kids do to have fun in the thirties?
—What were schools like in the thirties?
—Write your own question about the thirties.

- Then he asks students in teams of two to figure out what it must have been
  like to drive to Alabama in the 1930s.

- He gives maps to each team and has his students map out the route with
  crayons, but use two lane roads rather than highways.

- Then Ron tells stories about the 1930s. He has his students actively listening by answering the following questions based on his stories and information they find in the books and articles (Figure 7.2):

Ron asks his students to answer in writing about five of these questions.
Ron discusses the answers with his students, which often leads into a general
discussion about race in America then and now, and how the book portrays
these issues.

Historical Connections

About half-way into the novel, Ron reveals the historical connections of the
book. He tells the story of the Scottsboro Boys and how Harper Lee based
the novel on this tragic racial event of the thirties where several young black

males were falsely convicted of raping two white women. This story sets up the trial scene of the book. He also tells his students about the interesting story of Harper Lee, growing up with the writer Truman Capote.

The Trial

After the trial scene has been read by his students, Ron holds a dramatic reading of the trial scene in class. He assigns parts for his students to read from the trial and sets up his classroom like a courtroom. Ron has to be really careful to edit the words from the scene in a way that will not cause embarrassment or anger. So Ron is very careful about which scenes to select and what his students will read.

The Discussion—Response.   After the book has been completed, Ron requires one last guided writing and then opens the discussion. The first time Ron taught the book, his class insisted on talking about race right after the first reading workshop. One of Ron's African American students, Lynette, objected vehemently to the derogatory racial term used throughout the book.

"I hate that word. We shouldn't read a book with that word in it," Lynette tearfully exclaimed. Ron admired her courage for speaking out so forthrightly in a mixed racial class. The class was silenced by Lynette, but Joanne bravely said that she felt bad about the term, but that's the way people spoke then. Ron said he felt the word was used so innocently that it was shocking to read. Lynette silently cried in her seat. After class Ron talked to Lynette and gave her the option of reading something else. Ron told her she could read another book without anyone knowing. Lynette told Ron she would stay with *To Kill a Mockingbird*.

Ron felt not only terrible but confused as to the right response for Lynette. Ron may have experience as a teacher, but he still confronts inexplicable dilemmas every year. Should *To Kill a Mockingbird* be removed from the classroom because of the racial nature of the book? Are the portrayals of African Americans so passive that they represent a negative image for today's African American kids?

Ron doesn't have all the answers to these questions, but he believes in the book enough to keep it anyway, and for the final discussion of the book that year his students never hit on race at all. Instead, they discussed family, friendship, loyalty, and love.

Extensions

Comparing the Book to the Movie.   Ron likes the movie version of *To Kill a Mockingbird* a lot, enough to use with the class. Ron uses the movie partially to reinforce his movie unit. What he does is have his students draw selected scenes as storyboards from the book. And then Ron shows the film. The students relate extremely well to the movie, which adds dimensions to the book itself.

Ron's directions to his students are as follows:

Storyboard the following (draw cartoon panels showing how you would film one of the following scenes):

The Opening
Jem on the Radley Porch
The Jailhouse Scene
The End of the Trial
The Attack on the Kids
The Last Scene

In groups you are to do the following:

- Each group will draw a cartoon of the scene to present to the class. You will receive a grade based on the following with every student in the group doing one of the following activities:

    1. Drawing the scene (up to three illustrators with each panel signed).

    2. Describing the drawing under each panel based on the book (up to two describers with each description signed).

    3. An outline of the storyboard (up to two contributors dividing the storyboard in half).

- Each group will present its storyboard. After each storyboard is completed, we will watch the Academy Award-winning movie *To Kill a Mockingbird*.

Ron's Other Extension Activities.
These are the activities Ron offers his students as extensions on the book.

Activity Choices:

Racism and Prejudice

1. Dramatize a scene that reflects the townspeople's prejudices.

2. Hold a panel discussion on whether Tom would have been found guilty in a modern court.

3. Use quotations from the novel to create a collage of images representing racism.

Justice vs. Injustice

1. Write an article for the *Maycomb Tribune* summarizing Tom's trial. Then write an editorial in which you express your opinion of the jury's decision.

2. Design a book jacket illustrating the novel's condemnation of injustice.

3. Present an opening argument in defense of Boo's actions on Halloween night.

Courage
1. Write an essay describing the most courageous character from the novel.

2. Write a letter to Dill from Scout in which you describe the events of Halloween night.

Coming of Age
1. Interview Scout and Jem 20 years after the close of the novel.

2. Create a mural illustrating Jem's coming of age.

Reflections on Teaching Classic Novels

Ron worries about imposing one "great book" on an entire class. In fact, Ron believes this is the most difficult and potentially least rewarding literary teaching experience. That is not to say that classic texts cannot be taught. But novels are another story. In college English classrooms, a novel is assigned, and students are told to have it completed on a certain date. There are no chapter-by-chapter breakdowns, no endless quizzes, and no two-week long units. Ron does not believe that breaking a novel down into chapter-by-chapter readings can work. The drudgery of this approach will kill any novel. Differing reading rates and styles must be ignored; students will lose the larger context of the novel because they get so bogged down in the reading.

Therefore, Ron believes it is very important to select the right novels very carefully. Are *The Great Gatsby*, *Huckleberry Finn*, and *To Kill a Mockingbird* the right novels? They can be. But they are confusing works, with racist and elitist sentiments that are tough to set aside that may repel a modern, fair-minded reader. Ron does the right thing by bringing up these issues, and the discussion ends on the right note when Ron allows his students to express confusion and uncertainty about the books. Ron certifies that his students' opinions, even if they reflect tentativeness, are valid. As a result, his students feel more confident as readers. Ron's openness to student analysis allows his students to explore difficult and complex literature. His students know they will be given a fair hearing and thus they are willing to offer ideas that may be risky. When Ron is uncertain about his interpretations or feelings about a book, he will tell his students. Thus, Ron models for his students how even a mature reader may have trouble with difficult literature.

Perhaps this class is an uneasy alliance between meaning-centered theory and traditional English teaching. Or perhaps this class displays how the classic teaching texts can be adapted for English teaching for our time. You decide.

Teacher as Researcher

Questions

- What is "classic" literature?
- Should classic literature be taught in secondary classrooms? If yes, why? If no, why not?
- What classic literature did you have good experiences with in junior and senior high schools? Why were the experiences good?
- What classic literature did you have bad experiences with in junior and senior high schools? Why were the experiences bad?
- What are the problems with teaching the classics, particularly the same work to an entire class? How would you try to overcome these problems?
- Would you be able to tell if your students are reading your assignments without giving quizzes? How?
- How would you make assignments on a classic novel? Explain your approach.
- What would you do when students tell you they do not understand and/or hate the assigned book?
- *The Great Gatsby* and *The Adventures of Huckleberry Finn* are two of the most frequently taught books in American high schools. Do you agree that these books should be taught in secondary schools? If yes, why? If no, why not?
- Do you find moments in these books to be racist or elitist? If yes, how would you deal with these aspects of the book? Would you have trouble using these books in multiethnic classrooms? Are these just "dead white male" books that have passed their time, or do *The Great Gatsby* and *Huckleberry Finn* have messages for the great variety of students in classrooms today? Explain. How would you lead a discussion on *The Great Gatsby*, *Huck Finn*, or *To Kill a Mockingbird* in a multiethnic classroom?
- Are there any books that are commonly used that you feel should no longer be in a classroom? Explain why.

Activities

- React to the story. Give your impressions and thoughts.
- Make a list of classic literary works that should be part of the secondary curriculum. Explain why you selected these works, why they would work, and how you would teach them to young adults.

- Rent the movie "The Great Gatsby." Discuss how true the movie is to the book. Did the movie change how you felt about or interpreted the novel?
- Plan thematic units that pair classic novels with young adult novels. Plan introductions and activities for the units. Here are two unit examples: Journeys—The Adventures of Huckleberry Finn and Homecoming by Cynthia Voigt; Friendship—Of Mice and Men and Bridge to Terabithia by Katherine Patterson.

IRA/NCTE Standards for English Language Arts for With Performance Benchmarks for Chapter 7

Standard One

Students read a wide range of print and nonprint texts to build an understanding of texts, of themselves, and of the cultures of the United States and the world; to acquire new information; to respond to the needs and demands of society and the workplace; and for personal fulfillment. Among these texts are fiction and non-fiction, classic and contemporary works.

Performance Benchmark for Standard One

Students will read classic American novels.

Standard Two

Students read a wide range of literature from many periods in many genres to build an understanding of the many dimensions (e.g., philosophical, ethical, aesthetic) of human experience.

Performance Benchmark for Standard Two

Students will read classic American novels.

Standard Three

Students apply a wide range of strategies to comprehend, interpret, evaluate, and appreciate texts. They draw on their prior experience, their interactions with other readers and writers, their knowledge of word meaning and of other texts, their word identification strategies, and their understanding of textual features (e.g., sound-letter correspondence, sentence structure, context graphics).

Performance Benchmark for Standard Three

Students will be introduced to many scaffolding methods in order to distill and understand classic novels.

Standard Four

Students adjust their use of spoken, written, and visual language (e.g., conventions, style, vocabulary) to communicate effectively with a variety of audiences and for different purposes.

Performance Benchmark for Standard Four

Students use a variety of media to communicate about classic American texts. These media include journals, critical response papers, storyboards, and other written activities.

Standard Six

Students apply knowledge of language structure, language conventions (e.g., spelling and punctuation), media techniques, figurative language, and genre to create, critique, and discuss print and nonprint texts.

Performance Benchmark for Standard Six

Students apply language and media knowledge to create a variety of responses to critique and discuss classic novels.

Standard Seven

Students conduct research on issues and interests by generating ideas and questions, and by posing problems. They gather, evaluate, and synthesize data from a variety of sources (e.g., print and nonprint texts, artifacts, and people) to communicate their discoveries in ways that suit their purpose and audience.

Performance Benchmark for Standard Seven

Students use a variety of sources to understand the social, political, geographic, and historic roots of novels such as *The Great Gatsby*, *The Adventures of Huckleberry Finn*, and *To Kill a Mockingbird*. These sources include print and nonprint material.

Standard Nine

Students develop an understanding of and a respect for diversity in language use, patterns, and dialects across cultures, ethnic groups, geographic regions, and social roles.

Performance Benchmark for Standard Nine

Students develop an understanding of and a respect for diversity in language use by participating in activities studying the dialects in *The Adventures of Huckleberry Finn*.

Recommended Readings

Applebee, A. N. (1992). Stability and change in the high-school canon. *English Journal*, 82, 27–32.

This is a survey of the literary texts used in American schools. Applebee discovers that the texts used in the schools come from a narrow band of the classics. Topping the list is *Romeo and Juliet*, with *Macbeth* and *The Adventures of Huckleberry Finn* close behind.

Day, F. A. (1999). *Multicultural voices in contemporary literature: A resource for teachers*. Portsmouth, NH: Heinemann.

This is a guide for using multicultural literature. The book describes authors and works as well as methods.

Johnson, C. D. (2000). *Understanding the adventures of Huckleberry Finn* and *understanding To Kill A Mockingbird*. Westport, CT: Greenwood Publishing Group, www.linincontext.com.

These electronic resources represent the wave of the future since they are online. Each of these collections presents background materials and resources for the study of these novels. For instance, the *To Kill A Mockingbird* site includes audio and newsreels about the Scottsboro Trial, and *The Huckleberry Finn* site includes a narrative of a slave auction.

Peck, D. (1989). *Novels of initiation: A guidebook fox teaching literature to adolescents*. New York: Teachers College Press.

This is a guidebook for using novels, both classic and new, in the classroom. The first section of each chapter contains an analysis of each novel. This is followed by a section or guide on how to teach the novel.

Phelan, P. (1990). *Literature and life: Making connections in the classroom*. Urbana, IL: National Council of Teachers of English.

This is a collection of essays that explores ways of connecting literary experience with the students teachers face.

Simmons, J. S., & Deluzain, H. E. (1992). *Teaching literature in middle and secondary grades*. Boston: Allyn and Bacon.

This text is a comprehensive view of literature instruction in middle and secondary schools. The book includes a section on reader-response techniques.

Whaley, L., & Dodge, L. (1999). *Weaving in the women: Transforming the high school English curriculum*. Portsmouth, NH: Heinemann-Boynton Cook.

This book is a helpful guide on using literature about women in high school English classes.

Often Taught Classics

Romeo and Juliet
Macbeth
The Adventures of Huckleberry Finn
Julius Caesar
To Kill a Mockingbird

Of Mice and Men
The Great Gatsby
Lord of the Flies
The Scarlet Letter

chapter EIGHT

Teaching Writing

Introduction

Getting Started

I see writers everywhere I turn. When I was a high school teacher, my students would not only hand me poems they had written, but also more than one turned in a full-length novel. I am always encountering adults from all walks of life who have squirreled away, in their attics or basements, novels they have written. When my daughter was in first grade, even she was a writer. She would spend entire Sunday afternoons at the typewriter, using one finger at a time, laboriously composing stories that were only middles filled with invented spellings.

A Writing Classroom

Bob Sanderfelt (Chapter Four, "Discussing Books") has students who are writers. They are usually writing something, or reading another student's paper, or talking to a classroom neighbor about a piece of writing. These kids do not hesitate to read a piece of their writing out loud, and many of them have entered writing contests. They speak the language of writers, understanding the place of voice and style and the need for clarity and structure. They know how to overcome writing blocks and understand the purpose of free writing. These are students who write all the time and in all kinds of modes. They write in journals at the drop of a hat. They write about readings, class discussions, and events. They are given topic choices and write on those, or they find their own topics. Much of the work is bulk writing, skimmed by the teacher and graded only for quantity. Some early writings is read and responded to in an informal way. Some writings go through several drafts before they become public, either read by the teacher and students in class or by an extended public reached through writing contests, the school newspaper, and letters.

Some kids talk a great deal about what they write and like to share it. Others allow only the teacher to look at their work. Everything these students write is placed in folders or journals, all of which are kept in boxes in the front of the room. Each student has a personal record of what he or she writes, including a chart describing each piece. An outside evaluator could pick up a folder and get a sense of that student's accomplishments as a writer.

These students seem to prize freshness and style or voice. They understand the need to communicate with vigor and grace, and they applaud fresh writing when they read it or hear it. They feel the other ingredients, structure and correctness, are the scaffolding that holds up the rest of the work. Correctness is dealt with on an individual basis. The teacher identifies a problem and goes after it or delivers lessons based on class errors. All in all, students have a complete and full sense of writing, of how to go about doing it and how to make themselves into writers. (Principles of writing workshops can be found in Chapter One.)

Introducing the Lesson: Preparing for Writing

Bob hates that school starts in August. "What's wrong with the Tuesday after Labor Day?" he muses. There is a psychological distastefulness to teaching in August that drives Bob crazy. "Maybe that will change with the next-generation teacher," he says, "when year-round schools are common." But Bob still believes that school should start the day after Labor Day.

For all teachers, the first week of school is critical. They have to set a tone, establish their authority, and lay down guidelines for the class. For most teachers it is a very tough week. Bob uses a good part of this first week to acquaint his students with his writing program, which he believes is unusual and complex enough that many students need an orientation.

Bob assembled some supplies for this class before the first week of school. He has boxes for the portfolios his students will keep, folders that will function as the portfolios, and notebooks that will serve as journals. (His school supplies him with these items, at least at the moment.) Bob's classroom is set up as a writing workshop to facilitate students' work (Figure 8.1).

Bob introduces his writing program to his 10th graders on the third day of class. He saves the first two days to go over class discipline rules, acquaint students with other parts of his program, and pass out materials.

Bob divides his writing orientation into two main points: writing and record keeping. The students each get a copy of his guidelines, and Bob reviews them with the class (Figure 8.2). He takes his time answering all questions.

figure **8.1**

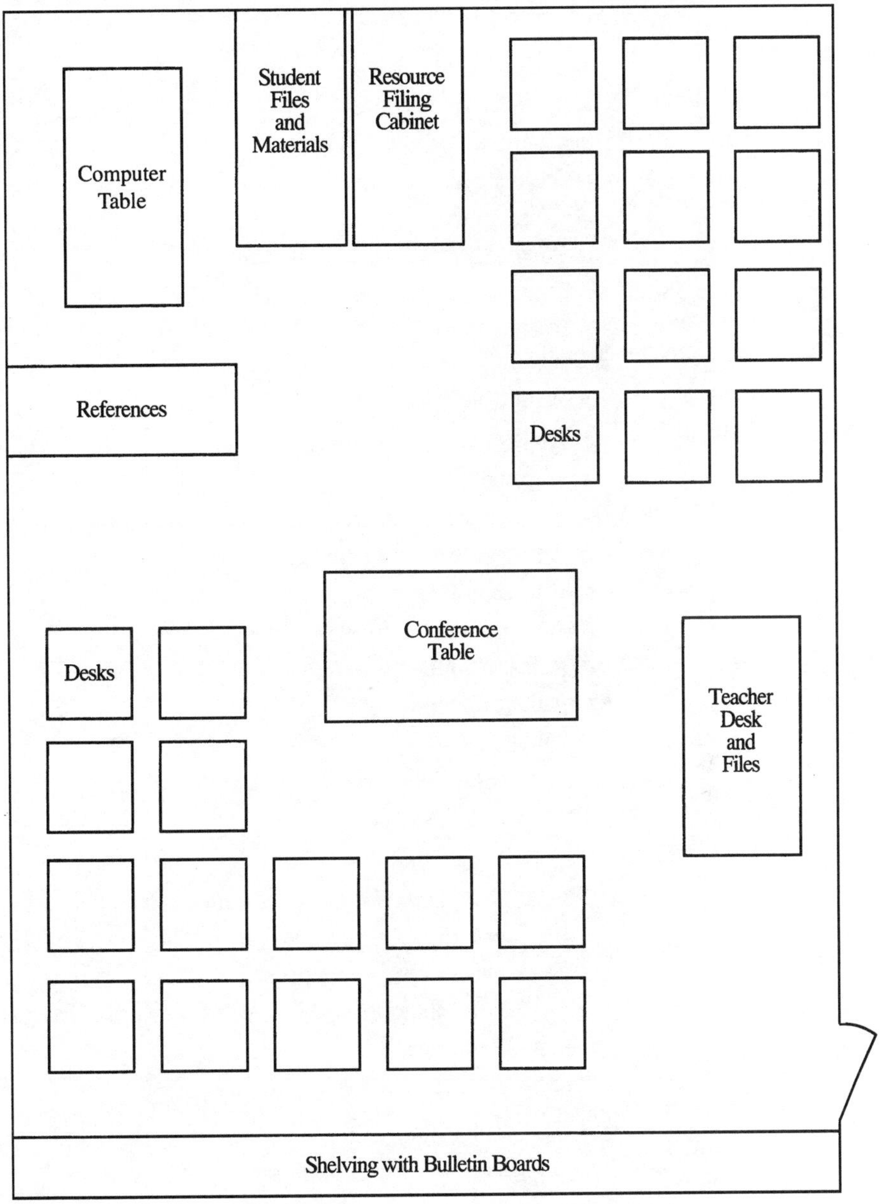

Computer
Table

Student
Files
and
Materials

Resource
Filing
Cabinet

References

Desks

Desks

Conference
Table

Teacher
Desk
and
Files

Shelving with Bulletin Boards

Free Writing (Informal Writing): You will be writing all the time in this class. Most of the writing will count if you have adequately completed it. You will do this in a journal I will supply you with.

- Journal assignments
- Poems
- Rough drafts
- Responses to readings
- Class topics
- Anything you want to write about

Public Writing (Formal Writing): This is writing you will develop for me and other readers such as your classmates. This is writing for an audience, writing that goes public.

- A personal essay
- An essay on a class topic
- A formal letter
- A newspaper or magazine article, feature, or editorial
- A short story
- A book critique
- A television, film, or play review
- A character analysis from a book or play
- A public speech
- Other

Public Writing Rules: You will be asked to turn in four completed papers—that is, papers that have gone through the following steps:

Step 1—Rough draft.

Step 2—Read and critiqued by a student. (You may use guidelines I provide. You must have a written critique attached to your paper.)

Step 3—Read and critiqued by me. This will count as pass/fail.

Step 4—Rewritten.

Step 5—Turned in to me. Graded.

Dates: (to be announced)

Paper 1	*Paper 2*
Step 1	Step 1
Step 2	Step 2

| figure ◊ 8.2 | (Continued) |

Step 3	Step 3
Step 4	Step 4
Step 5	Step 5
Paper 3	*Paper 4*
Step 1	Step 1
Step 2	Step 2
Step 3	Step 3
Step 4	Step 4
Step 5	Step 5

- At least two of these papers will be made available to your fellow students.
- At least one of these papers will be written for an audience outside the classroom.
- At least one of these papers will be on a subject or reading covered in class.

Grades: The completed public writing will be assigned a letter grade, based on the following (holistic scale):

5 = A   The writing shows a strong degree of organization, clarity, and thought. It is generally error-free. Above all, the reader senses the writer's voice. The writing has vigor and personality. There is strong detail and supporting evidence.

4 = B   The writing is clear, thoughtful, and organized. Errors are few and do not detract from meaning.

3 = C   Although there is paragraphing and basic organization, some of the writing errors may cause some loss of meaning or a general impression of sloppiness. The writing lacks voice and is flat and underdeveloped.

2 = D   The writing lacks structure. Some paragraphing may exist, but not much. The writing is characterized by a lack of coherence and organization at the paragraph and sentence level. Serious, debilitating run-ons and fragmented sentences are found in the writing. Errors occur that seriously hamper meaning.

1 = F   There is no clear structure to this writing. Paragraphing does not exist. Sentences seldom are complete or understandable. Errors are serious and frequent and greatly hinder meaning. The ideas are impossible to discern or are extremely superficial.

(The Step 3 paper may be graded on the same scale but will only count as pass/fail.)

figure ◊ 8.2 | **(Continued)**

You will receive an A/pass/fail grade for your free writing and your record keeping. An A will be given for having everything well done and in on time. You will receive a letter grade for your public writings. This grade will include all the steps outlined, as well as the holistic evaluation for your final copy.

Writing Workshop Guidelines
You may do the following during the writing workshop:

- Write, free write, draft, write final copy
- Read and respond to a classmate's writing
- Read your work aloud to a classmate
- Revise a piece of writing based on classmate or teacher suggestions

Record Keeping

Bob also tells his students what record-keeping procedures they are to follow.

I am going to pass out folders and notebooks to all of you. You will be required to keep all of your journal writing in your notebooks and all other writing in your folders, which we will call portfolios. These notebooks and folders must always be kept in these boxes up front in alphabetical order by last name, unless, of course, you have my permission to take your journal or some of your writings home with you.

Please place your name on the upper right-hand corner of your journal and on the tab of your folder. Also, I will ask you to keep a record of all of your writing and other projects on the record-keeping sheets you can find stapled on the inside of your portfolio. I might add that I will double-check your page counts.

At the end of this semester, I want you to do the following: Select your best public writing and select 5 to 10 pages of the best informal writing you have done. Place the public writing, with all of the drafts, and the best informal writing in the front of your portfolio and fill out the end-of-semester statement. These pieces of writing are your models, your statements, about the best that you accomplished this semester.

You will find record keeping sheets in your portfolios. I will show you how to keep these records. I will model their use throughout the class. Below you will find:

- Journal Writing: Writing Workshop—Figure 8.3
- Public Writing Record Keeping—Figure 8.4
- Additional Projects—Figure 8.5
- Reading Workshop Record Sheet—Figure 8.6
- End-of-Semester-Statement—Figure 8.7

Reflections on Getting Started

This ends Bob's introduction to his writing program; he and his students now know that school has started. His students will enjoy and understand the writing program once it gets under way. With this structure, they will undertake all the kinds of writing experiences, informal and formal, 10th graders should have.

The program allows Bob the freedom to assign a great deal of free, uninhibited writing. His students will spend a lot of time drafting and preparing statements, taking writing risks without fear of red-pencil retaliation, and generating ideas, thoughts, and images—in short, becoming fluent.

The program also allows Bob the freedom to generate ideas that can spur his students to write spontaneously about things meaningful to them. In essence, Bob plans for his students to write a great deal. His students will fill pages and pages on a variety of subjects, mainly themselves, of course.

But Bob also asks his students to control their writing, and he highly structures this part of his program. Bob knows that writing does not flow in one direction, that writers do not draft, revise, and edit in a strict order. What Bob hopes he is doing with the deadlines is showing his students a method of developing a piece of writing. He forces his students into drafting and revising at least some of their writing, and by doing this, he provides them with a system that someday they may adopt, modify, or reject. For Bob, it is important to help students systematize a chaotic and often inexplicable process.

Bob feels that the purpose of formal writing is to create statements for an audience to read, so he provides audiences for his students. He asks them to share at least two of their public pieces with each other. Bob does this in several ways. First, he has a reading day, during which finished papers are passed around the class for student reaction. These written reactions are not editing, but responses and queries to a finished piece of writing. Second, Bob places writing on the bulletin boards for casual reading. Every student is ensured of having at least one selection placed on the bulletin board during a semester. Third, Bob asks each student to submit a piece for a class booklet that is prepared at the end of

(*text continued on page 191*)

figure ◊ 8.3	Journal Writing: Writing Workshop

Date	# of Pages	Subject	Conf. Date	Reader's Comments	Reader's Name

figure ● 8.4	Public Writing/Record Keeping

	Step 1 Date/ Comments	Step 2 Date/ Comments	Step 3 Date/ Comments	Step 4 Date/ Comments	Step 5 Date/ Comments
Writing #1					
Writing #2					
Writing #3					
Writing #4					

figure ◑ 8.5	Additional Projects

Project Title	Comments	Date

figure ◊ **8.6**	Reading Workshop Record Sheet

My best piece of public writing is_____

I feel this is my best because:

My best informal pieces are:

I feel these are my best pieces because:

A note about myself as a writer:

figure ◊ 8.7 | **End of Semester Statement**

Date	Works Read	Pages	Responses	Comments

the semester, made available to any student who wants a copy, and placed in the library.

This class book fulfills Bob's requirement that at least one writing be made available beyond the classroom. However, many of his students fulfill this requirement in other ways as well. They send pieces about a book to the author, often getting responses; get essays in the school newspaper; send letters to public officials and others; and enter all kinds of contests.

Bob still must read a great deal of writing, but his system allows students to write much more than he has to read. And his holistic grading method simplifies, for both him and his students, the process of analyzing and critiquing the writing. Additionally, his method of grading echoes the message that the writing is what is paramount. The portfolios and record-keeping systems provide a semester-long view of his student writers, a view of them that is systematic, comprehensive, and helpful.

The Writing Workshop, Day One: Getting Ideas to Write About

For Bob, teaching *The Outsiders* is as close to a sure thing as he knows in education. "Kids like the book, and I know how to teach it," he will tell anyone. His 25 tenth graders have read *The Outsiders*, written critical responses, and freely discussed the book. Tomorrow, Bob and his students know, will be a writing workshop day, and although his students may write about anything, the stimulus Bob gives them is based on *The Outsiders* and the ensuing discussion. His students are filled with ideas, and they are thinking. However, rather than just send them to their journals, Bob feels he should provide them some kind of bridge to the writing. So following the discussion, Bob and his students brainstorm for questions they can use to help them start their free writing.

Bob begins the brainstorming by helping students develop a list of questions.

> Bob: "Nice discussion. So all kids feel like outsiders you explained. You could write about that on your writing day tomorrow. What other questions based on the book could you write about tomorrow?"

Bob and his students come up with this list:

> Who were the outsiders in the book and why were they on the outside?
> What were the characters in the book fighting about? What was the source of their anger?
> Could teachers have helped Ponyboy?
> Why was the poem "Nothing Gold Can Stay" so important to Ponyboy? Do you agree with the poem's premise?
> Write a letter to Ponyboy about your experiences.

Who were your favorite characters in the book and why?

What is an outsider?

Are there outsiders in this school? Who are they and why are they on the outside?

Do you ever feel like an outsider? When and why?

Writing Workshop, Day Two: Conferencing—Helping Students Get Started

When his students come in, they go right to the boxes at the front of the room. Each student takes out a spiral notebook and a folder. On the board are the questions Bob and his students posed yesterday. Bob reminds the class that this is a workshop day, and suddenly the chatter subsides and pencils and pens begin to move, talking turns to whispers; the workshop begins. Bob looks around to make sure the class is progressing. Because everything looks okay, he begins writing in his own journal, which has become a potpourri of ideas and thoughts, poetry and reminiscences, teaching ideas and concerns, lessons for the future, and critiques of those that have passed. Bob feels that it is important that he write also and not do other things, like grade papers. So, he writes for about 10 minutes and then wanders around the classroom, seeking those that may need his help.

"Need anything?" he asks Sam.

"Nope."

Bob moves on. Sarah stops him and asks if he would read what she wrote (Figure 8.8).

"Well, what do I do now?" Sarah asks.

"Nice stuff," Bob says, meaning it. "What do you and Marybeth and Jennifer do together?"

"I don't know, mess around, go to the mall on weekends."

"Why don't you write about one of your mall trips. Put in as much detail as possible."

"What do you mean?"

"You know, describe the store, what you look at. Do you buy anything? What do you eat for lunch? What do you wear? What do you talk about? Why these excursions are so nice."

"Okay. Thanks."

Bob gets up from the desk next to Sarah's and sees that George will do anything but write. George has his head on his hands on his desk.

"Hey, George."

"Mr. S."

"Blocking?"

"Huh?"

"May I help, George?"

figure ● **8.8**

> I love to be alone. I shared a room with my sister for years, but now she has moved out so the room is all mine. I go there to read or listen to music or write in my diary or journal. I like the solitude very much. I am never lonely. Sometimes at school, in classes, in the cafeteria, in the halls, I am surrounded by people, I am not alone, but I feel lonely. In crowds I often am sad and lonely. When I am with Bill I am not alone or lonely either, or when I'm with Marybeth and Jennifer I feel okay too...

"Help do what?"

"May I offer you some ideas to write about?"

George belongs to a class of students Bob and all teachers encounter in their careers: students who are deeply ambivalent or hostile to everything that goes on in school. These students seem to have complex inner lives that they never reveal and, in many cases, sad and often painful outer lives. George isn't motivated by grades and may or may not respond to Bob's gentle prodding. George may write for Bob on any given day, or he may not. George may fail the class or may decide to try and succeed. Bob, in the course of his career, will do the right things and the wrong things with his "Georges." He will communicate with some, while others will pass through with barely a word. Bob, like all teachers, would be better off if he were God, but he is not, and as a result of Bob's lack of omnipotence, he will not reach, motivate, teach, or transform all of his students. He will lose many of the most damaged, the most vulnerable, the students who most need to read and write.

Yet, Bob knows he is not trained to be a psychologist, so he is very careful not to pry or fool around with complex problems. Although he receives personal writing from his students, he handles the revelations they contain with a great deal of care. Bob's chief concern with George is to help him achieve

Dear Ponyboy,

I know how you feel. I am in this school with lots of groups just like you have. Here we've got the Socs but we call them "Chappies." They get the best clothes and they're the most popular kids — at least they think so. Then we got the jox — you know, the athletes who are also real popular and real stuck up and some of them are real dumb, too. Then we got the burnouts; you know, the druggies, guys with earrings and mohawks, and girls with nose rings (yuck) I don't belong to any of those groups and I'm happy about that and I got friends here that don't belong to any of those groups either.

We are like you, Ponyboy. I guess we are kind of a group; an ungroup, you might say.

literacy. The teacher knows he is not fully equipped to help George with his problems.

George puts his head back on his arms, which are lying flat on his desk. He will not write today.

Jim is wildly flailing his arm, gaining the attention of Bob, who walks over and reads the proud young writer's journal entry (Figure 8.9).

Jim's journal entry continues for a bit and Bob finishes it with a smile and "nice" to Jim, who smiles back.

Bob has time to read a few more entries and suggest a new idea to a stuck writer before he needs to end the workshop.

"It's time to log your entries," Bob tells the class, breaking the workshop mood. A new noise takes over the classroom, the rustling of bringing this activity to conclusion. His students make the proper notations on their record-keeping sheets and then put their portfolios back in the boxes right before the bell rings. It will take Bob about 20 minutes to check the entries for record-keeping accuracy, to skim the journals, and to comment on some entries that ask questions.

Reflections on the Writing Workshop

The process has started. Bob's students have begun to write—the important first step. The informal writing belongs to his students. They are free to choose what they want to write and how they want to write it. They are free to make mistakes and to be disorganized. They are free to drop topics and start new ones. Bob sees this freedom not as license, but as an important step in becoming fluent. Through selective revision and editing, Bob's students will create public pieces. But those pieces are only possible if his students have a body of work, a discovered corpus of ideas and stories that only come about with free and fluent writing.

When Writing Goes Public

Rough Draft—Bob Writes for His Students

Bob feels October is the most beautiful month of the year: warm days, cool nights, colorful leaves, lots of sunshine. By the middle of October, his 10th grade class has bonded. He needn't worry too much about class discipline, although individual behavior problems will crop up all year, as is usual. His students have read *The Outsiders*, read self-selected novels, looked at some poems. They are completely accustomed to the writing workshop. Most of his students have written over 50 pages in their journals on all sorts of topics and themes. His students enter the classroom familiar with each other and comfortable with Bob, who will introduce the first piece of public writing.

"Your job now is to find a section of your journal that you feel you would like to prepare for others to read. Let me give you a personal example. I did some journal writing of my own during the writing workshop, and I would like to publish a portion of it. Let me share it with you.

"My First Flight"

I do not love to fly, but I do it anyway. My family and I were traveling abroad for the first time, to France for a visit with distant relatives. The first part of the flight left from Cleveland and was supposed to leave about 2 p.m. It was TWA. We got on the plane and were about to leave when we were told that thunderstorms would delay our flight to Kennedy airport, so we got off and waited for an hour in the terminal. We knew some people that were also on the flight, so we talked to them in the lobby. About 3 p.m. we got back on the plane and it took off. A lot of passengers were worried that they were going to miss connecting flights. Most people on the plane were going overseas because this plane was landing at the International Terminal at Kennedy. We were not worried because our flight to France wasn't scheduled to leave until about 11 p.m. that evening. We had plenty of time. The ride was kind of bumpy and our friends on the plane complained a lot about the delay, although the stewards and stewardesses fought back insisting it was the weather. When we arrived at the TWA terminal in New York, the weather was ominous, soon breaking into one of the worst thunderstorms I had ever seen. We went to the International Terminal where we planned to wait the six hours for our chartered flight on a small, unknown airline where comforts are short but seats are cheap. We got to the International Terminal by bus provided by the airport. On the way we passed the famous Saarinen-designed TWA terminal. I enjoyed looking at the different terminal buildings. When we got to the International Terminal we were the only ones there except for airline personnel. It was obviously a cheap airline because the terminal was poorly decorated, kind of barren and depressing. We were lucky in that we were able to check in this early, but we had not much to do until the plane was scheduled to leave at 11 p.m. We had packed our dinner, so we went to an empty bar-restaurant and ate our sandwiches, watching the activity of the airport from the big glass windows. After dinner we went back to the main area of the terminal where more people were arriving and it was filling up with lots of kids running around. I went to a candy shop in the terminal where the clerk advised me that the plane was going to be delayed for hours. I went back to my family despondent at the news. 11 p.m. came and went but by now the terminal was crowded with the people that were going to fill this 747. We soon heard a rumor that buses were going to take us to a Holiday Inn where we could spend the night, although the flight was now scheduled to leave about 6 a.m. The bus scene was awful. Too few buses for too many people. I was separated from my family who were taken first and then I was put on a crowded bus where I had to stand in a crowded aisle and wait on the hot bus. Finally I was taken to the Holiday Inn where I was reunited with my family and we tried to check in. Much to my dismay I discovered that the airline was not putting us up for the night at all. They were just giving us a banquet meal, a meal I absolutely did not want and could hardly eat. By now it was 2 a.m. My family and I found an empty conference room. My children and I slept on the floor while my wife wrote a letter. At 3:30 a.m. the buses arrived we were told by a screaming person who jarred the children and myself awake. My exhausted family and myself trudged to the buses that took forever to load. By 3:45 a.m. we were back at the terminal and in line to board the plane. The only problem was there seemed to be no plane. We waited for an hour and twenty minutes until this line moved. I was angry at this point and asked for my money back from an airline representative, who promised to look into it, but disappeared permanently. Finally, at 5:30 a.m. we were on the plane, a cramped 747, but we had a blanket and pillow nicely wrapped in plastic bags. We settled in and fell asleep as soon as the plane took off. Not quite 55 minutes into the flight I was awakened by this announcement. Because of flap problems, we have to turn around and go back to New York. I turned to my wife and remarked casually, "I don't think they can land the plane without flaps." My wife looked terror stricken. Basically the passengers around us were fairly calm. I asked a stewardess if it was going to be a rough landing and she said no. Fifty-five minutes later we landed smooth as silk at Kennedy where we were kept on the plane for about a half hour before we were allowed off. It was midmorning by now and I really wanted out of this flight. I went to the airline agent screaming to refund my money. I wasn't the only one. A man quietly told the agent that he feared for the health of some of the elderly passengers. Meanwhile, people were passing around juice and cookies to the exhausted passengers sprawled out on the terminal floor. It was like a scene out of a disaster with Red Cross workers trying to help. I wanted to walk out of there and rent a car to drive home. But we stayed. By 10 a.m. a new airplane arrived and by 11 a.m. we were all boarded. My children slept for the entire flight. I slept through most of it, having nightmares about endless long lines that went nowhere.

Bob looks around the room after the reading; his students look both amused and sad for him.

"It's a true story," Bob says. "This is a really rough draft. I will use this as an example of how a piece of writing develops from step one, the rough draft, to the final copy. Please keep this in your portfolio because we will be developing my story as an example as we go along.

"Now it is your job to find a piece of writing that you will develop and turn into a piece of public writing.

"I am now going to place you into groups of three. Your job is to help each other select a portion of the journal that you would like to use for your rough draft.

"Here are your group roles:

"Person one either makes a selection or asks for advice from persons two and three. Keep switching roles until all three people have selected their piece.

"When you have selected your piece, copy it, rewrite it, or continue writing it and turn in two to four pages on Friday."

Bob goes from group to group offering suggestions. The letter to Ponyboy that Jim wrote is going to go public. Tom's group convinces him into using his broken-arm story. Sally decides to enhance her response to *Roll of Thunder, Hear My Cry*: "Why every student should read this book." The bell rings.

Reflections on Rough Drafts

Bob has spent a great deal of time helping his students become fluent. Up until this point, they have written without being subjected to judgment or criticism. Now Bob will help them shape their first piece of public writing, using his own story as an example. He intentionally wrote it quickly. Although he did not insert mistakes, he did allow his writing to ramble, so that the story is a bit understructured. He will develop this piece at each step of the process.

His students have to turn in a rough draft of something, which is all they are required to do. Bob will take them through each step until they have a finished piece. Bob grouped his students and gave them a relatively low-level project so they can get used to working with each other. He based his groupings on what he knows about his students and how well he feels they will work together. Bob hopes that these groups will be permanent and that they will become full-fledged writing support groups.

Bob allows his students a great deal of freedom in their writing. The class has spent a lot of time on what Bob considers prewriting activities (he also considers them thinking activities). These activities consist of the books, poems, stories, and plays the students read and discuss. Bob's classroom is the scene of a great many stories, images, ideas, and characters, and his students are allowed to write free of editing and interruption. Only after Bob believes that there is a sufficient amount of this completed journal writing does he ask his students to take a small piece—he hopes a jewel—from the free flow of writing in their journals and turn it into a public statement. His students get to select the journal topics (even though he aids them in this), the public statements they wish to make, and the structure of the writing (no thesis statements required). However, Bob does provide his students with an increasingly critical readership to help them shape their writing for public consumption. For Bob, the next step is to help his students begin to shape and structure their rough drafts.

Training Student Readers: Rough Draft Read and Critiqued by a Student

"Take your rough draft out," Bob requests. "You will need to read each other's work and offer some suggestions on how to shape the writing for clarity and understanding. I recommend that you consider the following questions when you read another student's work:

- Is the writing divided into paragraphs that make sense?

- Is it understandable and clear?

- Do you recommend that some parts be cut?

■ Do you recommend switching some of the writing around?

■ Are there places where writing needs to be added?

■ Are most of the sentences clear and understandable?

"These are questions that you may use as guidelines to help a classmate shape her or his writing. I have made copies of these questions that I want you to keep in your portfolios.

"Each of you is required not only to place your rough draft in your portfolio, but also to write some comments, either on a classmate's rough draft or on a separate sheet of paper. Sign these and turn them in with the rough draft.

"Okay. Once again, at the end of this, place your rough draft in your portfolio, along with your classmate's comments.

"Here, let me show you what I mean. Take out my story that I gave you, 'My Worst Flight.' Let's read some of it together to see what suggestions you may offer me. What are some comments you would make to me on this piece of writing?"

Sally raises her hand. "The story is just one big paragraph."

"So what would you recommend, Sally?"

"I would make a new paragraph at 'The first part of the flight left from Cleveland.' and at the 'The ride was kind of bumpy,' and at 'When we arrived at the TWA terminal.'"

Bill raises his hand.

"I don't agree with Sally on some of her paragraph ideas. She's creating a lot of one-sentence paragraphs for you."

"Okay, Bill. "What are your ideas?"

"I would place the first paragraph at 'We got on the plane and were about to leave,' and I wouldn't start a new paragraph at 'The ride was kind of bumpy.' But I agree with Sally on her third paragraph placement."

"All right Bill and Sally. Thanks. I'll take both your suggestions under advisement. Any other ideas for improvement?"

No response.

"Is the piece understandable and clear throughout?"

"Yeah."

"The sentences are kind of choppy."

"There are a lot of details."

"I guess I'll work on my paragraphing and try to make my sentences more interesting. I'll check over the details and see if I get wordy and cut some, maybe. We'll take a look at my story again after I go back over it."

"Now," Bob stated, "move into your writing groups and begin reading each other's papers. Remember to be friendly and positive, but consider a helpful dialogue based on the questions you have. You'll have the rest of this period and all of class Monday."

Bob works the room. Some of the groups request that each member be allowed to read his or her rough draft aloud, with the two remaining members providing the critique. Bob consents, of course. Some groups have each member read silently and then comment. When the period ends, Bob's students are at various levels of completion of this task.

A Class Analysis

Bob passes around a rough draft of a theme that a 10th grader wrote for him many years ago (Figure 8.10).

He had the piece read aloud by various students while the rest of the class read along. Then Bob had his class analyze the draft based on the questions he gave them.

"Is the writing divided into paragraphs that make sense?" Bob asks.

"Yes."

"All right. Is it understandable or clear?"

"Yes."

"Okay, do you recommend some parts be cut?"

Sally raises her hand. "That part about 'Yum, yum, it isn't every day you get food like this. Oh, look...' makes my skin crawl."

Laughter.

"Can't we be a bit more delicate, Sally?" Bob admonishes. "What do you mean?" "I don't know. It just doesn't feel right."

"I know what Sally means," Billie adds. "Like in the second paragraph where she writes, 'Let's go across the street and have something to drink.' That's yucky."

"So," Bob says, "you don't like where the writer talks directly to the reader. You want to change the writer's voice here, make it more like a story. I agree. What would you suggest this writer do?"

"Change it," says Sally.

"How?"

"While we are waiting, my friends and I go across the street and have something to eat," Billie answers.

Now Sally has her hand up again. "Get rid of the 'Yum, yum' and the 'Oh, look.'"

"Good. What would you add there?"

Sally looks stumped, but Tom has an idea. "Begin the paragraph, 'I don't know which I like better about these amusement parks, the rides or eating until you are about to explode.' And then," Tom continues, "do this: 'For lunch I ate french fries and Coke and still found room for a coney dog. I guess I didn't have room for all that food, so I better work it off on a couple of rides.' How about that?"

The perfect day for me would be an exiting, fun-filled day. I could go to an amusement park with a bunch of my friends. I would defenately take friends, because I hate to be alone. I would leave very early, pick-up my friends and away we'd go. We would have breakfast at a restaurant along the way, and arrive at, let's say, Disney World, at around 8:30.

The amusement park doesn't open until 9:00. I can't wait! Well, while we are waiting lets go across the street and have something to drink.

"O.K., gang it is about ten minutes until 9:00, so lets go." I can't decide what I want to ride on first, so I'll ride on them all at least once.

We would probably split up into groups of two, according to who wanted to go on which ride. "O.K., It's agreed then, we all meet back here at exactly 12:00, no ifs, ands, or buts, see ya later."

I love riding on all the rides they have especially the Rollercoasters. As soon as I get off of one I'll turn right around and get in the same line, again. Speaking of the lines. I can't stand them. You wait and wait and the longer you wait the more nervous you get. So finally when you get up to the ride, you are almost too scared to get in. But, I guess that's what makes them so fun. Well it is about time to meet everybody else for lunch.

figure ◊ **8.10** | **(Continued)**

> Lunch, I don't know which I like better about these amusement parks, the rides or eating until you are abot to explode. All the french fries, cokes, and, well, to sum it up "junk food." Yum, yum, it isn't everyday you get food like this. Oh, look, they have coney dogs, I guess I have enough room for one. Oh, I guess I didn't have enough room for it. Well, what better way to work it off then to ride a couple rides.
>
> Another thing I like about these parks is they have these games that look so easy but they really are impossible. You can play one for hours and never get any better. If you do, totally by luck, happen to win you can get the huge stuffed animal. They are really nice to look at but to try to lug them around for the rest of the day is shear murder. The smart thing to do is not to play until late in the day when there is not that much time left.

"Nice," Bob says. "That takes care of the 'speaking directly at us' problem. This author needs to make changes like that throughout the entire piece. Next question: Do you recommend switching some of the writing around?"

"Not really. Kind of flows. Goes from one event to the next in the order of the day," George offers.

The class concurs with this, so Bob moves on to the next question: "Are there places where writing needs to be added?"

No response.

"I feel this could be better if the writer used more details," Bob adds. "You know what I mean? What rides? What were the rides like? What happened in the lines? What was the weather like."

"I'm not sure about the weather, but I see what you mean about the details," Jennifer says.

"Could you describe a Disneyland ride for me?" Bob asks.

"Star Tours, so cool." Brian blurts out.

"Tell me about it."

"You get in this room, see, and it's a movie, but the room moves."

"Putting detail like this in the story, I think, makes it more interesting," says Bob. "I recommend the writer add descriptions of some of the rides like Brian is doing. Brian, describe Star Tours, and Bill will copy it down on the board while you do it."

"Well, it's this movie," Bill copies, "about a space flight. You're strapped into your seat and the spaceship in the movie falls into space and the room moves when it falls. You know, it's based on *Star Wars*. R2D2 is the pilot. His robot is in the room and not in the movie, you know what I mean?"

Bob has to admit that the class does look a bit puzzled.

"Anyway," Brian continues as Bill copies, "this flight gets attacked and lasers and everything are right in the room. You really get jerked around. It's awesome."

"I think they use flight simulators, the kind they train pilots on," Sue offers. "Thanks, Brian and Bill," says Bob. "We have a good start on some more details in this writing. But Brian told us about the ride, so it reads just like Brian talks."

A snicker from George draws a dirty look from Brian.

"This is the same thing you changed already," Bob explains. "The writer wrote talking, not writing. So all we have to do now is to change Brian's talking and make it more like writing."

"Okay, how's this?" says Jennifer, who goes to the board and writes the following:

> My favorite ride was Star Tours. They put us in a room with a movie screen. The movie was a ride through space and the room moved with the action, which included a spaceship free fall and an intergalactic battle. Lasers and lights blaze through the room during the battle. The room that this ride used was actually a flight simulator that they use to train airline pilots in. It was awesome. The class breaks out into applause and Jennifer takes a bow.

"Good, Brian and Jennifer. You did it. You created a paragraph with a lot of interesting detail, which will make this piece of writing more interesting. Where will it fit into the story?"

"How about after 'so I'll ride on them at least once'?" responds Billie. "Seems to fit," says Bob. "Anyone else?"

As usual, a question like "anyone else?" is a complete conversation stopper, but Bob wants to bring this discussion to a close.

"We are on the way," Bob says, "to improving this draft. We have changed the voice from directly speaking to the reader to make it more like writing. We have to make our new voice consistent throughout. We are also adding detail, some specifics to give it more body. I wish we had the writer here who may want to defend some of the writing we are changing. But although this will be a different piece of writing, I believe it will be a better piece of writing, more like writing, with more details, and less like talking. You can help each other by using the questions I have given you to help shape your rough drafts. See you tomorrow."

Bob's Turn: Critiquing the Draft

Bob has done everything he can to train his students to develop and revise a piece of their writing. He has taken them, by using examples, from topic selection through a peer reading. Now it is time for Bob to give his initial feedback. It is his hope that the drafts have all been read and critiqued well by his students. Bob has provided a model for how to do this, and he has aided in the group process. So far these steps—producing the rough draft, reading a neighbor's, incorporating changes into it—have only been for a credit grade. This next step, Bob's first reading, will include his evaluation system, which will lead to ways of changing the draft. Even though Bob will critique the draft, it will only count for credit. This gives his students every opportunity to revise, change, and improve without penalty. Bob will now comment on errors. Everything, including correctness, will finally be an issue.

Bob gives his students one more workshop day to improve their rough drafts. He helps them if they ask, and at the end of the workshop, collects portfolios for his first home reading of the year.

Bob uses the scale that he outlined for his students in the introduction to the writing section of the course. Every student will get a numerical value based on the scale, plus an explanation, and many students will get questions or even some guidelines to aid in their rewriting. For Bob, this is hard and unfriendly work, but at least he has the satisfaction of knowing many, but, unfortunately, not all, of his students are going to revise based on his direct and positive systems.

For Bob's students, the joy of free writing has turned into the discipline of rewriting and revising. They are being asked to learn how to discipline their writing. Writing instruction on discipline and control is not irreconcilable with effective English teaching. The creation of fluent and controlled writers who are able to communicate with style, grace, clarity, and correctness is an important goal of secondary English teaching. How to get there is at issue, but where to go is not. Bob believes teachers get there by engaging students in whole writing tasks and providing them careful and controlled editorial assistance much like the kind offered professional writers. Bob feels he must also get students accustomed to the kind of measurements and evaluations they will face with increasing frequency, holistic evaluations that evaluate a whole piece of writing. Bob has some qualms about making sweeping judgments about students as writers from controlled writing samples. However, Bob believes that holistically evaluated writing samples provide part of a picture of a student writer.

Rewriting

On the next workshop day, Bob asks his students to prepare their writing for the public copy to be turned in in two days. On this day, he tries to give his students very specific help. Bob does one of the following with all of his students:

■ He ignores those whose themes may need nothing more than recopying. For instance, he merely smiles at Kim, who wrote the story about removable high heels. These are the students who have earned 5s on their rough drafts (Figure 8.11).

■ He pairs students who will help each other. For instance, he places Tim and Bill together in case they need aid and advice from a classmate.

■ He helps as many students as he can, based on who he feels needs him the most. For instance, he sits down with George and sees if he can get him to expand his piece called "The Perfect Day" (Figure 8.12). Bob can't. George won't.

Bob goes over to Tim, who wrote the piece on baseball, and offers to show him how to straighten out one of his sentences (Figure 8.13).

"Okay, read me this sentence aloud, Tim."

" 'But a ballpark is also a place of excitement.' "

"Read me the next sentence."

"The excitement of baseball."

"Not exactly a sentence, is it? Why don't you attach that last phrase to the sentence before. Use a comma."

"Like this? 'But a ballpark is also a place of excitement, the excitement of baseball.' "

"Yep. Read me another one. There."

" 'Hitting baseball is the hardest thing to do in any professional sport.' "

"Now read me the next one."

" 'A baseball, approximately 2 inches in diameter.' "

"What are you going to do about that fragment?"

"Attach it to the sentence before it?"

Bob points out to Tim that this is slightly more complex. "If you merely attach that phrase to the previous sentence, you will be saying that professional sport is approximately 2 inches in diameter. So you have got to put that phrase in the middle of the sentence, where it belongs, next to what you are describing, which is the baseball."

"Okay," Tim says. "Like this."

"Yes. Now wrap commas around it," Bob replies.

" 'Hitting a baseball, approximately two inches in diameter, is the hardest thing to do in any professional sport.' "

Bob wishes it was always this easy. Tim is a very cooperative kid.

figure ◗ **8.11**

The Wonderful, Indispensable, Totally New Idea of
REMOVABLE HIGH HEELS

Many women in the world travel to work each morning wearing "oh so painful" high heels. Have you ever really thought about the idea of removable high heels? Chances are, you probably haven't. The fact is, about 9 out of 10 women who wear high heels too work have blisters on their painful feet by the end of the day. Well, I've thought of a solution that would prevent those terrible blisters, and that solution is removable high heels!

The whole idea of my invention is so that women can convince people that they are wearing high heels all day when they really aren't. The removable high heel would look like a regular high heel but have a "secret velcro strip" on the side where it would be attached to the rest of the shoe. The velcro strip has a special adhesive that is very strong, yet lets go when the woman pulls it off. When the woman is walking to and from appointments, or just to her car, she would remove the high heel, and PRESTO! Her shoes would be transformed into flats which are much more comfortable. Then, when she arrives at the appointment she attaches the high heel back on to her shoe, and then,

figure ◦ 8.13 | (Continued)

> So much of your writing here is really good. You provide lots of information that is interesting; and your description of baseball is filled with the love of the game. This would be a wonderful theme for our class magazine. But you will need to clean it up first. Some of your sentence are not sentences. I have checked those. You have some spelling errors. I have starred those. And you have a number of punctuation errors. I have Xed those. Have Bill help you and bring back the clean, ready-to-share theme on the final draft day and this 3 will become a higher number.

Public Writing

Bob takes great pride in the fact that almost all of his students exhibit development from the journal writing stage to public writing. Now the numbers count, and Bob hopes that his students will have the three major traits he has been helping them to develop: voice, structure, and correctness.

Bob believes that many of his students need to develop their voice first, unencumbered by concerns about structure or correctness. That is why he asks for free writing before public writing. However, when the writing is to go public, he helps his students develop a sense of structure and correctness. Bob does this not only because he believes writing develops this way, but also because this is how his students will be evaluated on the state competency test.

For the first public writing of the year, Kim gets a 5 for her inventive piece about high heels; George gets a 2 for his four-sentence effort; Tim gets a 4 for his baseball theme.

Errors

Bob loves to teach, likes his students, and feels he is a very good English teacher. Yet, there is something missing in him. He cannot get crazy when a student commits a writing error. You know how the public thinks English teachers are supposed to get—livid, horror-stricken, and repulsed by the subject-verb disagreement, the run-on, the famous fragment, or the misspelling of misspelling. Bob cannot count the times he has heard a stranger exclaim, upon hearing Bob is an English teacher, "Better watch what I say!" And even though Bob tries to care, he just cannot bring himself to worry whether the guy sitting next to him on the airplane dangles a modifier. That is not to say that Bob doesn't care deeply about some things. He just does not get worked up about split infinitives, a mistake he has a tendency to make himself.

Yet, Bob does not condone mechanical writing errors. He understands errors create writing problems. The major problem errors can create is to cloud the meaning of the writing. Certain kinds of errors and a sufficient quantity of some errors can obfuscate what the writer is trying to say. Another problem with many errors is that they stop the readers who notice and condemn them, undercutting the credibility of the writer and the message she or he is trying to convey. Therefore, Bob sees that part of his job is to help his students write cleanly and free from mechanical errors. He uses three basic approaches to accomplish these goals.

First, Bob believes that direct teaching of at least simple grammatical terms is necessary, so that there is some common ground for discussion between his students and himself. So, throughout the course of the semester, Bob will spend 20 minutes of class time, on several occasions, reviewing the most basic definitions and usage examples for terms such as nouns, verbs, and adjectives, and rules for common punctuation marks.

The second approach Bob takes to help eliminate errors is to identify those made by several students and then have his class do some usage-based exercises in class. For instance, Bob may find a plethora of sentence fragments in several students' writings. In that case, he may spend some time going over some simple "find the fragments and turn them into complete sentences" exercises. Bob also tends to find misplaced modifiers and subject-verb disagreements, which he also will teach through usage-based exercises.

However, Bob puts most of his effort into a third approach: He works with each student based on his diagnosis and remediation schema. Bob bases his diagnoses of mechanical errors on the following principles:

- Errors in written composition are not all equal in seriousness.
- The most serious errors are those that interfere with the message.

- Some errors are a result of risk-taking and should not be discouraged.

- Some errors should be ignored, with the teacher concentrating only on the most serious types.

- Those errors that jump out at the reader should be considered for analysis and remediation (Foster & Newman, 1990).

For the most part, Bob circles errors before the final draft and asks the students to fix them. Errors are usually minor and caused by inadequate experience with community language standards. Bob's students need experience with and exposure to the ever-shifting but expected language standards that give a writer credibility. For instance, in this phrase, "Now the purse don't have to be big," Bob will circle "don't," with the expectation that this young writer will change the verb to the correct "doesn't." Sometimes Bob will change it for the writer and tell her why her choice was wrong. Subject-verb disagreement that springs from the way his students talk is one of the most common errors Bob encounters. So he tends to spend some time directly teaching subject-verb agreement.

Most of the errors Bob finds are spelling errors. These are real problems to break, and Bob knows of no great ideas to conquer all the misspellings he encounters. He explains to his students that no matter what they write, their credibility will be nil if their spelling makes them look stupid.

"Let's say," Bob tells them, "that an interested person is reading my theme about the airplane experience. They read this sentence I've put on the board: 'It was obviously a cheep airline because the terminal was poorly decorated.' Suddenly, my reader stops in her tracks, sits up, and shouts, 'That is not how you spell cheap. You spell cheap C-H-E-A-P. What a bozo writer.' Of course," Bob says, "I have lost her. She no longer trusts me as a writer. That's what the most blatant grammar and spelling mistakes do."

Some of Bob's students are rolling their eyes at this didactic little speech. Some are laughing. Perhaps some of his students are actually taking it in. But he believes in what he told them, and he hopes he can convince at least some of them.

Bob takes one of three actions with spelling errors:

1. He circles the word and asks his student to spell it right in the next draft.

2. He has his student write the word correctly five or ten times on a sheet of paper.

3. He makes the student keep a spelling notebook with these categories: correct spelling, my spelling, why my spelling, how to remember correct spelling (Figure 8.14).

figure 8.14

Correct Spelling	My Spelling	Why My Spelling	How to Remember Correct Spelling
restaurant	resteraunt	Because I pronounce the word quickly to sound like the way I spell it.	I will break the word into three pieces, rest au rant, and remember these three pieces.
castle	catsole	Because I spell it the way I say it	I will remember to add le to the word cast.

(Van Deweghe, 1982, p. 102)

figure 8.15

1. My theme topic deals with my love for the game of golf.
2. The closest place to Heaven must be a beautiful golf course.
3. Rising of dusk anticipating the rising of the sun over the quickly fading trees.
4. The smack of the first golf ball indicates the beginning of another Saturday.
5. Reaching into your bag. Looking throughout your scattered clubs.
6. As your clubs, Hogan and Titleist now become your best friends.
7. The precious lessons and practice now must be drawn out by your abilities.
8. Setting goals and achieving them is what life is all about.
9. My Walter Mitty dream would be to play against some of the greatest golfers.
10. Tom Watson a money winner on the PGA tour.

Bob does the best he can with these three approaches; however, trying to eliminate misspelling is a never-ending battle. Bob hopes for an occasional victory and really hopes that he seldom slips up in front of his students by revealing some of his own spelling problems.

The Worst Errors

Once I tried to sew a shirt, but got so frustrated decided not to do but when I thought how I was depriving myself from doing something picked up from where I started from and attained a certain feeling about myself.

With Bob's system, it would be hard for a student to get to the final draft with this piece, and in Bob's career, he has seen very little of this kind of writing. But when Bob does see it, he gets worried because he considers this an example of the worst kind of errors students can make. The problems seen in this example obliterate comprehension. He cannot understand what this writer is trying to tell him. Most of the errors he usually sees, subject-verb disagreement and misspelling, may make the student writer appear foolish, but they seldom put up huge blocks to communication. The errors seen in this example are basically sentence problems, either long convoluted run-ons or fragments, and they make it impossible to understand the writer. Bob gets a little worried when the controlling ideas of a piece of writing disappear so completely. Sometimes this kind of problem is created by a topic so out of the experience of the writer that she or he cannot control it at all. Then all Bob has to do is to convince the writer to stick to topics that are within her or his grasp.

However, the topic in the example is about as concrete and easy to handle as it can get. When Bob runs into this kind of problem, he will allow the writer to do the journal writings, but will suggest that for the public writing phase, the student consider a different kind of writing activity, beginning with more list making, categorizing, and direction writing.

By asking these students to make lists, Bob is aiming for clarity. He hopes he will have time to do the next step with these students, which is to turn the lists into groups. Then they will turn the groups into paragraphs.

Next, they will combine the sentences and build prose statements. For instance, one of Bob's students who loves golf created the list (Figure 8.15).

Notice that this student has trouble with sentences. Bob points out the differences between sentences 1, 2, 4, 6, 7, 8, 9, and phrases 3, 5, and 10.

The next time around, this student, choosing a whole new topic, produces this list (Figure 8.16):

figure ● 8.16

> 1. How many human beings can the earth support?
> 2. What kind of world are we willing to live in?
> 3. Limited supplies are quickly dwindling away.
> 4. A enormous amount of industry will be required.
> 5. Prices will continue to rise.
> 6. Land will become scarce.
> 7. Food prices will be out of site.
> 8. Today 10 percent of the land area is unoccupied.
> 9. Civilization has covered 3.5 billion acres.
> 10. The increase is destined to reach 6.5 billion by the turn of the century.

From that list, the student created this paragraph (Figure 8.17):

figure ● 8.17

> How many human beings can the earth support? What kind of world are we willing to live in? Limited supplies are quickly dwindling away. An enormous amount of industry will be required. Prices will continue to rise. Land will become scarce. Prices will be out of sight.

From that paragraph, Bob teaches this student to combine sentences. Bob wonders, however, if so much structure is a good idea. He has squeezed the voice and spirit out of this writer to come up with this paragraph, but at least it is clear. He is grappling, trying to solve one of the most difficult problems he confronts teaching writing: helping his more troubled writers make clear

> and I would be playing which things I like to dow on the field at that time and have number 1# draft picks on are team that I really got to now real good while I was there I would help the team win games by the was I played and the things I had did the way I ran with inerception...

statements. Perhaps Bob could try extended conversations with these writers—language experience activities in which Bob records narrative that the student dictates. Perhaps some of the finest adult literacy computer programs would help. At least he has identified the problem and created a quick and dirty solution for remediating it. As is true with most of the finest classroom teachers in this country, he is doing the best he can with what he knows. And yet, "is it good enough?" he thinks as he reads the first writing sample about football from Scott, his new student (Figure 8.18).

Dialects and Writing

Bob's students are an ethnic, racial, and regional mix, and this is reflected in the language they speak and write. The variety of life experiences adds a great deal to class discussions and writing. Bob's students share stories about customs, holidays, meals, and trips.

Bob discusses and deals with different dialects. Bob loves the range of dialect in his room. He loves to hear the rich regional and cultural languages his students bring to class, and he gives them plenty of opportunity to use them. They write plays and radio spots. They perform rap using different dialect. They create TV commercials in dialect and perform them. Everyone has a great time. But Bob has a hidden agenda for all this sport, which is to make dialect a classroom issue that is open for discussion. For instance, after the television commercials are performed, Bob asks his students what they think about the activity.

Sue: "It was a lot of fun."
Toni: "I liked the West Virginia accent the best."
Bill: "Yeh, they were pretty funny."

> Maryann: "No one would buy anything from them."
> Susie: "Unless, they're from West Virginia, too."
> Jerri: "I thought the black rap was real cool."
> Toni: "So did I. But how can anybody rhyme like that?"

Bob has two very difficult and long-term goals. First, he hopes his students will learn about and respect the dialects that are represented in his classroom. But Bob also hopes his students learn the appropriateness of dialects—that different languages serve different purposes at different times. Bob's objectives are that his students will be able to use and appreciate dialects when appropriate, but will also be able to shift to a community language when appropriate. This is a slow and tough process, one dealing as much with attitudes as with skills, and Bob spends much time listening to his students as well as talking to them.

Bob makes it clear that in their writing, dialect-based language is perfectly appropriate in the journals, in poetry, in appropriate fiction writing (plays and stories), and in some cases, public writing aimed at specific audiences. However, Bob makes it very clear that in most of the public writing, where dialect-based language interferes with community standards, it is not appropriate for the intended readers.

Yet, Bob is aware that some of his students only have a private language and do not know how to shift to a community language. One of Bob's former students, an African American now in college, wrote a letter about this very matter. Bob keeps a copy of this letter handy and rereads it at least once a semester. Occasionally, he shares the letter with his current students.

> Dear Mr. Sanderfelt:
>
> I have been doing a lot of thinking about different ways to approach dialect. It seems a little hard to put into words, but I'll try it anyway.
>
> The first problem I see is sensitivity. As hard as they may try, most people are not truly sensitive to the dialects of other individuals, i.e. the students in my college classes who cannot tolerate incorrect grammar. It's not their fault, though. Most of them come from middle- to upper-middle class homes where Standard American English (SAE) is heavily enforced. Because this is their environment, they haven't been exposed to much else. I wish there was some way to let these (I'll call them SAEs) SAEs switch places with a person of another dialect for a while so that they could experience the feelings of inferiority and inadequacy when a teacher or a person pokes fun of or rips apart the way you talk.
>
> I have a friend who is from St. Louis who doesn't speak the greatest English in the world. His dialect is slightly different because of the area he is from. He has to take a business English class next semester and is dreading the thought of it. Why? Because teachers constantly criticize

him when he speaks or writes. He told me that he has a hard time speaking and writing "proper English." Since he moved to Ohio, no one has really made any attempts to help him improve. They just continue to criticize. Being a business major, he understands the need to speak clearly and correctly and if he works *real hard* at it, he can do a pretty good job. It's just that once he gets started talking fast, he slips into his St. Louis dialect. Fearing rejection or ridicule, he will simply not respond.

RE: Black English

Well, I've pretty much expressed my opinion of this term to you. I don't think I would use this term in my classroom if I could help it because I think black students will be offended. Like I said before, this term has a negative connotation and is looked down upon by many individuals (most don't recognize it as a language, just bad grammar). These negative connotations bring a feeling of inferiority with the term. I think this is partially due to prejudice. Let's face it, SAE is viewed as a language created by white men, who at one time persecuted black men. I think black students think about this and the fact that many times blacks (and other races for that matter) are looked at as inferior. They see SAE as a way to rob them of their identity. I don't have a lot of ideas of how to deal with this problem in a classroom, but I feel the topic should be addressed in all schools. The best way to do this would be to use journals. This way students will write what they genuinely feel. Besides that, you don't want a racial debate in your class.

In the past your discussions have helped me to see that even I am not always sensitive to the dialects of others (then again, I'm not perfect either).

I think this is the first time I have expressed my complete and true feelings on these topics (THANKS!). If you want to talk to me more about it, let me know. I got a call about a job yesterday, so it looks like I will not have to consider leaving college (yea!).

Have a nice "rest of the summer" (smile).

Debi

While Bob sees Debi's point, he is also aware of the impact of a writer who cannot overcome prose like this:

in the morning of the year 1891 John asked me to go with him and then in the after noon I would be at work at my office aterny-of-law and my scecetary came in and he told me that I was the top lawer in the whole U.S. and that all the outher lawers quite thier jobs because of it and then I told hem to get a contrat out and mack braches all over the state. In the evning me and my best frend went the whole way we went to

Fredrec's of Hollywood and spent 77,000,000 wourth clothes and ev. then we flue down to New York and eat. when I got home John ask me to marry hem. and then I change the office to Mrs. Mr. aternies-of-law.

The problems in this theme are not just dialect-related, but many of them are. Most of the misspellings relate to dialect-driven pronunciations: wourth, aterny, lawer, outher, hem.

Many of the verb problems relate to dialect-related structures as well:

"Then we flue down to New York and eat."
"John ask me to marry hem."

Yet, the writing is basically clear, has detail and voice, and contains a strong personality. There is definitely an intelligence behind this piece, even better, a budding lawyer. But it will take all his effort and skill to convince this young writer of her need to know how to reshape her writing so she can shift into the norm. Bob will need time and patience, and he will have to be believable. This young writer will have to trust Bob. If she does, and if Bob makes the right moves, it is very possible he may, eight or nine years from now, attend her law school graduation.

Bob's students confront the many and varied problems a writer faces when writing goes public. Bob, through examples and with sensitivity, helps his students shape and mold from their free writing the most appropriate selections for an audience. His students have to face the difficult problems of logic, structure, organization, grammar, and correctness. Now Bob's students need to develop the ability to write in a public format for others.

English—A Second Language

Bob has always had students from many different countries in his classes. Although he has had some coursework in English as a Second Language, he has relied heavily upon the school's ESL teacher for help. He has found that most of the techniques that work for his native born kids generally work for his second language users. After all, his error analysis approach comes directly from ESL practice. Also, allowing his students to generate writing without having him bleed all over it allows his ESL students the same opportunity to gain a fluency that his native speakers have.

Yet his second language users come with special kinds of problems. For instance, Hiep Nguyen entered his class in February. Hiep moved to this country in July and lived in Los Angeles until his family moved to be closer to relatives in the community where Bob teaches. Hiep brought with him a movie review he wrote for his California school (Figure 8.19).

figure   8.19

1. Plot: In 1939 Cuiquao lived in Northern China (around Yellow Earth). She lived with her younger brother Hantlon, and her father. One day the army Cu Qing visited her house. He wanted to find somebody whose sings was good.

    China is system of government communism. So they don't have freedom. So they were poor. When they are lonely or angry or happy, then they are singing the songs. Sometimes they sing about communist.

    Cuiquao walk some miles to get water from Yellow river every day. One day Cuiquao's father wanted to Cuiquao get marry, but she didn't want. So when Cu Qing live a Yellow Earth, she said she want to live there, too. But he said he will come Yellow Earth again and he just left. She was sad so she sings a song. She met one man who will marry with her but he was 70 years old. After that she really doesn't wanted to get marry so she decided to live Yellow Earth. So she acrros the Yellow river. It was sad about her life.

2. Theme: They show a girl's life and her family in Yellow Earth. Their life was pretty tough.

3. Characterization
    Cuiquao: She is around 14 years old. She live with her father and brother Hantlon in Yellow Earth. She doesn't have mother so she did all house work and she walked some miles to get some water from Yellow river everyday. She like to

figure ◊ 8.19 | (Continued)

singing. She doesn't want to marry. That's why she left Yellow Earth but when she acrros the Yellow river she died.

Cuiquao's father: His wife and first doughter died. He is farmer.

Hantlon: He is Cuiquao's brother. He doesn't like to talk.

Cu Qing: He is army. He wanted to find who sing good. He visited Cuiquao's house later when he left he promis to a Cuiquao and he said she will come her house on April.

4. Acting: Cuiquao show her mind with song Hantlon doesn't talk a lot.

5. Special Effects: We saw Chines marrige. They show us Yellow river and people who live in the Yellow river.

6. Sound Track: I'm not sure that sound track is not clear or the songs are different than other songs. I mean their voice are litter bet higher than other people and it sounds strong. I think I don't like Chinese songs.

Not bad for a student who has been using English for less than a year, Bob thought. Bob takes the paper to Carol, his ESL teacher buddy, and asks her what to do.

"Hiep's analysis is fine. He has good control and a large writing vocabulary for such a new speaker and writer of English," Carol tells Bob.

"His verb tense errors, preposition mistakes, and lack of articles are very typical for a Chinese speaker. This paper is a great example of how a Chinese speaker adapts to the English language. His mistake patterns represent the differences between Chinese and English."

"For instance," Carol continues, "how does this sound?" She reads:

"He is army. He wanted to find who sings good. He visited Cuiquao's house later when he left he promes to Cuiquas and he said he will come her house on April."

"You can hear him speak in that section. He is a very good writer who needs encouragement to continue to tell his stories and write his essays. When he has a desire to learn standard form, which will come, then work on his language patterns. Slowly, one error at a time, you can begin to show him the difficult verb patterns of English. Introduce him to using past tense first, then go to irregular conjugations. However, you may want to start with his prepositions."

"Do not overwhelm him. Take the error work slowly, step-by-step," Carol repeats. "Use his papers as a basis for correction. Too many rules and workbook exercises will only confuse him."

Carol makes one last comment that intrigues Bob.

"You may find that it will be easier for Hiep to change to standard English than for many of your native speakers. After all, Hiep has been using nonstandard forms for only a year. Your native speaks have been doing it for their entire lives."

"Interesting," Bob replies thoughtfully.

Computers in Bob's Classroom

Bob has managed to gather five computers in his classroom. He has four PowerMacs, vintage 1994, and one 2000 version iMac. The iMac is Bob's third generation classroom Macintosh, having had available an Apple IIe for 10 years. However, it was the PowerMacs that changed his classroom. Now most of his students will use a computer for their public writing.

"It sure makes editing easy," Lashawna tells Bob. "The problem is that I seldom save rough drafts. Now I just edit over them."

Lashawna is a student who loves to write. Bob helps her with ideas and serves as a friendly reader. Most of the time Lashawna uses workshop time on her own, composing not only for Bob, but for the myriad writing contests she enters and occasionally wins.

Lashawna is one of the students who owns a computer at home. She has a Compaq and she hates the Macs. But at least the iMac will let her use her PC disks.

Because Bob has only five classroom computers, he can allow only a few students to use them at any given time. To get the use of a computer, a student

figure ◊ **8.20**

Computer Request Time

Name:
Date and Period of Request:
Reason for Needing the Computer

---

must fill out a nasty piece of bureaucracy that Bob thought up, his Computer Request Time Sheet (Figure 8.20).

Bob accepts any reason as long as the computers are free. When more than five of his students request computer use, editing wins over drafting. Bob's school has a computer lab, and he sends students to it if the lab is unoccupied at the time. To find that out he sends a scouting party. His students know better than to con Bob into sending them to the lab when they plan to go somewhere else. Bob's favorite cliché, "The first time you con me, poor you. The second time you con me, poor me."

However, Bob does play favorites for using the computer. His students who have the most trouble writing need the computer the most. For one thing, on the computer they can read what they write, which is so often impossible with their terrible handwriting skills. For another thing, they can use spell check, which Bob permits without any reservation.

"I don't care where my students get the correct spelling. You can sue me, but I allow my students to use this tool. Computer spell checks, as we all know, are not invincible," Bob explains. "They sure don't catch words that are spelled wrong but are still words. And they do require the judgment of the writer to determine which is the correct spelling." On the other hand, grammar checks are so clumsy and so often difficult to use that his students seldom use them.

Almost all of his students are skilled enough to use computers, even those who do not have computers at home. Most of his students have encountered computer training from elementary school through high school. Of course, students with computers at home do have the advantage with their ease and comfort with the technology. Student assignments have never looked better now that computers are available.

Bob plans to have at least 10 computers in five years. He keeps bugging his principal, and he will probably succeed.

His iMac is networked on the broadband system the local cable company provided for the school system. So his students use the iMac when they have research needs. Most of the time Bob allows them to use a state educational search engine that has none of the trash, yet has a plethora of sites available. Freedom of speech has never been so tested as it has with the Internet. Bob figures that his computer savvy students use a greater variety of sites at home than they use at school. Bob isn't sure if he wants to know what sites his students visit.

But overall he loves his computers. They have made writing easier by eliminating handwriting as a negative unreadable factor and by making editing so simple and even fun. The best of the Internet provides fast, up-to-date information that is so much more accessible to teenagers than hunting for information in books in a library.

Reflection: Bob as a Writing Teacher

Each fall on the first day of class, Bob faces a room full of total strangers. As always, they look ragged and ominous to Bob, a disquieting mass. Bob's voice cracks and is uneven. But gradually, as the semester continues, this mass transforms into individuals, kids Bob comes to know and know well. Bob will come to know most of them from an impression as distinctive and private as their thumbprints—the writings they do in his class. His trick, the professional trick of the master English teacher, is to conjure from them honest and heartfelt statements, real stories, honest emotions, innermost thoughts, imaginings, and opinions of the head and heart, and gradually help his students shape these statements into polished and crafted writings. Bob knows that, for most of his students, the statements come first, and the polish comes second. Bob knows that he has to provide his students with the motivation to write. He has to provide ideas and stories that interest and provoke his students. He has to provide readings that lead to writings, talk that leads to written reflection.

Bob knows that the honest writing will only come if his students are free from evaluation, the dreaded red pen. So he allows his students the freedom of journal writing—free, unrestricted statement-making. He spurs them with credit for filling pages, but he knows that more is happening than that. For in some of his students' journals, he reads stories, some crudely written with many conventional errors, but powerful accounts of real and often troubled lives. He reads stories about kids who are growing up far too quickly; he reads stories about imperfect people, quick to judge and filled with prejudice and generational, bestowed hatreds. Yet, through the clutter of errors and bad handwriting, Bob reads intense and honest texts. He hears the voices of a nation's youth, troubled and in danger, both sensitive and cruel, there in the journals like thumbprints.

Bob has a special set of ears to hear these voices that not all teachers have. But Bob knows that his job is not just to listen. He must also respond and question, respond and comfort. He must also help shape these voices, clear away the clutter, create articulate and polished spokespeople. So Bob asks for public statements. He gives his students a format to create these statements, a kind of writing ladder to build clear and clean writing. He helps them create statements that are unencumbered by disorganization and errors. He helps them learn the skills required to become literate citizens.

Yet, all his writing instruction is meaning-centered. Even the work Bob does with traditional grammar is meaning-centered, based primarily on the errors he encounters in his students' texts. The central question Bob asks of his students is, "Can I understand your writing? And, if not, what can we do about it?"

Bob tries to accomplish his goals realistically, shaping his work load in a way that makes sense. Bob feels he must not evaluate every piece of writing his students produce. If he did, he would drive his students crazy, and he would slowly diminish the amount of writing he allows them to do. Yet, when he does read, he has a goal in mind, whether it's just to be a supportive reader or to help shape a piece of writing for public consumption. Despite Bob's careful control of writing assignments, he still takes home too much work, and he looks enviously at the math teachers. Yet, by offering his students a regular, in-class writing workshop, Bob can do much of his reading in informal and formal class conferences. By carefully training his students to serve as each other's readers, he has formed a corps of surrogate teacher-students who provide each other additional response to the writings.

Bob would pass muster with the "skills" people, who demand accountability. Bob's portfolios provide plenty of accountability. And Bob's holistic evaluation can provide all the performance objectives a steely behaviorist desires. Here are two examples:

Students will be able to:

- Develop in writing several paragraph statements that are logical and organized with few errors, and almost no errors that detract significantly from the meaning of the text.

- Write simple, declarative, active sentences with 100% accuracy.

Bob could go on and on developing performance objectives for his writing program. But in his heart, his most important objective is to create an enthusiasm among his students for making statements in writing that are meaningful to readers. In short, his goal is to create whole and vital communication. For Bob, English teaching, at its best, elevates the social dialogue to its highest possible levels.

Teacher as Researcher

Questions

- How are the principles of writing in Chapter One reflected in the writing section?
- What discipline problems might occur in the writing workshop, and how would you solve them?
- How would you approach the different dialects in your classroom?

- How would you aid students, whose second language is English, with writing?
- Would you use portfolios as a method of evaluation? How?
- Is there a place for computer technology in an English classroom? If yes, explain where and how. If no, justify your answer.

Activities

- React to the story. Give your impressions and thoughts.
- Create some prewriting activities. They can be prompts, topic-finding activities, or responses to literature.
- Develop a set of rules for a writing workshop. How would they be like Bob's and how would they differ?
- Make a plan to conduct in-class writing conferences. How would you be able to reach all of your students? What would the rest of your class be doing while you are conferencing with a student?
- Design a plan to train your students to peer edit.
- List potential audiences and topics for the public writing your students will do.
- Create a grammar lesson that is meaning-centered.
- Write a letter in response to the author of the dialect letter that Bob received.
- Design a plan to keep records of all the activities that would go on in your class.
- Write pupil-performance objectives that would satisfy state authorities, yet relate to meaning-centered.
- Create free writing that you would share with a class. Develop a plan to share the writing with a class.
- Develop some ideas to get students to share their writing with each other.
- Design your workshop classroom. How would desks be arranged? Where would supplies be kept? Where would you be?

IRA/NCTE Standards for English Language Arts with Performance Benchmarks for Chapter 8

Standard Four

Students adjust their use of spoken, written, and visual language (e.g., conventions, style, vocabulary) to communicate effectively with a variety of audiences and for different purposes.

Performance Benchmark for Standard Four

Students write for different audiences and purposes during writing workshop.

Standard Five

Students employ a wide range of strategies as they write and use different writing process elements appropriately to communicate with different audiences for a variety of purposes.

Performance Benchmark for Standard Five

Students use many different strategies as part of the composing process to communicate with different audiences for a variety of purposes.

Standard Six

Students apply knowledge of language structure, language conventions (e.g., spelling and punctuation), media techniques, figurative language, and genre to create, critique, and discuss print and nonprint texts.

Performance Benchmark for Standard Six

Students apply knowledge of language structure and language conventions by composing written works for different audiences.

Standard Eight

Students use a variety of technological and informational resources (e.g., libraries, databases, computer networks, video) to gather and synthesize information and to create and communicate knowledge.

Performance Benchmark of Standard Eight

Students are given the opportunity to use computers in the composing process.

Standard Nine

Students develop an understanding of and respect for diversity in language use, patterns, and dialects across cultures, ethnic groups, geographic regions, and social roles.

Performance Benchmark for Standard Nine

Students learn that language is situational; different audiences require different language use. Students learn that diversity in language is a useful tool.

Standard Eleven

Students participate as knowledgeable, reflective, creative, and critical members of a variety of literacy communities.

Performance Benchmark for Standard Eleven

Students are taught respect for the language of their peers, and they are given opportunities to use a variety of languages in a variety of settings.

Standard Twelve

Students use spoken, written, and visual language to accomplish their own purposes (e.g., for learning, enjoyment, persuasion, and the exchange of information).

Performance Benchmark for Standard Twelve

Students are given the opportunity to select what they will write and for whom they will write.

Recommended Readings

Carter, C. (Ed.). (1982). *Non-native and nonstandard dialect students*. Urbana, IL: National Council of Teachers of English.

This collection of essays provides helpful advice, including methods of peer teaching and reading and writing instruction for non-native speakers.

Coles, W. E., Jr. (1974). *Teaching composing: A guide to teaching writing as a self-creating process*. Rochelle Park, NJ: Hayden.

This book describes a college writing class based on 30 assignments that require students to reflect on a host of ideas, particularly learning and teaching. This book provides many good assignment models based on critical and reflective thinking.

Elbow, P. (1973). *Writing without teachers*. New York: Oxford University Press.

This is one of the earlier writing-process books, but it is still well worth the time to read how Elbow designs his "teacherless" writing classrooms.

Farrell, P. B. (Ed.). (1989). *The high school writing center: Establishing and maintaining one*. Urbana, IL: National Council of Teachers of English.

This collection of essays focuses on practical advice from experienced writing-center teachers.

Gere, A. R. (1985). *Roots in the sawdust: Writing to learn across the disciplines*. Urbana, IL: National Council of Teachers of English.

This collection gives suggestions for writing instruction in almost all curriculum areas and provides additional insight on how writing is a form of learning.

Graves, D. H. (1983). *Writing: Teachers and children at work*. Portsmouth, NH: Heinemann.

This is one of the earlier attempts to apply the writing process to elementary-age children. Graves gives a practical picture of how children can write successfully very early in their lives. His theories are based solidly on psycholinguistic principles.

Harris, M. (1986). *Teaching one-to-one: The writing conference*. Urbana, IL: National Council of Teachers of English.

This book provides fairly comprehensive coverage of the procedures and problems of individualizing writing instruction.

Hillocks, G., Jr. (1986). *Research in written composition: New directions for teaching*. Urbana, IL: National Conference on Research in English.

This is a very comprehensive overview of the research compiled on the teaching of writing up to the time of publication. This book does not provide the final word on the subject, but it does show how complicated this subject is and how researchers attempt to solve problems.

Hoffman, E., & Scheidenhelm, C. (2000). *An introduction to teaching composition in an electronic environment*. Boston: Allyn and Bacon.

This is a description of many classroom activities used in a college composition course taught with computers. Many of the lessons are very interesting and can easily be adapted to a high school computer writing setting.

Kirby, D., & Liner, T. (1988). *Inside out: Developmental strategies for teaching writing* (2nd ed.). Portsmouth, NH: Heinemann.

This is a very popular, readable text with many ideas for secondary writing teachers.

Macrorie, K. (1984). *Writing to be read* (3rd ed.). Portsmouth, NH: Heinemann.

This book survives with its excellent ideas on how to free the writers inside students. Macrorie helped define the writing process.

McWhorter, J. (2000). *Spreading the word: Language and dialect in America*. Portsmouth, NH: Heinemann.

This book explains dialects as rule-governed language systems. The book is meant to explain how seeming errors are really just differences in usage and patterns.

Murray, D. M. (1985). *A writer teaches writing*. Boston: Houghton Mifflin.

Murray presents, in very clear fashion, a paradigm of the writing process. This book is a good handbook for teachers of writing.

Olson, G. A. (Ed.). (1984). *Writing centers: Theory and administration*. Urbana, IL: National Council of Teachers of English.

All the essays in this collection are aimed at the establishment of writing centers. Although this book is primarily for college or university writing centers, there is much that can be applied to the administration of high school writing centers.

Rief, L. (1992). *Seeking diversity: Language arts with adolescents.* Portsmouth, NH: Heinemann.

This book is a detailed account of a language arts program in an eighth grade classroom. This provides a description of language arts teaching ideas that go beyond writing. But the writing is so well covered here that this book is an excellent sourcebook for a writing teacher.

Rigg, P., & Allen, V. G. (Eds.). (1989). *When they don't all speak English: Integrating the ESL student into the regular classroom.* Urbana, IL: National Council of Teachers of English.

This book offers a nice combination of theory and practice for teachers who work with non-native English speakers. It is oriented toward meaning-centered psycholinguistic approaches.

Romano, T. (1987). *Clearing the way: Working with teenage writers.* Portsmouth, NH: Heinemann.

Romano gives excellent advice for working with teenage writers. His writing is clear and down-to-earth.

Romano, T. (2000). *Blending genre, altering style: Writing multigenre papers.* Portsmouth, NH: Heinemann.

Romano describes writing assignments that require students to take different stances and different voices. The book is filled with student papers.

Selfe, C. L., Rodrigues, D., & Oates, W. R. (Eds.). (1989). *Computers in English and the language arts: The challenge of teacher education.* Urbana, IL: National Council of Teachers of English.

The first part of this book describes computer-based classrooms and programs, and the second part suggests ways of developing model computer-based programs for English classrooms.

Shaughnessy, M. (1977). *Errors and expectations: A guide for the teaching of basic writing.* New York: Oxford University Press.

This book helped shape error analysis, which views writing errors collectively and reads them for what they tell about the writer's processes. Shaughnessy gives painstaking detail on the nature of errors, what they mean, and what to do about them.

Spandel, V., & Stiggins, R. J. (1990). *Creating writers: Linking assessment and writing instruction.* New York: Longman.

This book provides an overview of assessment concerns. All the models in this book are based on direct assessment (writing samples as opposed to multiple-choice tests). This text provides a comprehensive view of holistic evaluation.

Sunstein, B. S., & Lovell, J. H. (Eds.). (2000). *The portfolio standard: How students can show us what they know and are able to do.* Portsmouth, NH: Heinemann.

This shows a comprehensive view of portfolio systems for many situations, including writing assessment of course. This is a useful and comprehensive guide to portfolios.

Underwood, T. (1999). *The portfolio project: A study of assessment, instruction, and middle school reform*. Urbana, IL: National Council of Teachers of English.

This is a view of a portfolio-based assessment system piloted in California in response to State assessment policy. This book provides helpful information about large-scale portfolio assessment.

Wresch, W. (Ed.). (1991). *The English classroom in the computer age: Thirty lesson plans*. Urbana, IL: National Council of Teachers of English.

The lessons described here are organized for students with varying amounts of computer experience. The lessons represent a range of English teaching, including several lessons about literature teaching.

Yancey, K. B. (Ed.). (1992). *Portfolios in the writing classroom: An introduction*. Urbana, IL: National Council of Teachers of English.

All these essays discuss the benefits, problems, and methods of using portfolios as a means of classroom assessment.

Zeni, J. (1990). *Writing lands. Composing with old and new writing tools*. Urbana, IL: National Council of Teachers of English.

This book provides a practical look at how to successfully incorporate computers into a process-approach writing workshop.

Teaching the New Literacies:
Film, Television, and Computers

Introduction

> I called the course Media Analysis, and every student in school seemed to sign up for it. I found out later that the guidance counselors were telling students that there would be very little reading and writing in the course, "so if you are busy this semester, take Media Analysis." (This seems to be one of the stereotypes that plagues high school media courses.) But as unprepared as I was for the hordes of students who descended on the course, the hordes were just as unprepared for my opening-day introduction of all the reading and writing they were going to do. Legend has it that students camped out in front of the school office to drop the course. Regardless of the truth of this, the numbers did dwindle and eventually Media Analysis became just another English course with a nice mix of students and an enjoyable but "real" curriculum. I used more equipment for the class, the AV guy told me, than all the other classes in the school.

The School, the Students

West High School sits on a promontory overlooking an expressway. The outside of this large school, a light tan slate, looks new, but once inside, I found an old school with dark halls. The outer shell is merely a replacement for the old exterior. The neighborhood surrounding West High School is primarily Italian American and African American. Most of the students in this school come from middle- or lower-middle economic backgrounds.

The Teacher	
Maria Hernandez, age 37	Eleven years' teaching experience, all at West High School
Educational Background:	B.A., English, 1977; certified as postbaccalaureate, 1979
Approach:	"The new literacies of film and television are significant parts of our culture. My goal is to try to get my students to think about what they see. I want my kids to reflect on their culture.
Influences:	A lifetime of love/hate relationship with the media; a great deal of media literacy reading; many conversations with students.

Teaching Film and Television

Maria's Reasons for Teaching Film and Television

Maria Hernandez is intimidated by all audiovisual equipment. VCRs, computers, laser printers, video projectors, overhead projectors, cassette recorders, and CD players are all "machines" in her anachronistic lexicon, and they all have one nasty trait in common: they break just as she goes to use them in her classroom. Actually, Maria remembers the day the equipment did not break, the day the bulb worked, the tube turned on, the remote had batteries. On this day, the cart with the VCR and playback equipment (formerly called a television set) was too large to fit into her rather odd-shaped classroom door. Yes, Maria has seen it all. If a "machine" can fail, it will fail for Maria.

Yet, Maria is constantly in need of her "machines" because she believes passionately that her students need help in understanding, coping with, and appreciating the mass media that dominate so many of their lives. Maria has a love/hate relationship with radio, television, and films. She loves good movies, and she watches television. She is at the age where classic rock and roll is her favorite kind of popular music. She has been seen by students at a Celine Dion concert and at Jimmy Buffet's annual summer appearance. Maria is a child of the media, having grown up with Saturday morning cartoons, the Macy's Parade on Thanksgiving, and the Rose Parade on New Year's Day. But Maria also became a reader, a gardener, a traveler, and a lover of classical music. In other words, Maria sees the electronic media as add-on additional tools for her entertainment, educational, and esthetic needs.

Maria uses television and film, but she is not overwhelmed, dominated, or trapped by them. She loves what they add to her life, but she makes choices. She selectively watches television, only rents or goes to certain movies, and worries a great deal about what she considers the worst traits of the mass media: the romanticization of violence, the gross distortion of male/female relationships, and the promotion of materialism above all other values.

Maria also worries about her students' relationship with television and film. She doesn't see students exercising her selectivity. They seem to love it all, except, of course, *Live at the Met* on PBS, which, Maria concedes, is a form of selectivity on their part. She worries her students identify too closely with the fantasy elements of the media. She worries that many of her females believe they must look and act like the girls in *Dawson's Creek*. She is afraid that her male students use television and film as a training ground for their relationships with females. Maria has seen student pregnancies in her school increase fivefold since she started teaching there 11 years ago, and she wonders how television, film, and music have contributed to this. She worries about all the "things" her students own and their need to work to get them—designer everything, and cars, not just any cars, but really "hot" cars. "Why do they need all of this expensive junk?" Maria muses. "And what role does the media play in creating these value systems?"

Above all, Maria worries about the lack of pleasure her students get out of reading. Maria is a very good teacher, and she can get her students to write and appreciate books. But it takes her a lot more effort to get them to read enthusiastically than to get them to watch and love *Scream 3*. Maria knows that it's okay to see all kinds of movies, that it gives her kids pleasure. But is it okay to seldom pick up a book for pleasure? Is there a correlation between this electronic media bingeing she sees kids indulge in and their lack of reading? And does this lack of reading impact their ability to read? "All movies begin with written scripts," she tells her students day after day.

Okay, so Maria is a worrier. But Maria's worry is indicative of a deep-seated professionalism and love for her students. And, above all, Maria does something about it. She has made the New Literacies, the study primarily of film and television, a part of her curriculum. She makes her students reflect on the impact of the mass media.

Maria's Goals for Teaching Film and Television

Maria has always liked 12th graders. They appeal to her for the same reason many of her colleagues shun them. Many seniors are beyond high school; they no longer really care about it. Maria sees many of her students thinking about their futures. Her noncollege-bound students, particularly, tend to have dilemmas about "What next?" and "Where do I go from here?" Maria feels she can take this angst and use it to her advantage; that is, have her students read, write, and talk about things that really matter to them. And much of what these kids watch on TV and see in the movies really matters to them.

Maria has adapted goals for her film and TV units. The goals are stated in the curriculum guide, and she uses them to convince whomever needs convincing to let her incorporate media lessons into her English classes. These are the goals:

1. To transform students into discriminating viewers who can distinguish good from bad, exploitation from communication.

2. To sensitize them so they perceive how film and television are designed to influence and manipulate them.

3. To educate them to understand film and television visually and thematically, so they can analyze and critique the media they watch.

4. To develop critical awareness so students will pass up at least the very worst of the electronic media to read a book.

5. To develop an esthetic appreciation for the finest the electronic media has to offer.

Maria has developed several activities that she fits into her 12th-grade English class. She spreads them out throughout the semester. Her students will think, discuss, read, and write as a result of these activities, which are the systemic skills for all literacy.

Teaching Film

Vignette 1: Film Discussion

The room is dark, really dark because there are no windows. Twenty-seven 12th graders sit in two concentric semicircles intently watching the flickering images of the Civil War drama *Glory*. She uses the television version where the swearing and goriest scenes have been cut.

Although Maria considers *Glory* a prosocial film with very little that is controversial, she takes no chances and sent a letter to parents in advance.

Dear Parent or Guardian:

As part of my English course, we study television and film literacy. With the aid of a series of film and videotapes, we will probe how the electronic media informs, manipulates, and entertains. Students will participate in several activities that will help accomplish the major goal of this unit: to create visually literate and perceptive viewers who are capable of withstanding the constant barrage of media propaganda, viewers who are capable of understanding how the media shapes our world, and who can appreciate the media as a major artistic achievement of this century.

Included among the films I plan to use are *Glory* and *The Breakfast Club*. Both films are rated "R" and contain language and situations that may be offensive to some viewers. However, I feel it is important to analyze and understand how these powerful films impact upon teenagers, one of the largest film audiences in America. If you feel your daughter, son, or dependent should not see these films, please inform me as soon as possible so I can make alternative arrangements.

> Sincerely,
> Maria Hernandez
> Senior English Teacher

Maria's 12th grade class has a very nice and compatible racial and ethnic mix that includes several African-American students, one Hispanic student, two from Southeast Asia, and others with a variety of European backgrounds. Maria is very adept at dealing with potentially volatile subjects without allowing her students' natural animosities to poison the atmosphere. She manages to do this in several ways. First, she sets down discussion rules in writing:

- Everyone will be given a full turn to speak without interruption.

- All classroom remarks will be considered tentative. They may be challenged by members of the class but not attacked.

- Members of the class should consider the feelings of other students before making remarks that may hurt. I will stop a discussion if I feel it is creating too much pain.

- Discussions will only be held if the class atmosphere is friendly and positive.

- If rude and cruel remarks are intentionally made, the student who makes them will be eliminated from the discussion and penalized.

Some of these rules seem harsh and Maria doesn't mean to be, but she feels she must be firm in creating the classroom conditions conducive to talking about delicate issues. But it is not primarily the rules that allow Maria to conduct her discussions. It is her model of listening carefully, taking all of her students seriously, and her genuine interest and concern for them.

Maria's use of the film *Glory* is more than a study of a text, more than the study of a film. *Glory* is part of a thematic unit on Race in America. Maria's students have read and written on this theme, and they have discussed it. They have read Richard Wright, Langston Hughes, Nikki Giovanni, and Maya Angelou. They have written journal entries read only by Maria and have shared thoughts with their classmates.

Maria watches her students watch the movie. Many have seen the film. Many are inspired. Many are crying. Maria allows the credits to wind down before turning on the lights. Her students need time to reflect before they respond. Maria allows her students to use the rest of the period to write in their journals. Showing the film took two class periods. Maria will use the third period, tomorrow, to discuss it. Meanwhile, she has written some questions on the board that her students may use for journal writing.

- Did you feel the white officers treated the black soldiers with respect? Yes? No? Maybe? Why?

- Why were the black soldiers so motivated to fight?

- Could you tell from this movie why Civil War battles were so costly in lives?

- How would you describe the living conditions of the men during their training?

- Can you describe the music and how it created moods during the film?

- Do you remember how lighting and color were used to create viewer feelings in the last battle scene?

- How did movement (camera and crowd) increase the excitement during the battle scenes?

- Did you like the movie? Why or why not?

Discussing Glory

By this point in the semester, Maria has engaged her students in many classroom discussions. They wait expectantly in the circle Maria has formed. She hardly needs to ask a question, but she does.

Maria: "What did you think of the film?"
[Hands go up.]
Kevin: "I loved it. I thought it was great."
Maria: "Why?"
Kevin: "It was exciting. And there were neat battles."
Tony: "I wouldn't want to fight for a country where the white soldiers showed such little respect for me."
Bill: "Me neither."
Maria: "Did anyone answer the journal question on why the black soldiers were so motivated to fight?"

Suzanne: "I did."

Maria: "What did you say?"

Suzanne: "I wrote that they fought to help end slavery."

George: "It was more than that. Remember how the sergeant would talk about pride? These black soldiers were showing how much pride they had to the white soldiers."

Tony: "Yeah. They were saying, 'I'm as good a soldier as you are, even better. "This movie was so much better than *Driving Miss Daisy*, where a black man was nothing more than a tool of an old white lady. At least in *Glory* the black soldiers were independent and had pride like that soldier who was whipped. They whipped his back, but they sure didn't whip his spirit. Did you see how mean he looked at them?"

Annie: "They were still black soldiers being led by white officers."

Maria: "But that's the way it was. Even during World War II, there were black troops that were led by white officers. And those black troops were not given a great deal of opportunity to fight."

Suzanne: "I thought *Glory* was the best movie I ever saw in showing the bravery of black soldiers. I thought it showed how black men would react if given the chance to. My dad fought in Vietnam with lots of other black soldiers."

Jennifer: "Was this directed by a white or a black person?"

Maria: "*Glory* was directed by a white person."

George: "I saw *Boyz N the Hood* and that was directed by a black man."

Scott: "*Boyz N the Hood* was very cool. And no white person was the boss in this movie. Also, *Do the Right Thing* was made by Spike Lee, a black director, and the whites and blacks were equal in that movie."

Maria: "Spike Lee made *Summer of Sam* and *Malcolm X*. So you think *Glory* reflects a white man's view of the black experience?"

Suzanne: "In some ways. But it still made me proud. I don't believe that Denzel Washington would be in a movie he didn't believe in. And I felt prouder after seeing *Glory* than I did *Boyz N the Hood* because at least *Glory* showed the black spirit at its finest."

Tony: "But *Boyz N the Hood* showed it for what it's like today."

Maria: "I don't believe any film can be totally realistic. Do you?"

Jennifer: "No, not totally. But I know of films that I thought were pretty close."

Bill: "Such as?"

Jennifer: "Well, I can't think of any right now. But I know I've seen films that I thought were real life."

Maria: "What did you think of the music and the way the movie was filmed?"

Shawn: "The music was very inspirational. It gave me goose bumps."

Alissa: "The last scene was of the battle that was fought at night that had all those shells bursting, lighting up the screen. It was both beautiful and sad."

Maria: "Any last comments?"

Ben: "I liked the way the last scene was at night, all dark except for cannon bursts which lit up the sky."

Wendy: "And remember the first scene where he was crawling around and the camera angle was with him on the ground? It was like we were in the battle."

Bill: "It was a great movie. Thumbs up."

Reflections on the *Glory* Discussion.   This *Glory* discussion was similar in every way to a reader-response book discussion. The only difference was that a film was used as a text rather than a book. Maria does this for several reasons. First, she uses films because they are wonderful and powerful texts that are part of everyone's lives. Second, Maria wants her students to think about movies in a thoughtful forum like a class discussion. Maria believes that by making films part of her curriculum, her students will grasp the complexity and depth of movie experiences in their lives. Notice that her students brought other films into the discussion: *Driving Miss Daisy*, *Boyz N the Hood*, and *Do the Right Thing*. For Maria, this shows that her students are coming to grips with their relationships with films. This is her proof, the behavioral validation that her students are making the connections she wants them to make and the connection between the values they hold and the texts (films) they respond to.

Vignette 2: *The Breakfast Club* Trial

One of the major problems with using contemporary films in a classroom is how quickly they date. Fortunately, for Maria, *The Breakfast Club* has a staying power many other films do not. This film is set in a suburban Chicago high school library on a Saturday morning when five students gather to serve detention under the supervision of a vice principal. The film is about how young adults get trapped in group identities that exclude contact with outsiders and inhibit honest and sensitive communication.

Yet, the power of *The Breakfast Club* underscores the legitimate concerns of parents and teachers because the value messages young people receive from it are complicated and serious. The film seems to give approval to drugs and casual sex and promotes the view that adults are untrustworthy and unreliable, as indeed, some adults are. Themes that run through this film include ambition, family, love, career, anger, alienation, loneliness, cruelty, money, success, and justice.

For all these reasons, Maria finds *The Breakfast Club* an ideal film to use for a focal-point lesson on the media—a trial. She puts *The Breakfast Club* on trial. A trial, Maria figures, forces her students into a disciplined discussion in which arguments are presented in an orderly and logical fashion. Thus, she forces her students to seriously confront the impact a film may have on their values, beliefs, and actions. Also, this activity requires a great deal of thoughtful language use, primarily writing, and formal thinking. Once again, Maria uses the already cut-for-classroom-use TV version of the film.

The Classroom as Courtroom

Maria begins this activity with an overview of what the class will be doing.

"This classroom will become a courtroom where the movie *The Breakfast Club* will be put on trial. You will serve as the lawyers, the witnesses, the jury, and the judges. Here is the issue you will be deciding..."

At this point, Maria passes around copies of the following:

The Situation. The parents of a 15-year-old girl filed suit against the director of a youth group for showing the film *The Breakfast Club* at a youth group meeting. The parents claim that their daughter did not have permission to see this movie, which they feel is immoral and promotes promiscuity, drug use, and above all, a disrespect for grown-up authority. The parents feel this kind of film has led to the decline in values among American teenagers.

The plaintiffs, the parents, claim that teenagers should not be exposed to this film. They want the youth group director fired, and they are seeking damages of $50,000 from the youth group. The defendants, the youth group, and its director, claim they had the freedom to show this film and that the film is a positive statement for teenagers.

Note: Parents were not notified about the showing of the film ahead of time. The youth group director held a discussion with the teenagers after the film was shown.

Maria goes over this with her students and makes it clear to them that it is no disgrace to argue the side of the plaintiffs, the parents. Maria knows that her hardest job will be to convince her students to be fair about this, to argue this from the position of the parents. From experience, Maria knows that her judges will decide the case in favor of the youth group, but that is okay as long as the parents' side tries hard and provokes some thinking, and as long as those students who work on the parents' side are proud of the work they do. Thus, Maria is very careful whom she selects to work on the parents' side and keeps these students as productive and positive as possible. Maria makes it very clear to the entire class that those arguing the parents' side were appointed by her; they did not volunteer. At this point, Maria makes clear what roles are available in the trial. They are:

Two lawyers for the defendants, the youth group and its leader

Two lawyers for the plaintiffs, the parents of the teenagers

The defendant, the youth group leader

The plaintiffs, the parents

Two teenage witnesses for the defendants

Two teenage witnesses for the plaintiffs

A panel of three justices

The jury

Through written requests from students and by making appointments, Maria assembles her cast for the trial. She announces the roles and gives her students the schedule for the rest of the activity.

The showing of *The Breakfast Club*—two periods

Preparing for the trial—two periods

The trial—two periods

The discussion of the trial—one period

Maria explains that the procedures for the trial will be as follows:

Opening statements—five minutes each

Witness examination—five minutes per witness; five minutes cross-examination

Closing arguments—five minutes each

Jury deliberation/jury decision

Maria assigns every student a writing role in the trial.

Lawyers must prepare opening and closing arguments and questions for examination and cross-examination of witnesses.

Witnesses must prepare biographies to circulate to both sides.

Judges must write down trial procedures and instructions to the jury.

Jury members must submit written decisions. The majority decision will win.

This is fairly complex for a classroom activity, Maria acknowledges, but the trial has always worked for her, so she does it and enjoys it. Her biggest problem is not in motivating her students to do the activity, but in keeping them from overdoing the role playing. "Remember, this is only a game," Maria will tell her class many times before the trial ends.

Maria attempts to make the trial as serious as possible so that this activity becomes a memorable event for her students. She sets up her classroom like a courtroom—a table for the judges, a witness box, and prosecution and defense tables. She makes her judges wear robes (judge-like robes always appear). And, her coup de grace, she has the trial videotaped. She does this for two reasons. First, this gives her students a reason to perform well, and second, the videotape provides a worthwhile way of summarizing the experience.

Maria has a role in the trial; she is the bailiff. She welcomes the judges, swears in witnesses, and makes sure the judges keep the trial moving along on schedule. The trial begins with Maria walking into the classroom/courtroom, followed by the three judges.

> Maria: "Please rise. The Honorable Judges Ephraim, Brown, and
>   Gomez now presiding."
> Judge Ephraim (banging the gavel Maria provides): "Be seated."

At this point one of the judges reads the statement of what the trial is about and calls for the opening defense statement.

Courtney, the main defense lawyer, gets up, looks at the hushed and tense student spectators behind her, notes the camera pointed at her, and freezes. Courtney is too nervous to read her statement.

"Maybe the camera wasn't such a good idea," Maria thinks as she walks over to Courtney.

"Turn the camera off," Maria directs another student.

"I'm okay, Ms. Hernandez," Courtney says, and with a deep breath she begins reading her opening statement. The camera is turned back on without Courtney noticing.

> Courtney: "We believe that the evidence will show Bill Jones, the youth
>   group leader, has been leading the youth group well for six years.
>   He has been accused of corrupting youth by showing the film
>   *The Breakfast Club*. He is innocent. Through the evidence, we
>   will show that *The Breakfast Club* did not cause any harm to
>   Samantha Smith, a 15-year-old member of the youth group. We
>   will prove that Mr. Jones held a reasonable discussion following
>   the film, and in this discussion, Mr. Jones helped his youth group
>   to analyze and understand this film in a way that would do them
>   no harm."

Although Courtney reads quietly and occasionally stumbles over a word, her arguments are well thought out and she feels proud of herself when she is finished. She sits down with a sigh and to scattered applause, which Judge Gomez quickly gavels silent.

The prosecutor reads her statement without a problem and then the witnesses are called. The 15-year-old girl who caused all the problems is a fine witness. The student who portrays her came dressed in her most conservative outfit and refused to admit to any rebelliousness at all.

> Defense: "What was the last movie you saw?"
> Girl: "*Bambi.*"
> [The class laughs.]
> Defense: "You hear worse language in the halls of the school than you
>   heard in *The Breakfast Club*. Don't you?"
> Girl: "My friends never swear and that's who I hang out with."
> [The class groans.]
> Each side is allowed a closing argument.
> Here is the plaintiffs' argument, read by Faye:

> "Ladies and Gentlemen: *The Breakfast* Club is an R-rated movie. The contents of an R-rated movie are not meant to be seen by children under 17. Bill Jones did show this movie to a group of 15-year-olds. He also held a discussion without taking a moral stand on the issues. The damage inflicted upon the children has had a lasting impact. The community has a responsibility, a duty to protect its children from experiences such as this movie. How can Bill Jones live with himself? How can we even consider permitting this man to continue exposing children to this kind of influence? The Constitution protects freedom of speech, but it doesn't permit unfit material to be shown to minors under 17. Our duty as a community is to responsibly raise our children and keep them away from a bad influence like Mr. Bill Jones. Thank you."

After the closing arguments, Maria makes the class rise as the jury leaves the room. In about 10 minutes, the jury returns with its written statement in favor of the defense, upholding the defense position claiming the right to show the film.

The Verdict

> Judge Gomez: "Samantha Smith had many problems before she saw the
>   movie *The Breakfast Club*. Mr. Jones had no right to show an
>   R-rated movie without getting parental permission slips. We
>   require Mr. Jones to get a parent helper if he wishes to continue
>   to work with the teenagers. We also recommend Mr. Jones
>   apologize to Mr. and Mrs. Smith and Samantha and the parents

of the members of the youth group. Finally, we recommend that Samantha get counseling to help with her problems.

However, freedom of speech is a fundamental right in our society, and we do not find that Mr. Smith should be fired or fined for exercising this right. Case dismissed."

When It's Over

The trial goes just about as planned. The glitches are fairly predictable. The judges did not have as much to do during the planning stage as the rest of the cast, although Maria had them research, discuss, and plan trial procedure. One year she even had a lawyer buddy come in and give this group of students some help. Also, the witnesses have to be helped to keep their statements "of this earth." Teenage imaginations are interesting. Her students sometimes need aid developing examination questions, but television has made trial-lawyer behavior common knowledge. The parents' side needs some special care. But, for a complex activity, this one goes very smoothly.

The Breakfast Club Trial: Open Discussion

The trial ends, usually with a victory for the defendants, but not before members of the class have had an experience with disciplined thinking on the role of media in their lives. In the discussion that ends this activity, everyone wants to talk.

Vern: "No one smokes dope because of a movie. We know what's real and what's not."

Katie: "We make up our own minds. A movie can't make you do anything. Besides, I have a friend whose mom won't let her see anything. So she watches all these R-rated movies at her friend's house. Saying no is the worst thing you can do."

Michelle: "High schools are like this movie. There are groups and kids are in or out."

Billie: "Look at the way Mr. Scarpell (the vice principal) treats us. He considers us guilty and we need to prove our innocence, which is impossible."

Maria: "But not all adults are like that."

Chris: "Have you talked to any parents lately?"

Maria: "Come on, you're not being fair!"

Tonya: "Okay, not all grown-ups' hearts have died, but most grown-ups'."

Maria: "Also, if you were parents, at what age would you allow your kids to watch R films?"

Yolanda: "I wouldn't stop my kids at any age. They see whatever they want anyway at friends' homes."

Maria's students do not believe they are adversely impacted by the media. They claim they can separate fantasy from reality, and, in their opinion, these entertainment films are fantasy. Her students defend their right to see whatever films they want. Teenagers, Maria knows from experience, have an unblinking faith in their own maturity. On the other hand, most of her students see *The Breakfast Club* as an accurate representation of the cliques that can be found in high schools. As for the adults in *The Breakfast Club*, "lots of grown-ups are like that," one of Maria's students laments. "Yeah, but there are lots more grown-ups who aren't like that either," Maria says to a sea of skeptical and incredulous faces.

Maria fails in getting her students to admit to even the smallest change of perspective or point of view. But she is very content with the process to which her students have been exposed. Maria listed the educational benefits of this trial.

Students did the following:

- Created written and logical arguments
- Offered those arguments orally
- Wrote fictional biographies
- Developed questions to attack or defend an argument
- Asked questions to attack or defend an argument
- Spontaneously answered questions to defeat or support an argument
- Developed trial procedures in writing
- Created written decisions based on a critique of oral arguments
- Analyzed and probed a text for its influence and impact on their lives
- Participated actively in listening to and discussing a host of issues related to a text.

Maria scans this list, somewhat amused. "Not a bad use of a "teenpic," ' she thinks. Most important of all, Maria knows, is that she has made her students reflect on an experience that has the potential to be a powerful influence over them. That is at the heart of all good media studies—to create active participants in a passive environment.

Vignette 3: The Language of Film and Television

Maria loves film and the last thing she would ever want to do is to negatively impact the viewing experience for her students. Yet, she feels a need to train her students to become thoughtful and knowledgeable film viewers. "Film is not real. Film is an art," she tells her students over and over again.

Maria more than tells her students this. She conducts a lesson showing her students how film works to create the impact and send the message.

Field of Dreams

Maria begins this lesson with a discussion of baseball. She tells about her experiences growing up and loving the Texas Rangers. She relates how she would read the box scores every day.

"It was my mother who loved baseball and taught me the game," Maria tells the class.

"There are two kinds of baseball films in this world. One kind says baseball is nothing but a game. Two films from this camp are *Bull Durham* and *Major League*."

"The other kind of baseball film sees the game as larger than life, almost a myth of something very powerful. Two examples from this mythic side are *The Natural* and *Field of Dreams*."

"We are going to watch *Field of Dreams*, based on W. P. Kinsella's book, *Shoeless Joe*.

Maria shows the movie, the one she copied from television. Her showing takes three class days.

After the Movie

Maria tells her students, "think about the film for a while before we discuss it. I want you to write in your journals about *Field of Dreams*, but I want you to answer some questions that I will give you."

These questions concern not only what the movie is about, they also concern how the filmmakers use techniques to create meaning and feelings. Last, these questions ask you what the big meaning of the movie may be. You put together your answers concerning what *Field of Dreams* is about with the answers to the techniques questions, and you come up with a large interpretation of this film."

Maria's students looked a bit stunned at this point, but she tells them to try it anyway and see what they come up with.

Maria goes over each question (Figure 9.1) on the list with her students and at their request she shows the last 20 minutes of the film where they see the close-up of the handshake and the horizon line with the red sunset. They notice the beautiful baseball diamond outlined by lights and they see the umbilical cord of headlights leading toward the diamond as the movie ends.

As Maria checks the journals, many of them are grappling with the issues of the film. A few of her students conclude the larger meaning of the film deals with a son who gets the chance to recommunicate with his father through baseball, a game of catch that comes at the end of the movie. Some of her students do not see this film this way at all. A few of her students do not like the film. Maria will discuss this with her class tomorrow. She hopes that her students will begin to look at film through these three levels: the Literary, the Visual

figure ◊ **9.1**

Tips on Film and Television Viewing

Three Methods

I. Literary Level: the level of story
What is the film about?
What is the story?
What are the themes?
Who are the characters and what are they like?

II. Visual Literacy Level: the level of film art
What do you see?
What do you hear?
Describe the following:
> Composition: How the shot is put together, like a painting or a photograph
> Editing: How the film is cut and pasted; how the scenes change
> Movement: How the camera moves; how the objects in the scene are shown moving.
> Color: How color is used to create feeling and mood in the viewers.
> Lighting: How light is used to create feeling and mood in the viewers.
> Sound: How music and sound are used to create feeling and mood in the viewers.

III. The Superstory Level
The level of film and television myth (myths are stories and images that provide people guiding principles, values, ideas, and feelings—these often serve as moral and spiritual life guides)
> How do you connect with this film or show?
> What is this film or show really saying to you about life?
> What are the strongest feeling and ideas that this film or show conveys?
> Any other thoughts or feelings about this film or show?

Literacy, and what she calls the Superstory level. She will refer to these all semester because she firmly believes that this is the way to become intelligent, enlightened viewers, viewers who understand the art and craft of movies and television for that matter.

"I will never, ever ask students to look for these tips as they watch a movie. These are meant as guides to analyzing film *after* the viewing experience. But I have found most of my students find this to be a fun way to approach critiquing a film. And I have found this a sound method of creating the most educated viewers I can imagine."

Reflection

Maria has made film an important part of her curriculum. Her students read, write, and think about what they see, which she hopes helps her kids become intelligent viewers and thoughtful consumers of the mass media. Maria understands that school should not be divorced from the world around it. Rather, Maria sees school as a friendly place to study the world and gain mastery over today's complex and powerful network of communication systems.

Using the World Wide Web in the Classroom

Maria gets her wish. It's like winning the lottery for her. She is getting a newly remodeled technology room. This means the following: Maria's room will be next to one of the school writing labs, which has 25 computers and two printers. Her room has a door directly to the lab and the adjoining wall is just several large windows. This allows Maria to break her students into groups with one or more groups working in the lab under her not-too-distant supervision. Of course, there are days the lab is used by other students visible to her classes. But her students get used to this quickly, and there is only an occasional inappropriate exchange between a lab student and one of Maria's students. It's really a nonissue. Her students use the computer lab to develop most of their projects, which now come replete with graphics, charts, all kinds of visuals, including an occasional film or audio clip.

Best of all is the personal tech setup Maria gets in her class. Her desk is against a wall in the middle. Above her desk is a large TV clearly visible to all her students. At her desk she has a VCR and a computer with keyboard. She can run the computer screen off the television, and, of course, she is hooked up to the Internet with broadband access provided by the community cable company. Not only does she not have to drag TV and VCR carts anymore, now she can also do class demos of her writing or student writing and she can do lessons with Internet sites and web use.

The Web

Maria uses the Internet to enhance her lessons. For instance, when her class studied *Glory*, she found web sites about the film, but more importantly, about the real 54th Massachusetts Regiment, which the film recreates. After a search for film reviews, her students found many of them, some not so good. For instance, the *Washington Post* found the movie superficial, and Roger Ebert liked it a lot but questioned why the film was told through the eyes of the white officer. However, the teen critic called it the best Civil War movie ever.

Then Maria searched for information about the 54th. The first site she found was very powerful. The page from www.nara.gov/exhall/originals/54thmass.html gave a brief but moving description of the real regiment with pictures of proud African-American Union Army soldiers.

"I knew it was real, but seeing it is so fine," Nick remarked when the page appeared on the TV.

Next Maria clicked on the casualty page where the original list of those who died in the battle for Fort Wagner in South Carolina were recorded in the ancient-looking penmanship of the Civil War era.

"Can you read any of the names?" Maria asked.

"The first name is Audrey Burton, who is listed as a sergeant," Tammi replied after walking as close to the TV as she could get.

"I can see George Allison and Randolph Brandy, I think," Marsha responded.

"Back to the menu," Maria said. "Find the next site from this list."

"No question. Check on www.54thmass.org (Figure 9.2)," Carlos commanded.

What came up was a deep blue screen with the logo of the 54th on one side and a menu of options on the other, surrounding a picture of the monument shown in the last scene in the movie. A Civil War melody played in the background.

Maria searched through this site based on questions and the interests of her students. They were excited to see that there was a group of men from the Washington, D.C., area who role-played Company B of the 54th Regiment. These men are called Civil War reenactors, and they participated in the movie *Glory*.

Maria also found a book list for her students, some of whom have chosen to research the history of this regiment for their end of the year project.

Those students who were interested in doing the *Glory* history project will be back at this web site. They will spend time in the computer lab next to Maria's class researching this site and the links this site provides.

Tasha became very interested in the sculptor who designed the African-American Civil War Sculpture that is in Washington, D.C. She found out about Ed Hamilton and his art through the 54th web site.

Reflections on Using the Web in the Classroom

Because Maria has the equipment, she feels obligated to use it. As she continues with her web lessons she becomes increasingly more comfortable with them. Maria continues to find ways of making her web lessons interactive. Usually, her students tell her where to search, and most of the time she will have a student working her computer while she sits in the class with the rest of her students. Actually, many of her students are far more familiar with the computer and the web than she is.

figure ◗ 9.2

Now for every unit she does she will use the web for some pertinent information. It may be tracing a trip to Birmingham, Alabama, for her introduction of the Christopher Paul Curtis novel, *The Watsons Go to Birmingham—1963*. She also checks out the sites on the church bombing that killed four young African-American girls, which plays a large role in this novel, which Maria recommends as an independent workshop reading selection.

Maria will also search out what happened to the stars of *The Breakfast Club*. Naturally, her students love the entertainment sites, which are okay with her, as long as they use them in a way to support her television and film curricula.

Her students research sites using a specific search engine designed to weed out places the school does not want them to go. This search engine is from the State Department of Education, and students can find all they need using it.

There is a teacher in Maria's school who creates web high school courses, which students from anywhere in the world may take for credit with permission of their home high school. Maria's school is not quite ready to grant students access to web high school courses. Teachers are wary of the potential to eliminate staff if too many web courses are accepted for credit.

Reflection

"This is all so new," Maria says. "We are working it out. These are lessons under construction. Along with the benefits there are fears much of the staff has concerning computer use. This unregulated free speech medium is a challenge for all of us," she suggests in her nervous way.

However, for now, Maria is committed to offering her students the best and most technologically advanced education she has available. Maria is learning with her students, but she is not afraid to try, and she is secure enough in her classrooms to cross over to the new skills required for our time.

Teaching Television

Maria remembers when a media teacher's primary piece of equipment was a 16 mm film projector. Today, it is the videocassette recorder. VCRs tend to be easier to operate and break down less than the old movie projectors, enabling Maria to provide her students with a whole range of what she considers important media lessons. The *Glory* discussion and *The Breakfast Club* trial are activities based on strong film texts, but Maria believes that she has an obligation to explore the powerful, manipulative, and often far more banal texts of television. Maria feels that it is with TV, more than film, and certainly more than books, that her students spend most of their time as receptors, as nondiscriminating viewers. Maria wants her students to become aware of these television texts. She knows her students always will enjoy television, and she knows that many of them always will watch too much TV. But she hopes that with the tools she has as a teacher, she will help some of her students become more discriminating, more active viewers who are:

- less likely to buy something only because they saw it on television;
- less likely to be misled by the apparent ability of television to portray real life;

- less likely to believe that a happy, successful life depends on having the appearance or personality of a television star or character;
- less likely to believe that love as expressed on television correlates to love as expressed in life; and
- less likely to be desensitized by the constant barrage of murder and violence seen on television.

Above all, Maria wants her students to become intelligent viewers, viewers who can enjoy and appreciate a wide range of television experiences, including the best the medium has to offer.

Maria knows her goals are lofty, impossible for her to achieve by herself. But she also knows if media studies were woven throughout the educational lives of her students, these goals would emerge. But she is only one teacher.

Studying Television

Maria's unit on television consists of an increasingly complex set of activities. Early activities focus on the following:

- Children's commercial television (primarily Saturday morning fare)
- Children's television commercials
- Children's educational television (*Sesame Street*, *Mr. Rogers' Neighborhood*, *Reading Rainbow*, and so on)
- Adult television commercials
- Adult prime time shows (whatever is hot at the time)

Maria begins this series by taping samples from these categories. For children's commercial television and adult prime time, she has her students nominate programs for her to tape.

Before Maria brings the tapes to class, she holds a discussion on how to view the material, what to look for. After this discussion, she incorporates students' suggestions into a sheet of questions that she gives each of them for reference.

Maria tells her students that it is important to understand how the structural devices of film and television are used to create feelings in viewers. She tells them that this is particularly important in understanding how television commercials work. She provides her students with a technical analysis sheet (Figure 9.3).

Despite all Maria's preparations, analyzing the tapes is tricky because the images move so quickly. However, her students show a great deal of insight. They are particularly adept at pointing out how the commercials aimed at children are misleading when it comes to showing how toys perform. The prime-time adult programs are the least effectively analyzed because they are the least

figure ◊ 9.3

Film and Television Analysis Sheet

Structural Questions

How does the editing affect the mood of the viewer?

Does the lighting elicit a mood? How?

Does the movement excite or calm the viewer? Neither? How?

How do the images help create the mood?

How are colors used to create atmosphere or mood?

Do the music and background noises add to the general atmosphere?

How would you describe the rhythm of the work?

What elements were combined to create this rhythm?

Social Questions

How do the people dress?

What characterizes the behavior of the people?

How would you characterize the general appearance of the people?

How do the characters relate to each other?

What are the economic circumstances of the characters?

What methods do the characters use to solve their problems?

Describe the family situations that are shown.

Mythological Considerations

What does the program or commercial imply about the following? Consider any of the following:

love	play
death	men
sex	women
marriage	children
friendship	fun
family	adventure
teamwork	possessions
the individual	appearance
nature	leisure
success	reading
failure	knowledge
pride	home life
work	

figure ◊ **9.4**

Film and Television Structural Devices Critique Sheet

How did the images (pictures) affect how you felt about the movie or television program?

How did the images help you understand the story?

Did you notice how the piece was edited?

Did the camera move? Describe the camera movement.

Was there a great deal of movement within the shots (running, car chases, planes flying)?

Based on the total movement, would you describe this piece as fast or slow?

How did the lighting affect your feelings or mood?

How did the color affect the mood? Did any one color stand out?

Was there a great deal of background music? Did the background music help or hinder your enjoyment of the work?

Did background noises add anything to the piece?

Rating:

excellent   very good   good   fair   poor

Why did you give this piece the above rating?

(The New Literacy, NCTE, 1979)

---

interesting tapes. Her students feel the commercials are much more entertaining than the programs (Figure 9.4)

Vignette 1: Analyzing Television Commercials

Maria has a special place in her heart for this part of her curriculum. She feels no responsibility to protect TV commercials from emotional and judgmental teenagers.

She considers commercials manipulative in the extreme messages created by highly educated and overpaid adults aimed at bringing out the worst in teenagers in order to sell them mostly junk they do not need. Maria sees commercials as the enemy. She asks her students what they think about television commercials.

Ivory: "I love the Air Jordan one. That's my favorite shoe."

Henderson: "No, that Nike commercial with Andre Agassi. You know, the one where the television bounces all over the place. That's great."

Talisa: "Don't you get sick of people trying to sell you stuff—all that cheap garbage at high prices? How much do those shoes cost?"

Billie: "I got a pair of Air Jordans for eighty bucks. It was a great deal. They can cost as much as $110."

Talisa: "What about all those beer commercials? Huh? That malt liquor commercial. What's that called?"

Jerry: "Oh, yeah. That's that heavy-duty commercial that's black and white and has a real strong heavy-metal beat."

At this point Jerry begins singing the commercial while the class laughs. Maria watches and listens. She knows her students can and will discuss television commercials without her aid, so she lets them. Always, in these discussions, students will ask each other to think about the negative impact of television commercials. Maria takes note of what draws her students' attention. This year it is the shoe, beer, and car commercials.

Now Maria asks her students to take out their film and television analysis sheet. She goes over it with them and then says:

"I would like you to apply the analysis from this sheet, which you have worked with before, to television commercials that I am going to show you. I will be showing five TV commercials, and I would like you to write down comments for each. Take out five sheets of paper and number them one through five."

Tracy: "Do we have to answer all the questions?"

Maria: "No, Tracy. Select the questions or issues that strike you, that are most important to you."

Shelby: "Do we have to turn these in?"

Maria: "Yes. I will check them. They will count as one journal entry. And I would like you to keep them in your portfolios. Any other questions?"

Maria pauses, counting to 10 silently, to give her students enough time to ask questions if they have them. Then she takes her tape, a sampling of prime time and children's commercials, and slips it in the VCR.

"Okay. The first commercial you are about to see is a children's commercial for California Rollerbaby," Maria says.

Her students applaud; the tape soon lives up to their best (or worst) expectations. The commercial features a roller-skating doll in a skimpy leotard. A pseudo-Beach Boys rendition of *Surfin' USA* plays in the background as preteen girls dance with the doll. This is truly a disgusting commercial, Maria thinks.

After it is over, Maria stops the tape and has her students respond to the questions on the analysis sheet. Then she plays the same commercial again and has her students respond to the sheet again. She uses this system for the next four commercials, showing each twice because they move so quickly. This activity takes about half an hour, which brings the class to an end.

The next day, Maria returns the analysis sheets to her students. She spent about 15 minutes checking them, wrote a few comments, and gave students journal credit for them. Now, she begins the discussion by asking her class to deal with the California Rollerbaby commercial.

> Maria: "How did you analyze that commercial?"
> Talisa: "The editing was bam, bam, bam. It moved so quickly."
> Maria: "Why?"
> Talisa: "I guess to excite the little kids who are watching. You know, keep them interested."
> Alice: "They used all these bright, fun colors—you know, colors kids like and that make them feel happy."
> Chrissie: "I thought it was an awfully sexy doll."
> Andy: "Me too."
> Maria: "Explain, Chrissie."
> Chrissie: "Well, who is the doll being sold to? Little kids. Are they supposed to be dancing like that and wearing those sexy outfits?"
> Talisa: "I see little girls like that all the time. They're dancing away like they're teenagers."
> Chrissie: "That's great, Seven-year-old girls are going to have babies if this keeps up."

Maria has her class use the analyses they have prepared to discuss all five commercials. Catching a commercial is like catching the wind; they intentionally pass so quickly it is tough to consciously grab hold. But Maria is satisfied that her students have grappled with the often unpleasant nature of television commercials. Perhaps, Maria thinks, these young people will be a little less prone to accept the images in which television commercials would cast them.

Vignette 2: Analyzing Television News Programs

With the help of a friend, Maria tapes the newscast of two different networks on the same evening. In class, she gives each of her students a sheet similar to the following (Figure 9.5).

Maria assigns groups of students to prepare one or more of the entries on the sheets. She discusses each item with the class and holds a general discussion about television news. Her students have some disparaging remarks, particularly about local news programs and what they refer to as male "anchor hair" or the use of attractive women on news programs.

figure **◊ 9.5**

News Program Criteria Sheet
Compare

	Program 1	Program 2
Length of opening story		
Nature of opening story		
Number of commercials		
Time on anchor		
Time on newsfilm		
Number of stories		

News Analysis

Describe the set.

Describe the clothing of the anchor(s).

Describe the voice of the anchor(s).

What is the main story?

How is the main story depicted?

What is the most striking story
other than the main story? Why?

What is the softest story of the newscast?

How is that story covered?

Write a few adjectives that you feel
describe the newscast.

Describe the newscast in terms of
the following:

Editing

Composition

Lighting

Color

Sound

Movement

What kinds of commercials are shown
on the newscast?

Who is the audience for these commercials?

Then Maria shows the tapes, complete with commercials. The showing of each tape, and completing the work sheet, takes one period. She holds the discussion, based on the tapes and the analyses her students have written, in the third class period.

Maria leads the discussion by asking for comments based on each entry. Each of the groups presents its findings and the class comments on them. The differing anchor styles are some of the most obvious qualities of the newscast, and it becomes apparent to the students that the style is as important as the news. Maria's students begin to notice how the newscasts sell the anchors. They also notice how news stories are developed with voice-overs and interviews. And they become fascinated with how the same stories, treated differently on the two networks, create such different meanings.

Sample comments include the following:

Group one: "Dan Rather was wearing a white shirt and red tie while Peter Jennings wore a blue shirt with red pinstripe tie. Dan Rather was seen in close-up most of the time he was on camera. Whereas Jennings was often shot from midsection up. You saw more of Jennings who appeared softer and less intense than Rather."

Group two: "ABC had more news footage and less time on the anchor than CBS. ABC had three more stories than CBS, and ABC News was paced faster with more graphics."

Group three: "Both news programs must appeal to the same nervous people because they advertise the same products. Besides selling cars, they sell laxatives and antacids. Either the news is giving viewers bad stomachs, or they had bad stomachs to begin with."

All in all, Maria is very pleased with the results of this activity. The downside—some long moments watching two newscasts. The upside—a lot of thoughtful, insightful analysis on the part of her students.

Vignette 3: Newscast Simulation

The last activity Maria does in her media unit is the most complex. And because Maria hates "machines" so much, this activity is a particular burden because she has to use a video camera to record student newscasts. She has her students prepare newscasts, complete with anchors, remotes, commentary, sports, weather, and commercials. In some classes, she uses a published simulation that requires the students to prepare a parody newscast that can be quite funny (Beary, Salvner, & Wesolowski, 1977). However, in most of her classes, she has her students prepare a newscast based on newspapers and magazines, turning printed news stories and features into TV stories. They have to make editorial decisions based on the news of the day. When Maria does it the second way, she has two teams.

Newscast is an extended activity that takes at least nine class periods.

Introduction of Newscast, Period One. For Maria, the introduction of this activity is the hardest part of it. No matter how much she talks about it, her students will not understand the activity until they start doing it. "They love it once it is over, but getting them to do it is another matter," Maria explains. Because of this, she keeps her explanation short and concise: "You are going to prepare a newscast for television that will be videotaped for our viewing."

Then Maria divides the class in half and selects two anchors. She explains to the anchors that they will select roles for the other students in their groups. She gives each anchor the following cast list:

Anchor

Desk reporters (three)

Field reporters (three)

Editorial writer

Sports reporter (two)

Weather person

Commercial writers and stars (three)

Then Maria gives her anchors the following schedule for each newscast:

Anchor intro
    Report one
    Remote one

Anchor
    Report two
    Remote two

Anchor
    Commercial one

Anchor
    Sports report one

Anchor
    Report three
    Remote three

Anchor
    Commercial two

Anchor
    Sports report two

Anchor
    Weather

Anchor
    Commercial

Anchor
   Editorial

Anchor
   Close

Maria puts a lot of pressure on her anchors, but she chooses them very carefully and, of course, she helps them decide which students will take which parts.

She also provides each news team with a supply of recent newspapers and news magazines and explains that they are to carefully select the stories that they will write for television. Each newscast will last about a half an hour, so each report, editorial, remote, and commercial must last only about two minutes. Finally, Maria explains to the anchors their responsibilities:

- Supervise the writing of the stories, commercials, editorials, and so on

- Glue the newscast together with the opening, closing, and introductions of stories and commercials

- Help team members, when appropriate

- Organize the dress rehearsal

- Do whatever is necessary to make a smooth and interesting newscast

Newscast Writing Workshop, Periods Two and Three.   Students begin this project with a great deal of lethargy, Maria always notices. "What do you want to write about?" "I don't know. What do *you* want to write about?"

But left on their own, the project begins cooking. Soon laughter emanates from one of the groups, and Maria is being inundated with requests.

"Read this; is this okay?"

"We need magic markers, construction paper, and five empty milk cartons." "Ms. Hernandez, listen to my sports report, please."

Now Maria is having fun. She is everywhere, helping both teams and making sure the anchors are leading in such a way as to not create bad feelings. By day two of the newscast workshop, her students are basically on their own, finishing the writing of their parts.

Rehearsal, Periods Four and Five.   The rehearsal days take a bit of logistics because Maria needs two rooms, one for each team. She asks each team to try to get through the newscast at least twice to ensure smoothness. The anchors are in charge of the rehearsals, but Maria divides her time between both rooms to catch as much of these trial runs as she can. The newscasts contain serious news stories and some spoofs, particularly the commercials. Usually, the newscasts open with a shot of the TV station her kids have designed.

Taping, Periods Six and Seven.   The taping requires cooperation from Maria's principal because she tapes one team while the other one is in a different room, rehearsing one last time. Each team takes one class period to tape. Her students dress the parts, often wearing newscaster clothes from the waist up as that is what will be on tape. They learn quickly about the illusions of television. Something always goes wrong during the taping. Students forget their cues, a commercial prop isn't prepared properly. The glitches work to lighten the broadcasts for the participants.

Maria's students take the taping very seriously and exhibit a great deal of anxiety. They are very relieved and happy when it is over. Usually, part of the reason for their happiness is the pleasure they feel in having completed a successful project.

Showing Newscasts, Periods Eight and Nine. All Maria does during these two periods is show the entire class each of the newscasts. After all the work, this is the payoff and her students enjoy the videotapes immensely. No one criticizes anyone's on-camera performance, but the class critiques the overall nature of the videos and compares the "look" with that produced by professionals. Many of her students make suggestions of what they might do differently— look into the camera more, punch the words, pause after each paragraph—but the viewings are basically very entertaining.

Maria has done the taping herself but she has had help from students and the school media director who know how to run the equipment. One year, Maria took her class on a field trip to a television studio, where they were professionally taped on a real news set. Because she did not want to scare her class in advance, this was a surprise to her students until they walked into the studio, when many of them turned to her and said, "We have to go to the bathroom." The TV studio was an unforgettable experience for Maria's students, but the tape was the stiffest, most rigid performance she has ever encountered with this activity.

The newscast is an important activity in her media studies because it gives Maria's students a sense of what producing a show is like. They all take careful note that it begins with writing clear and cogent prose, and continues with articulate and literate speech. So, Maria ends her media studies with an activity that requires as much reading and writing as anything she asks her students to do all semester. The newscast simulation is a fitting tribute to how all the language arts interact and reinforce each other.

Reflection

Maria loves books, but she knows that her students live in a world where the written word is seriously challenged. Maria tries to level the playing field for books by making media more comprehensible, less mysterious. Her goal is not to make kids hate film and television, which would be impossible, but to make them more active consumers of the media, more selective in what they watch and how they watch it. And Maria truly wants her students to know how to use computers in the best possible ways. Maria incorporates her media activities into her English classes so that computers, films, and television programs are studied along with books, short stories, and poems. All texts in Maria's classes interact, reflecting the dynamics of the super mediated global culture of the new century.

Teacher as Researcher

Questions

- Is the description of Maria's technology realistic? Explain.
- How well does Maria incorporate web studies into her class?
- How can you teach Internet use without the resources Maria has?
- How else can you use computer technology in an English classroom?
- How do the new literacies impact reading and writing?
- Should English teachers be responsible for teaching the new literacies? If yes, why? If no, why not?
- How would you justify to parents and administrators teaching film and television in an English class?
- What are the risks Maria takes in teaching the film *Glory*?
- Is it advisable to have discussions about race in an English class? If yes, how would you conduct them? What materials would you use? What are the dangers of these discussions, and what would you do about these dangers? How would you prepare for these discussions?
- What other "trials" could you hold about media? What other trials could you hold in an English class?
- What films have had an impact on you? Why?
- How do you feel about the value systems promoted by television for teenagers? Explain.
- How do current film and television shows portray teenagers? How do you feel about these portrayals?
- Have you had any film and television lessons? If yes, describe them?
- When and why do you watch television? What do you get from television?
- Do any television shows or feature films have value systems that trouble you? Which one and why?
- How do you feel about the "real life" television shows? How do these shows merge reality with fantasy?
- How does advertising on TV influence teenagers? How does it influence younger children?

- Has television been good or bad for the political life of this country? Explain.
- How are children harmed by television?
- How are children aided by television?

Activities

- React to the story. Give your impressions and thoughts.
- Design other web lessons for English classrooms.
- List web sites that are useful for English teaching. Divide your list into web sites for students and web sites for teachers.
- Develop a technology wish list for an English teacher.
- Develop a rationale for the purchasing of computer equipment for your classroom.
- Make a list of films that you feel deserve classroom attention. Justify your choices.
- Describe other activities involving the new literacies.
- Describe your experiences with using AV equipment in a classroom. Prepare for equipment problems.
- Describe a unit on the globalization of America. Consider telephones, fax machines, satellite dishes, cable television, national newspapers and magazines, airplanes and airports, motel and hotel chains, bullet trains, superhighways, and business chains like McDonald's.
- Keep track of your television viewing. Analyze why you watch what you do.
- Take a survey among your friends. Determine what are the most popular shows of your peer group and figure out why.
- Describe the kinds of TV shows you would like to see aired.

IRA/NCTE Standards for English Language Arts with Performance Benchmarks for Chapter 9

Standard One

Students read a wide range of print and nonprint texts to build an understanding of texts, of themselves, and of cultures of the United States and the world; to acquire new information; to respond to the needs and demands of society and the workplace; and for personal fulfillment. Among these texts are fiction and nonfiction, classic, and contemporary works.

Performance Benchmark for Standard One

Students read film, research the web, and watch television to build an understanding of texts, of themselves, and of the cultures of the United States and the world; to acquire new information; to respond to the needs and demands of society and the workplace; and for personal fulfillment.

Standard Three

Students apply a wide range of strategies to comprehend, interpret, evaluate, and appreciate texts. They draw on their prior experience, their interactions with other readers and writers, their knowledge of word meaning and of other texts, their word identification strategies, and their understanding of textual features (e.g., sound-letter correspondence, sentence structure, context graphics).

Performance Benchmark for Standard Three

Students develop a knowledge and understanding of the various ways the electronic media uses textual features to create meaning and feeling in viewers and users.

Standard Four

Students adjust their use of spoken, written, and visual language (e.g., conventions, style, vocabulary) to communicate effectively with a variety of audiences and for different purposes.

Performance Benchmark for Standard Four

Students make media news productions to communicate with a variety of audiences for different purposes.

Standard Six

Students apply knowledge of language structure, language conventions (e.g., spelling and punctuation), media techniques, figurative language, and genre to create, critique, and discuss print and nonprint texts.

Performance Benchmark Standard Six

Students use the language of film and television to create a television news program.

Students use computers to generate compositions.

Standard Eight

Students use a variety of technological and informational resources (e.g., libraries, databases, computer networks, video) to gather and synthesize information and to create and communicate knowledge.

Performance Benchmark for Standard Eight

Students use video equipment to create a newscast.

Standard Twelve

Students use spoken, written, and visual language to accomplish their own purposes (e.g., for learning, enjoyment, persuasion, and the exchange of information).

Performance Benchmark for Standard Twelve

Students use the language of film and television to create an informative, entertaining, and persuasive work.

Recommended Readings

Alverman, D., Moon, J. S., & Hagood, M. C. (1999). *Popular culture in the classroom: Teaching and researching critical media literacy.* Newark, DE: International Reading Association.

This book addresses media literacy and contains ideas and methods for incorporating media literacy in the classroom.

Carey, J. W. (Ed.). (1988). *Media, myth, and narratives: Television and the press.* Newbury Park, CA: Sage Publications.

This series of essays takes television seriously and offers a great deal of useful information for teachers of this medium.

Flood, J., Heath, S. B., & Lapp, D. (Eds.). (1997). *Handbook of research on teaching literacy through the communicative and visual arts.* New York: Macmillan.

This is a huge collection of essays about the use of media in classrooms. Much of it is aimed at elementary classrooms.

Foster, H. M. (1979). *The new literacy: The language of film and television.* Urbana, IL: National Council of Teachers of English.

This book is an account of how film and television work on the emotions of viewers. The second part of this book provides visual literacy lessons for secondary classrooms.

Foster, H. M. (1984). The new literacy: Television, purveyor of modem myth. *English Journal, 73,* 26–30.

This article shows how television conveys powerful, allegorical stories and discusses their impact on viewers.

Gruber, S. (Ed.). (2000). *Weaving a virtual web: Practical approaches to new information technologies*. Urbana, IL: National Council of Teachers of English.

This book offers twenty essays on using the Web in classrooms. The Web can be a complicated issue so this is a useful guide to classroom teachers who incorporate technology into the classroom.

Jensen, J. (1990). *Redeeming modernity: Contradictions in media criticism*. Newbury Park, CA: Sage Publications.

The book is about the belief systems that dominate our thinking about the media. Jensen explores the nature of media criticism in relation to modem society.

Masterman, L. (1985). *Teaching the media*. London: Comedia Publishing Group.

This thoughtful work offers questions and issues for media teachers. The book deals more with abstract issues than concrete lessons.

Winn, M. (1978). *The plug-in drug*. New York: Bantam.

Winn's anti-TV bias is strong, but the book provides powerful evidence of the dangers of too much viewing with too little knowledge about this medium.

Grading and Assessing

Introduction

> If Carrie has any philosophy of grading it is "the more grades the better." That is, the more ways her students can earn a grade, the better off everyone is. Carrie does this because her students desire grades, a kind of surrogate paycheck for the work they do. Carrie also does this because the more ways she has of assessing their performance, the closer she is to some kind of honest and accurate final evaluation for report cards. On the other hand, the more grades she gives, the more she has to read and evaluate student work. And the more she reads and evaluates, the less willing her students are to experiment, take risks, and write, speak, and perform without inhibition. Carrie gets a headache thinking about all these variables. But she resolves these contradictions by giving a great many simple, credit/no-credit grades.

The School, the Students

I have two impressions of Main Street High School: first, there is no neighborhood; second, there are no windows. The school is situated on the edge of downtown in a mid-sized city with no discernable places where people live. Where the kids come from is a bit of a puzzle. Actually, most of these kids live in the scattered housing, some old, some new apartments federally funded, surrounding the downtown. These are city kids.

The school is a red brick structure apparently without windows until you look at the third floor. For some reason, third floor classrooms have large windows that look upon a cityscape.

The Teacher	
Carrie Hanigofsky, age 43	Twenty years in teaching, all in the same city system at five schools. Teaching at Main Street High School for the last 12 years.
Educational Background:	Graduated from local state university with B.A. in English Education and Special Education. Earned master's degree in secondary education.
Approach:	I have had no formal training in new methodologies but the needs of my students led me to meaning-centered classrooms. However, I still believe in traditional grammar teaching and its efficacy.
Influences:	Her son's learning style is a major influence. He has trouble learning and has difficulty reading. Carrie believes he needs motivation, real reading experiences, and selected skills work. However, she has worked closely with a university English Education specialist who has convinced her that portfolios and writing assignments that are meaningful are the best way of teaching writing. Carrie is intuitively a fine literature teacher who knows how to relate literary experience to the needs of her students.

Semester Grades

Carrie uses a plan like this one:

Informal Grades—30% of final grade

- Journal writing — A/pass/fail—based on quantity and effort

- Responses to class reading — A/pass/fail—primary trait: Did the student read the work? A's given to especially strong readings or opinions about the work

- Poetry writing — pass/fail

- Poetry selection — pass/fail

Basically, these grades are simple check-off grades, and Carrie's grade book is filled with passes. Her students must perform to earn this 30%, so these activities are meant to be motivational, a way of keeping students actively engaged without too much fear of criticism.

Carrie's overall grading plan looks like this:

Informal Grades	30% of final
Journal writing	A/pass/fail
Responses to class readings	
Poetry writing	A/pass/fail
Poetry selection	pass/fail
Semiformal Grades	
Responses to books	A/B/pass/fail
Responses/records of independent reading	A/B/pass/fail
Play performance	A/pass/fail
Special projects	
Television and film projects	A/B/C/fail
Peer editing and group work	A/B/C/fail
Oral presentations	A/B/C/fail
Panel presentations	A/B/C/fail
Film and television critiques	A/B/C/fail
Grades for Public Writing	35% of final

Completion of steps (rough draft, read and critiqued by student, read and critiqued by Carrie, rewritten, final copy) and

■ At least two of the papers made available to class

■ At least one paper written for audience outside classroom

Holistic Evaluation	A/B/C/D/F 20%
Portfolios, maintenance, and record keeping	5%

Portfolios

All of the class work Carrie requires goes into portfolios, folders that Carrie supplies all of her students. Carrie also requires that her students use a notebook that they keep as a journal. Both the portfolios and the notebook are kept in boxes (file cabinet size) next to her desk, alphabetized by last name. In each portfolio, Carrie has stapled her record-keeping sheets.

Carrie considers the portfolios a crucial part of her process. These portfolios are a cumulative record of each of her student's writings and as complete a picture of this semester for her students as any. Carrie would like these portfolios to travel with her students each year and serve as a growing document on her students as language learners. Carrie is doing her best in trying to convince other department members to consider this system, and she will keep trying. But for now, at least, Carrie has a record she can turn to that indicates the potential and progress of each student. And her students' end-of-semester

---

figure ◊ **10.1** | **Journal Entries (pages/dates)**

Student Name	Entry number	1	2	3	4	5	6
Erik Rodriquez		5 pg. 2/15	3 pg. 3/15				
Joan Davis		7 pg. 2/15	3 pg. 3/15				

statements, along with the samples her students select as their best writing, are tangible evidence of growth and progress.

Carrie's classroom is a fairly complicated place that has a great deal of activity. Carrie must be organized to keep it all running smoothly. So along with her grade book, she keeps master sheets to help her know who is doing what and when (Figures 10.1, 10.2, 10.3).

Using Computers for Final Drafts to Assess

Carrie has four Compaq computers in her room. So many of her students are computer literate that Carrie can rely on students to teach students who want to learn how to use the computers. During every writing workshop, all her computers are in full use, with a waiting list of students. Through the computers, her students make final drafts that are ready for her evaluation. These are so much easier for her to read, assess, and recommend changes.

Carrie has another, even better resource that she uses. Main Street High School has a computer lab replete with 20 fairly new Compaqs and two laser

---

figure ◊ **10.2** | **Conference Record**

Student Name	Conf. 1	Conf. 2	Conf. 3	Conf. 4	Conf. 5
Erik Rodriguez	10/2—Good entry on "Outsiders" Develop into public writing				
Joan Davis	10/2—Needs focus on trip to Grand Canyon. Suggest she consider just writing about mule trip.				

figure ◊ **10.3**	Public Writing

Student Name	Paper 1	Paper 2	Paper 3	Paper 4
Erik Rodriguez	11/2—"On the Outside" Excellent voice, strong emotional account of coming to America. Needs spelling and grammar check. Will be a 4.			
Joan Davis	"Mule Trip into Canyon" excellent. Quick pat on shoulder. Score: 5.			

printers. Once a week Carrie conducts her writing workshop in the computer lab. Carrie provides every opportunity she can for her students to write using computer technology. In one of her journal entries, Carrie provided a list of computer-use pros and cons. First, the pros:

- Writing on a computer can be faster and easier than with paper and pencil.
- Students who have difficulty with handwriting often improve because they can read the computer-generated copy but not their handwriting.
- For many students, writing on a computer is just plain fun as opposed to the laborious task of writing by hand.
- Spelling and grammar programs make life easier for many students.
- Large-scale editing tasks and revision are greatly simplified on computers.
- A printed final copy is more like a "real" publication than a carefully handwritten copy.

But Carrie has her list of cons as well:

- The time spent adapting to the technology often sets back the concentration involved in composing.
- The technology is more complicated than it appears, so students spend a great deal of time trapped in technology problems such as inadvertently moving parts of a text that should stay put.

- Some students see the computer as a toy and worry more about "type style" than the written messages they are composing.

- Reading a computer screen is not the same as reading a page of writing on a piece of paper. The difference between the two takes adaptation and may lead to writing problems for students unaccustomed to computer screens.

- In short, Carrie feels computers in a classroom are a mixed blessing. But she feels the benefits outweigh the problems, and she plans to continue to help her students adapt to the ever-improving computer technology.

A Course in Testing

Carrie, like all teachers, faces an increasingly hostile and suspicious public. The outcry is for accountability, performance objectives, and tests of all kinds. Carrie's state has initiated so many tests that she has lost count of them. "The portfolios are test enough for me," Carrie states. "These portfolios give a comprehensive picture of the work a student has produced over the course of the semester. No standardized test, not even a holistically scored writing sample, provides a longitudinal picture of writing capabilities as accurate as my portfolios. But, of course," Carrie laments, "it takes time and effort to prepare and interpret portfolios, so we are stuck with less expensive forms of testing, such as the relatively cheaper computerized, standardized tests like the SATs."

Actually, Carrie feels her students are being more than adequately prepared by her class for the State Proficiency Test because it is a relatively expensive, holistically scored personal writing sample. Carrie does not worry too much about the other tests her students must face for one very good reason: All her students take a course offered by Main Street High School called Test Taking. "This course has no pretense," Carrie claims. "The sole purpose of it is to prepare our students to take and score well on the multiple local, state, and national tests they face. In fact, I like to teach the course on occasion because it relieves other teachers from having the bulk of the burden of preparing students for standardized tests."

Test taking is not the course considered the most fun in the curriculum. Test taking is a course based on modern, political realities. Students in this course do the following:

- They write holistically scored essays just like those the state gives. They review and analyze their scores and rewrite.

- They take a myriad of practice standardized tests in subject areas. These computer scored tests include math, science, English, and social studies.

- They take practice tests similar to PSATs, SATs, and ACTs.
- They practice various standardized test-taking strategies.
- They analyze and study questions on standardized tests, and they become familiar with scoring methods.

Although test taking is not meaning centered, Carrie and her colleagues are vehement defenders of the course. "Test Taking protects our students from forces beyond their control, and it allows us to teach our other courses the way we feel is best," says Carrie.

A Proficiency Test Story

"You know how many kids showed up?" Carrie challenged after proficiency test makeup day. "Five. If the kids don't care what can I do?" Carrie, like all teachers that day, was in charge of a makeup group for the State Proficiency writing test. These were not Carrie's students. She never met them before. They were assigned to her room to take this makeup after failing at least twice, once in 9th grade, once in 10th grade. Some of Carrie's students were seniors who were not going to be allowed to receive a diploma unless they passed the test. Basically, Carrie was in charge of 12 students.

"Five came," she said again. "I want the state reps to see this. We have these kids who just aren't going to do it no matter what the state does."

Passing a State Writing Test

Carrie is aware that these tests are referred to as high stakes tests, and she knows why. Fail them and you do not graduate from high school, with a full diploma. Almost all states have these tests now and the trend doesn't seem to be diminishing, although there are some voices of dissent among angry parents who see too much of the curriculum devoted to these tests. And Carrie has seen flaws in the system. For her most academically able students, these tests are minor hurdles to be passed asap in ninth grade, the earliest grade they are made available. This works well for these students as long as they are tracked into classes where the curriculum goes way beyond the proficiencies. For her struggling students, the proficiencies are a never-ending nightmare with potential success if the student will show up, and the teacher, or in many cases, tutor teaches the test.

"What's this tell us about these kids?" Carrie reflects. "I guess these tests measure some level of aptitude. Who knows. These tests are here and will be here for the rest of my career," she concludes.

Carrie's State Proficiency Unit—The Writing Relay Game

Carrie knows what her students need to do. They need to practice taking the writing test and meeting the criteria. So she turns it into a game. The writing test asks students to write on two topics or prompts. These prompts are always on personal issues such as describe your hero and tell why. Or what is your favorite object in your room, explain. Or what extracurricular activity do you participate in and why. So students are given two of these topics to write on and they will have two hours to complete two essays. The state says it is only interested in students producing a rough draft but there is a criteria for the grading of these exams.

Proficiency Writing Test Criteria

Students must

- write on the topic;

- show a sense of organization, have a beginning, middle and end;

- be clear; and

- exhibit knowledge of the conventions of writing; that is punctuation, and spelling.

So, what Carrie does in October is require her students to play this writing game (Figures 10.4, 10.5).

Carrie scores each essay and requires a score of 3 or higher to continue If a student does not score a 3 or more Carrie does another reading and uses a trait

---

figure ◊ **10.4**

Rules of Writing Relay:
Teams are composed of three students. The goal of each team is to arrive at the end of the game board by rolling a pair of dice and landing on a topic circle. There are five topic circles. Inside each topic circle team members will find about a half a dozen prompts. Each member must write on one topic and turn it in in their portfolio to Carrie. She will then score it based on the state rubric which is as an analytic scoring rubric. Once all members of a team pass, they can move to the next topic circle. Teams who complete the entire board will receive a pizza party later in the semester. Carrie makes sure all teams succeed eventually.

figure ◊ **10.5**

State Writing Test Rubric
5: written on topic; organization very evident; strong sense of voice and purpose; strong command of language conventions.

4: written on topic; organization evident, sense of voice and purpose; command of language conventions.

3: written on topic, organization somewhat evident; command of language conventions.

2: any or all of the following—not written on topic, no evidence of organization; little command

1: unreadable

---

rubric. This rubric looks for specific traits that can be analyzed to help students pass (Figure 10.6).

Once Carrie determines why her student scores below 3 she determines a program to help her student overcome the difficulty.

This is all done during writing workshop so she can help every student individually as long as the majority of her students receive a 3 or better on the state rubric during her practice session. However, if many of her students do not receive 3 she will teach a class lesson on the skills her students need, whether it is grammar or organization or other skills. Almost always, all of her students will complete the game and earn the party.

Modeling the Test

Regardless of the class, however, Carrie models writing a state test. In some ways she hates doing this because she is giving a dull drill-oriented formula, but she feels her students need to know this to pass the state test.

After the game is over, Carrie gives her students several practice tests under the same conditions they will encounter during the proficiency. So Carrie's students write timed essays using the prompts from past state tests.

After she evaluates the essays, she goes over the simple formula for passing a state proficiency test. She also writes a model for her students. Then she gives them another practice test, all over again. Her formula is simple and tacky, the five-paragraph theme: thesis statement, opening paragraph, three supporting paragraphs, closing summary paragraph.

"If you do follow this simple formula you will pass," Carrie explains to her students, and they will, those that come to class. However, Carrie teaches in

figure ◊ **10.6**

Trait Rubric
Check one of the following:

written on topic_____

somewhat on topic_____

not on topic_____

Organization and clarity

5: Excellent at the paragraph and sentence level. Strong evidence of a beginning, middle, and end

4: Strong evidence of beginning, middle, and end.

3: Some evidence of organization.

2: No strong evidence of organization. No sense of paragraphing and/or lack of sentence cohesion.

1: No organization

Conventions

5: Excellent punctuation and spelling.

4: Good sense of punctuation and spelling with few serious errors.

3: Sense of punctuation and spelling; errors do not often interfere with meaning

2: Lack of understanding of conventions; many errors in punctuation and spelling; as a result, text difficult to read.

1: Serious lack of correctness.

a district in which over 40% of her students move in and out during a school year.

"These kids may be poor, but they're not dumb," she explains. "But remember Jacqueline from last year? Her mother moved out in December because she was afraid of Jacqueline's father. Trust me, during this period of intense stress, I could not get Jacqueline to care about in any way the state proficiency test. She failed it of course. Didn't even show and who knows where she is now.

"Last year I had 12 kids in my seventh period 11th grade English class who had failed the writing proficiency in 10th grade. I worked with them half the semester, and had students from my 12th-grade class tutor them. Two of the kids wouldn't do a thing. One of them, Kim from Korea, didn't speak much English. But the other nine tried, including Sergie from Bosnia. Sergie and Kim passed by the way. Kim flunked the first time because the question was about a circus, which she had never seen.

"The state has no idea about the lives some of my students lead that make them indifferent at best to these tests," Carrie finishes.

Reflections on Binding and Assessing

Carrie cares a lot. She has spent a lifetime teaching difficult kids for most teachers. They listen to her. She gets to them, and they trust her for the most part.

And Carrie's grading system works for her most of the time. It may be a little too complicated for some of her students, but her system allows for a variety of literature projects and various kinds of speaking and writing without always sacrificing structure. Carrie is a little too unmathematical to control a point system, so she adopted this percentage basis for giving grades. Carrie hates to give grades but she knows she has to, and she has learned to use grades as one of her incentives.

But even Carrie cannot mend broken lives; she cannot cure poverty; she cannot put broken families back together again; she cannot overcome the deeply depressed hearts and minds of her most damaged students. Grades may matter for many of her students, but for most of these kids, state proficiency tests are as important to them as sunspots. Carrie tries and does save some. But she has to be content with low percentages and she also sees worthy kids, who will some day make it in this world, scarred by these tests, which prematurely brand these kids as losers.

Second chances. That is what Carrie hopes these kids will get. It is so sad that a 15-year-old kid will need a second chance, but that's the way with so many of these beautiful but harmed children Carrie faces on a daily basis at Main Street High School. She loves these kids, but the state does not. These kids are test scores to be published in the newspaper to convince the community how poorly Main Street High School educates its kids.

In fact, adults like Carrie are for so many of her students their last hope before the choices of adulthood. Maybe Carrie cannot bring all of these kids into a world of opportunity right now. But for many of them, she plants the seeds of good choices to be made at a later date, that is, if they can overcome the branding they will receive at the hands of the state testers.

Carrie has grit; she does one of the toughest and noblest and most invisible jobs in America. She is an inner city school English teacher. She is neither large nor scary. She lives in a suburb and is very much like her neighbors.

But she has a moxie, a determination and self confidence that is precious. I have been told by her friends that it is her religious convictions. I have also been told by her friends that she has a son who has had difficulty learning. Whatever it is, she is an American hero. If only people knew.

Teacher as Researcher

Questions

- Is Carrie's grading system practical? Explain.
- What would you change about her grading system?
- Do you agree with her use of pass/fail grades? Why or why not?
- What would you weight differently?
- Is there too much or too little emphasis on correctness in writing?
- Are the literature experiences and special projects given enough weight in Carrie's grading system? Explain.
- What are problems you will encounter giving grades? How will you try to overcome these problems?
- How can you use your computer to help you keep track of your grading system?
- How do you feel about proficiency testing in schools? Explain.
- Do you support minimal standards tested in schools? Explain.
- Do you support tough standards tested in schools? Explain.
- What kind of entrance or exit tests have you taken? How do you feel about your experiences?
- Do standards testing help or hurt the English curriculum in schools? Explain.
- Are there any kind of tests that are more appropriate to test English skills than others?
- Should teachers be paid more if their students do better on proficiency tests?
- Besides testing, what other ways are there to assess student achievement?

Activities

- Read to the story. Give your impressions and thoughts.
- Chapter Ten deals with grading. Yet most of the previous chapters present some models for assessing the foci of the chapters. Find the models in previous chapters and develop a grading system from those models.

- Create your own grading system for an English class.
- Convert Carrie's system to a point system. Develop clear guidelines on how to explain points to your students.
- Critique Carrie's system of grading with a positives list and a negatives list.
- Develop a philosophy of grading in the English classroom.
- Match all the benchmarks in the IRA/NCTE sections at the end of each chapter with a method for evaluating the benchmarks.
- If you are for proficiency testing, prepare an argument to convince parents who are against testing that it is a good idea.
- If you are against proficiency testing, prepare an argument to convince parents who are for testing that it is not a good idea.
- Design a unit plan to prepare students to take and pass a proficiency test in English. Prepare a list of test taking advice to give to students who will be taking a high stakes test.

IRA/NCTE Standards for English Language Arts with Performance Benchmarks for Chapter 10

Chapter 10 is about the processes of grading and assessing. There are no standards that deal specifically with evaluation. Rather, evaluation systems are meant to ensure that the standards are met. Chapter 10 serves as the summary of how evaluation systems may operate in the stories that precede this chapter. Thus, the grading and assessing procedures are means of determining how well students achieve all the benchmarks.

Recommended Readings

Falk, B. (2000). *The heart of the matter: Using standards and assessment to learn.* Portsmouth: NH: Heinemann.

This book examines how standardized testing and assessment can be incorporated usefully into the curriculum. If you can't beat it them, you might as well join them. Although this book deals with younger students, it is helpful for all teachers who have to face testing.

Taylor, K., & Walton, S. (1998). *Children at the Center: A workshop approach to standardized test preparation, K-8.* Portsmouth, NH: Heinemann.

This book serves practical advice on how to prepare children for testing. The workshop approach can be applied to older children as well.

Tchudi, S. (1997). *Alternatives to Grading Student Writing*. Urbana, IL: National Council of Teachers of English.

This text offers a series of essays describing alternatives to traditional grading practices.

Wolcott, W., & Legg, S. (1998). *An overview of writing assessment: Theory, research, and practice*. Urbana, IL: National Council of Teachers of English.

This book deals with the issues of writing assessment. The text provides an overview of assessment theory and practice.

part

3

BECOMING AND STAYING A TEACHER: REFLECTIONS AND RESOURCES

Introduction to Part Three: A Guide to Using the Reflections and Resources

Section One of Part Three includes the following:

"Preparing for the Encounter: On Becoming a Teacher" (Chapter Eleven)

- Finding a mentor
- Coping with fatigue
- Handling discipline problems

   "Planning for the English/Language Arts Classroom" (Chapter Twelve)

- Long-range planning
- Weekly and daily plans
- Making plans for the principal
- A discussion of goals and objectives

   "Remaining Alive in the Classroom" (Chapter Thirteen)

- How to be a reflective teacher
- Doing something new in a classroom
- Faculty development
- Attending conferences
- Reading about teaching
- Connecting with a university

Each of these chapters is followed by activities, questions, and a list of resources.

You may wish to use the following questions as a way of examining Section One:

■ Are these stories realistic?

■ How do these stories match what you know about teaching?

■ What are the problems in becoming an effective teacher?

■ What are the rewards in teaching?

■ How do you stay an effective teacher?

The chapters in this section show effective teachers dealing with a wide range of issues, from discipline problems, to planning concerns, to remaining alive as a teacher. All the teachers in these stories have two traits in common: they intend to be effective meaning-centered teachers, and they reflect about their teaching.

In Section Two, Fundamentals, Plans, and Terms, you will be given help with the technical side of teaching English. The following two chapters will aid you with the fundamentals of preparation and pedagogy.

"Three Sample Unit Plans" (Chapter Fourteen)

■ Samples of unit and lesson plans for several of the stories of Part One of *Crossing Over*.

■ Plans for teaching *A Midsummer Night's Dream;* teaching poetry; teaching *To Kill a Mockingbird*.

"What Every English Teacher Needs to Know" (Chapter Fifteen)

■ A glossary of terms and teaching strategies suited for English Language Arts Teachers.

These chapters are meant as resources for your use in your planning. You may wish to think about the format of the plans in Chapter Fourteen. You may also decide to develop a glossary based on Chapter Fifteen. What would you cut? What would you add?

chapter ELEVEN

SECTION ONE: Reflections

Preparing for the Encounter:
On Becoming a Teacher

Introduction

On my very worst days, I wonder if I have learned anything about teaching. I amaze myself at the quantity and quality of classroom mistakes I am capable of making, even after 20 years. I have always found teaching to be a tough profession, full of an ambiguity of results that is truly maddening. But just as a parent loves a bad child, I've always loved teaching. It is so interesting, so difficult, and so new every semester and every class. On my better days, I can see what I have accomplished, and I do not need test scores to lift my spirits. I feel the ambience of a good class; I see it in the eyes of my students. I hear the hum of a finely tuned machine. On my good days, I feel I have made an occupation as difficult as tightrope walking seem as effortless as breathing.

But then . . . there was that first year! I am sure, among all the teachers in this country, there are some who would claim their first year in the profession was a cakewalk, no sweat. But I have not yet met one teacher who found the first year easy, fun, or rewarding—a learning experience, maybe, but one not to be repeated.

I was once told by a veteran teacher that if you do not make any really stupid mistakes your first year of teaching, consider yourself successful. I have always felt that it takes three years before one can experience, on a consistent basis, the pleasures of the classroom, particularly an effective classroom, which requires so much student participation. The lessons I learned in those first encounters as a teacher still guide me in subtle and not so subtle ways. What follows is the story of one person's first year of teaching.

George Gets a Job

George Myers got lucky. When he was student teaching, he met the sister-in-law of his supervising teacher, the assistant superintendent of a suburban district on the other side of the city. When George and the sister-in-law chatted at the supervising teacher's home, she told him of the need for an assistant soccer coach at a high school in her district. George volunteered to coach soccer for the school until year's end. In May the school's principal announced an opening for an English-reading teacher/soccer coach for the fall. After several interviews with various parties, George got the job.

George was hired to fill the position of a 15-year veteran who decided to leave the profession. Because George was a replacement, he was told, he would inherit his predecessor's schedule. It was a good one, cultivated with 15 years of political experience and friendships. George was told he would teach five classes: 10th-grade reading, 11th-grade honors English (three sections), and 11th grade creative writing. He was given textbooks, a school handbook, a student handbook, a handshake, and a "see you in the fall." George was a happy young man with a great, carefree summer ahead of him. He was motivated and ready to be a great teacher, suffused with ideas encountered during his training.

By George's standards, his summer was terrific. He worked part time on a road crew for the state, he played league softball, and he prepared his classes for the fall.

At the beginning of August, George was given a date and time in late August for new-teacher orientation; he had to fill out some financial forms and get a chest x-ray. On the appointed day, George pulled into the high school parking lot and found his way to the Learning Resource Center, where four other neophytes sat quietly, sipping coffee. When the principal arrived, orientation began with introductions, followed by a slide show about the community and the school.

In retrospect, George remembers only two events from the two-day orientation. The first occurred in his first English department meeting when schedules were given out. Remember the classes he was promised in May? Well, George was surprised to learn that his real schedule included two sections of 10th grade English, two sections of 9th grade reading, one 9th-grade honors English class, and one 9th-grade English class. George's first-year schedule not only would not include one class he was promised, he would have to teach six classes instead of five. Actually, George was more than surprised; he had a panic attack when he realized that not only would his summer preparation go to waste, but also now he was unprepared to face the six classes he would have to teach the next day.

"What happened?" he sputtered to himself. "But I was promised." Too bad, George. Welcome to your first real-world lesson. Remember in your college courses they kept telling you, teachers need to be flexible? This is what they meant. Be flexible.

But how could this happen? Simple. When George was told in May what classes he would teach, the principal assumed George would take over the schedule of the teacher he replaced. The principal is a busy person with a million things on his mind and hadn't put a great deal of thought into what he told George. Shortly after George was hired, the English Department held a meeting to discuss schedules for the next school year. All the courses George thought were his were divvied up among the veterans, who felt they should get these plums.

At this meeting, George was labeled as Teacher X and received the courses that were left over. Summer came. No one thought much about fall, and George was never informed until he got his schedule the day before his first day of real teaching.

George's second real-world lesson came shortly after lunch that same day when he was told what rooms his classes would be in. When George went to find his textbooks, he found what seemed to be the rattiest, oldest copies of books in the school. Already feeling like a character in a Kafka novel, he was not surprised this time. George sought out the other 9th-grade teacher, John Bishop, who put his arm around George, took him into his classrooms, and showed George the glistening, new sets of class paperbacks he had.

"George," John said affably, "after I am done using these books with my students, they are yours."

At this point George knew that meant he would get some copies of *Hatchet* by December. "Be flexible," he thought. "Help!" he screamed to himself.

George's First Year

The first day of school came and went, and George and his students survived. George even made it through the year, but it was difficult. His students tested him at the beginning of the year and found him to be a pushover, so that by the middle of the semester, exactly when he should have been loosening up, he was tightening his discipline. So he never did manage his classes the way he would have liked. Planning, time management, and discipline were his biggest worries, and he never really mastered them. George felt overwhelmed by the job. If he wasn't teaching, he was grading papers, planning for his classes, or supervising after-school activities. Also, he was in charge of a cafeteria study hall where he had to keep 75 teenagers relatively quiet and seated.

George was on his feet all day; his throat was parched and his voice cracking by the end of the day. He spent his evenings planning and grading papers, and although he saved one weekend day for himself, the other was consumed with schoolwork.

And yet, during this teaching year from hell, George had very positive experiences. He made some teacher friends, including his assigned mentor, who helped him with his problems. George really thought his mentor, Sally Liebler, was a wonderful teacher.

George's Mentor

The law in George's state requires that every new teacher have a veteran, a mentor teacher, to help her or him during the first year. Not all states have mentoring programs, nor do all assigned-mentor relationships work. In this case, George was lucky. However, if George had not been assigned Sally, he should have been smart enough to seek her out. First-year teachers who have a veteran friend as a role model are in much better shape than those who do not. Therefore, a first-year teacher would be wise to find a mentor on her own if she has to.

Because most good veteran teachers are helpful, it is a matter of finding the teacher the novice feels would serve as the best role model. A new teacher soon learns who best exemplifies a mentor. That new teacher should express interest in how the selected veteran teaches. With some luck, a strong mentoring friendship will start. The veteran will appreciate the attention, and the novice will gain invaluable support. Nothing spreads effective teaching as rapidly and as well as strong veteran teachers mentoring and training first-year teachers.

Sally, an 11-year veteran, was assigned to help George. Sally teaches five 10th- and 11th-grade classes and advises the school newspaper, which is considered her sixth class. Sally exhibits the quintessential meaning-centered approach in her classrooms. Her students read, write, see, hear, and speak about ideas and events that engage them. In a nine-person department, Sally and one colleague are most committed to these ideas. The other English teachers run the gamut from process-writing teachers, to traditional product-oriented teachers, to those who are literary canon-oriented. George got lucky in having Sally appointed his mentor because she practices what he believes in. George, who is fresh from a teacher education program, is filled with innovative ideas. Rather than have these ideas ridiculed by colleagues hostile to change, George got a veteran teacher who would nurture and support his ideas, but also temper his enthusiasm and youthful need for instant gratification. New teachers need to learn the nuts and bolts before trying more interactive or innovative activities.

Discipline: Sally Teaches George About Controlling a Class

"Develop a seating chart; be businesslike, but not unfriendly; and pass around a set of class rules that you will stick to," Sally advises George.

"But I thought I would introduce myself, and..."

"Develop a seating chart; be businesslike, but not unfriendly; and pass around a set of class rules that you will enforce," Sally responds, smiling.

"I know, Sally. You're right."

figure   ◊ **11.1**

> **Class Rules**
>
> For Students:
>   I will arrive on time.
>   I will pay attention to all class proceedings.
>   I am capable of working by myself without supervision.
>   I will undertake the independent tasks as directed.
>   I will cooperate with my classmates, and I will treat them with
>   the respect I expect.
>   I will be patient if mistakes occur, such as equipment failure.
>   I will do my best to learn.
>
> For the Teacher:
>   If the above rules are respected, I pledge to give you full responsibility
>   for your participation in this class.

"They will test you, George, particularly because you're new. Look, I am not advising you to be mean. I am just advising you to hold off on your open class discussions and classroom plays for a while. Gain some respect first. Go slow."

Sally no longer needs to follow her own advice; her reputation precedes her. But she knows how first-year teachers are treated. And Sally knows that for George to maintain his own ideas, it would be better if he did not fail with them early on. So she advises George to go slow. "Introduce your procedures; tell them about the class," Sally says. Even Sally uses seating charts at the beginning of the year and goes over her class rules with her students (Figure 11.1).

As for seating charts, she points out to George that "you need to be able to refer by name to your students before you know their names by heart. Trust me on this. There will come a day when you are talking, and one of your students will be tapping his desk with a pencil and making a very loud noise. It will be nice if you can say, 'Bob, please' instead of pointing and grunting toward the fourth kid in the fifth row."

"George," she tells him, "the trick is to be positive with your kids. Build a relationship with them. Reward them for doing well. But don't let them walk all over you. If you create a respectful atmosphere in your class now, it will carry over to your class discussions later."

George Observes Sally

"Sally makes it look so easy," George thinks after he observes her. Certainly, Sally's experience shows. She oozes confidence in the classroom. She takes it easy at the beginning of the year—passing out books, explaining her rules and grading policies, and going over class procedures for workshops, writing, and discussions. Generally, her students are very quiet at the beginning. They sit in rows for the first week or two, and then, after Sally knows the names of her students, she shifts their desks to a horseshoe configuration. Sally has a diagram of what her room looks like at that point (Figure 11.2).

Initially, however, Sally's classroom feels and looks very traditional. She enforces rules at the beginning of the year that she eases out of after a while. For instance, when her students make their first forays into making comments or asking questions in class, Sally insists they raise their hands.

Also, Sally does not allow whispering. All she does to stop this activity is to look at the guilty student and quietly say "shh."

"You know why I stop my students from whispering?" Sally asks George. "Because I do not want any discipline problems in my class greater than whispering. I cannot always keep my students intently working and interested in what we are doing, so when they have to act out, I want them trying to figure out how to whisper in my class, so they are not trying to figure out how to throw books out the window or screaming out swear words."

"Wow," George says, very impressed.

"Discipline problems grow," Sally explains. "When you see a class that is completely out of control, you know that the teacher did not make her students fight just to whisper to each other."

"But I thought you wanted students who interact, who express themselves, who feel free to give their opinions," George responds.

"I do," Sally says. "But it takes time for the rapport in a class to grow. And meanwhile, your students push and prod you to find your weak spots and exploit them. This testing only lasts for a little while, but it is important to be prepared for it."

Actually, George notes, there really isn't much testing going on in the classes he observes. For the most part, Sally's students know about her through the usual high school ISCN (Informal Student Communication Network). Her students know that Sally is an experienced teacher and that she knows how to control her classes.

Also, George notices that Sally and her students are having dialogues without hand raising more often than Sally realizes. An astute observer would notice, George thinks, that the bonding Sally talks about is taking place a lot more quickly than she realizes. After only one week of class, her students are greeting her informally as they walk in. "Hi, Mrs. Liebler." Sally cracks a joke and her students laugh as the atmosphere slowly relaxes.

But George knows a veteran teacher can do things that no rookie ever dare do. So George maintains his own aloofness a bit longer, although he can't wait for the day his classes become like Sally's "family," always bickering and at each other on the surface, but together and unified deep down. And George knows

figure   11.2

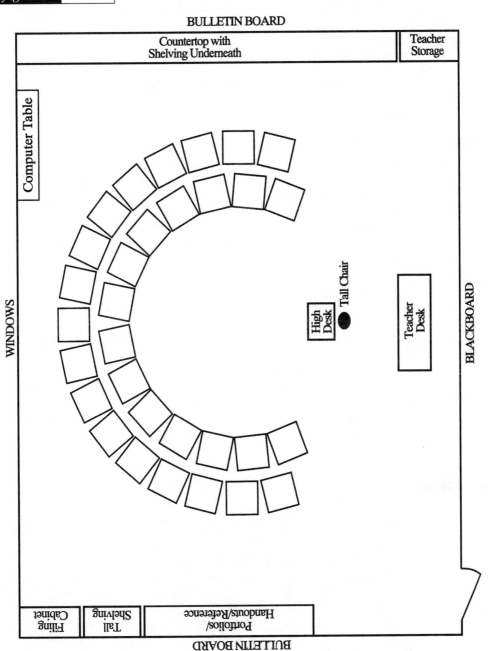

that an effective teacher has a controlled classroom in a structured environment. Only a well-disciplined class can enjoy the freedom.

Sally's Classroom

Sally's reading and writing workshops went very smoothly the year she was George's mentor. She was well organized and capable of keeping track of everything, and George unabashedly borrowed some of her organization and record-keeping ideas.

The skill that most impressed George was the way Sally listened to students. When a student had a comment to make, she would beam her eyes on her or him. George could almost feel Sally listening. She almost never interrupted a student, and a small halo of silence encapsulated most comments by her students. Sometimes, Sally would follow up with a comment or a small remark; sometimes she would repeat what she felt the student was saying; and sometimes she wouldn't say a thing. Many times, other students would comment on what a peer was saying. George could tell that Sally's students were very comfortable with class discussion.

Much of what George learned his first year came from Sally, whose classroom he would visit whenever he could. Sally trained her students for class discussions and made sure they knew her rules (Figure 11.3)

Sally seldom used anything but open-ended questions. "How do you feel about it?" and "Why?" were more common than "What happened?" And she was rarely judgmental about comments her students made.

George knew how lucky he was to have Sally. Also, he knew that had she not been assigned as his mentor, he would have eventually linked up with her. They were kindred spirits, compadres, comrades-in-arms. George knew how important it was to have a supportive friend, because he knew how quickly his

---

figure ◗ **11.3**

Discussion Rules
1. Be polite.
2. Allow others to discuss-be generous; do not hog.
3. Listen to complete statements—do no interrupt.
4. Disagree, but politely.
5. Ask questions based on responses—listen to answers and probe.
6. Respect teacher's need to flow control of discussion. Please understand if you have to be passed over to let others speak.

best ideas could be snuffed out by colleagues hostile to his approaches. George learned a few things his first year by keeping his eyes and ears open and his mouth shut.

George Confronts a Serious Discipline Problem

"What did he call you?" Sally asks.

"I heard him muttering under his breath, 'Such a ****,' " George replies.

George is worried about Robert. He saunters into the classroom ever so slowly, takes his sweet old time to sit down, and recently has been muttering to himself. Robert obviously senses George's rookie vulnerability and plans to win some points with his costudents. Thanks to Sally, however, George is ready.

"I don't know what you're talking about," Robert explodes loudly in class during an explanation of free-writing rules.

"What would you like explained?" George counters.

"Nothing. You make me sick."

George's class is stunned silent. George is silent, somewhat stunned, but much more prepared for this than Robert had anticipated. George makes no reply to Robert and continues with class. Robert feels like a winner. He got away with it—until the bell rings.

While his students file out, George goes to Robert, looks at him and says, "I wish you would give me a chance. You are to go to the office now, Robert, and see Ms. Wilson (the vice principal). Robert, don't ever do that again," George says before turning and walking away.

George and Sally had prepared Jane Wilson for Robert, so it was no surprise when George reported the incident. Robert was given a fairly unpleasant 3-day in-school suspension, which solved the Robert problem. He became a fairly cooperative student after this incident. The other students in George's class, who assumed George had lost this battle to Robert, knew what happened when Robert did not show up for class the next day. Most of George's students were very relieved that the teacher had won the battle with Robert, knowing what a hell a classroom becomes when a student tyrannizes it.

Sally's Advice

Sally figured that Robert was going to test George and test him big. She has seen it before. She has seen students calculatingly attack a teacher, and she has seen students lose control in class. The central principle of handling these situations remains the same, Sally believes: *Do not allow the incident to lead to a classroom confrontation.* Students who calculate an attack need to be punished. Sally and George prepared the vice principal for Robert's fairly predictable assault, and the vice principal agreed to a swift and severe punishments—3-day in-school suspension—if it came to that, which it did.

To prevent a confrontation, George was wisely advised to avoid having words with Robert in front of his classmates, where Robert, for teenage male-ego reasons, would feel compelled to win. Rather, George was told to confront Robert after class, without other students hanging on every word. George handled the incident this way and was successful.

Sally explained that students with short fuses who lose control in a classroom without calculating are much more difficult to deal with. These situations need to be defused. Students who have lost it need to be distracted, cooled down.

"Better to deal with these situations when all your students have left class as well. But you need to calm these students down, to listen and only proscribe punishments later, if warranted, when the students become more rational," Sally explains.

"One other thing, George," Sally continues. "If you feel a student may become violent or dangerous, and I have only seen this happen once in a classroom, get your other students out of any danger and seek adult help. Do not try to handle it yourself."

Sally notices George's discouraged look.

"All professions have their difficult and painful sides, George. Once you catch on, most of the hours you spend in teaching are very rewarding."

George tries to believe this, but wonders and, for now, worries.

Reflections on George's First Year

George's incident with Robert was as tough as any he would encounter all year. The rest of the year had its frustrations, but nothing quite as dramatic. George tried writing workshops in his class but got inundated with papers and lost track of who was doing what when. Many of his students spent many happy moments, not writing, during his workshop time. Yet, he received some fresh and lively writing from many of his students, and Mattie Rose told George at the end of the year that he had taught her how to write. His worst teaching unit was *Great Expectations* with his 9th graders. The text was an abridged version of the novel, in one of those high school literature anthologies. As hard as George tried, he could not generate enthusiasm for the book, and eventually his students won him over to their point of view by wearing him down. "I, too, hate *Great Expectations*," George thought.

But George did hold some good discussions on poetry, and he had his 10th graders act out scenes from *Our Town*. Everyone had a good time with that project. George published a book of class writings, and he held a cabaret day during which his students read selections from their writings to each other.

George's main problem his first year of teaching was fatigue. He felt like he never had any time for himself during the school day, and he continually planned and graded on nights and weekends. George felt he was always surrounded by masses of kids who were demanding one thing or another. Questions, questions, questions. It never stopped. Noise all day. Crowded halls. Fire drills. Teenage energy in bucketsful. But George got used to it. By the end of the year, he had learned valuable lessons about pacing his teaching. He learned that on some class reading and writing days, he could also read and write. George learned how to operate his study hall on automatic pilot (after the first 10 minutes). Also, he began using his preparation period more efficiently, on some days to drink coffee and rest, and on others to plan or grade papers. Even his planning and grading had become more efficient by the end of the year. His plans became more outline and less prose. As for grading, George stopped reading and responding to everything in every journal—he skimmed more, and he found his students could live with it. He used holistic evaluation more effectively as well, giving an overall impression for his students rather than meticulously almost rewriting their papers, which did his students no good at all.

Sometimes, many times, when he tried his hardest, he faced students who seemed just not to care. No matter what he did, he could not motivate some of his kids to do anything—read or write or speak. By midyear, he began noticing that some of his students looked a little more tired, a little more ragged than some of the others—like Andy, who always wore the same Uniwear baseball cap and untied basketball sneakers. Andy was very quiet in class, and when George approached him, the teacher could see in his eyes, surrounded by his dirty, broken-out face, that Andy was a million miles away. Whatever this student's life was like away from school, George knew it lacked the essentials to provide him the ability to concentrate and learn.

The next most vexing problem for George was the apathy he found among his students. "Let's face it," George thought. "I am new. How interesting can I be?"

George began to notice the other "Andys" in his class; the dullness of their eyes gave them away. These kids were glazed over by something more powerful and primal than George could overcome. These kids, George knew, were in a fight for survival. Finding food, clothes, housing, love, and a safe haven from violence and fear were the lessons these kids were learning, but not in school. Some of George's "Andys" would tell their stories in their journals, leaving George feeling both hopeless and gratified. He felt hopeless because of the overwhelming problems these kids carried with them. "What can I do about it?" George thought. But, at the same time, George was gratified these kids would write to him. Perhaps he could help some of these kids use writing to express their problems, to communicate their lives to others, and to relieve some of the pain. Perhaps. "But I am no psychiatrist," George thought, "so I better be careful."

Most of his "Andys," however, remained silent and oblivious to George's best efforts to make them readers and writers. "How can I reach kids who do not come with their minimal needs met?" he lamented on the phone to his mother one tired Tuesday evening.

So it was in his first year that George noticed the damaged goods in his classrooms. Much of the apathy George found he attributed to these sad and growing readiness problems. But he also knew there was a strain of apathy he faced that had more to do with his teaching than with his students. Thus, George prayed that with experience he could learn to rid his classes of some of the first-year dullness that on occasion plagued his classes. George had a good start on becoming the teacher he planned to be.

Teacher as Researcher

Questions

- Ask some teachers about their first year. How do their experiences compare to George's?
- Many schools are formalizing the mentor relationship by requiring that new teachers have mentors. Do you think this is a good idea? Explain.
- Whether or not a mentor is required, how does a new teacher find a compatible mentor?
- What if you could not find a kindred-spirit mentor? What would you do?
- Why is teaching at first so physically draining? How is it possible to overcome the exhaustion of teaching?
- On what does Sally base her view of controlling classroom behavior?
- Is it possible to implement Sally's approaches in the first year of teaching? How?
- Is it possible to implement Sally's approaches in all schools with all kids?

Activities

- React to the story. Give your impressions and thoughts.
- Develop a set of rules you would give your students the first week of class.
- Design your ideal first-year teaching schedule.
- Design an ideal high school English department schedule. Explain why it is ideal.
- Describe successful classroom discipline plans that you have experienced.

chapter TWELVE

Planning for an English/Language Arts Classroom

Introduction

This story may be apocryphal or it may be true: Alfred Hitchcock felt his movie scripts were perfect, so when he actually put a film into production, he felt he was presiding over the erosion of a perfect work of art. The reality of the film could never live up to the perfection of the concept.

I have always felt teaching is like that. I see teachers as the creators of two major works of art. The first is the creation of the plan. The second is the act of teaching. No matter how perfect my plans, my execution of them is different than I had imagined—not always worse, but different. However, I find both acts, teaching and planning, to be extremely rewarding, artistic creations in which I can take great pride. And like Alfred Hitchcock's movies, the teaching I perform begins with the script, my plans.

Planning Process

Planning, like writing, is a process. For Joanne Adler (Chapter Three), planning is more important than the plans themselves. She knows of veteran teachers who walk into a classroom with virtually no written plans, but who teach great classes. Years of planning and mental preparation make such feats possible, although Joanne would not recommend a beginner try to teach without written plans. Yet written plans are mere guideposts. The act of thinking them through by writing them is everything for her.

This is why Joanne cannot use anyone else's plans to teach. No matter how beautiful the curriculum guide, no matter how perfect the published plans, Joanne cannot use them unless she has made them.

As with most experienced teachers, Joanne's plans do not begin from scratch. She builds on her previous plans, even if it's a new course. If an anthropologist could study her plans to understand her as a teacher, the scientist would find an evolution of ideas and thoughts about English teaching. The scientist would also see the development in her classes. Some years her courses change more than others. For instance, her reading and writing workshops were developed at a summer teacher's institute. But generally, the change in her classes has been gradual, but over the years, significant.

Joanne begins with her overall plan for the semester, usually 16 weeks. She breaks the overall plan into three broad sets. First, she determines what workshops she will be doing and what her workshop rules will be. Next, she determines what she will base grades on.

Finally, Joanne decides what units she will teach during the semester. For instance, Joanne may teach any of the following to her 9th graders:

- Poetry reading and writing
- *Roll of Thunder, Hear My Cry*
- Newscast
- Newspaper reading and writing
- Performing *Romeo and Juliet*
- How to watch television
- Reading and writing short stories
- Taking and passing tests
- Writing children's books
- Writing oral histories through the eyes of the elderly
- Reading about science (with the science teacher)

Once Joanne decides the content of three basic elements of her class—the workshop rules, the grading plan, the units—she has a view of the overall structure for the semester. For instance, Joanne's class will be doing reading and writing workshops two or three times a week when possible, so almost 50% of her class time will be workshop time. Her workshops will cover the following:

Reading Workshop

- Book talks (students and teacher)
- Book swaps (among students)
- Reading time
- Group discussions based on books
- Journal writing about books
- Book review writing

- Book review reading and book selection
- Reading record keeping

Writing Workshop

- Topic discussions
- Writing demonstrations (teacher and students)
- Journal writing
- Student-teacher conferences
- Rough drafting
- Free writing
- Rewriting
- Grammar demonstrations
- Error analysis
- Class readings
- Class publications
- Evaluation seminars
- Proficiency test preparation

Much of Joanne's work helping her students create reading and writing will be done in workshops. But Joanne will also spend time with her special units. She will not do the entire list; she will pick and choose based on what she learns about her students and what her students want. For instance, Joanne will not ask her students to produce both a children's book and an oral history. Instead, she will select one of those units based on what her instincts tell her about her students and which of these her students prefer.

Joanne also must decide in what order the units will come and how long they will take. For instance, she would never start the semester with her *Romeo and Juliet* or her *Roll of Thunder, Hear My Cry* units. Both these activities require a well-integrated group of students who will work together, listen to each other, and have a rapport with the teacher. Joanne starts, of course, with her introduction to the class, where she presents her rules and her procedures. The first student-centered activity will be the quiet task of journal writing rather than the noisy task of play performing, which she will do much later in the semester. So, Joanne spaces her units according to the nature of the activity and the time of year. She starts out doing most of the talking in class and builds to student-dominated activities later in the semester, such as performing *Romeo and Juliet* and discussing *Roll of Thunder, Hear My Cry*.

Based on her experience, Joanne determines how long each unit will take. She assigns four weeks to *Romeo and Juliet* and three weeks (with workshop interruptions) to *Roll of Thunder, Hear My Cry*. She bases this schedule on time she has left over from her workshops. For some of her more complicated activities, such as performing *Romeo and Juliet* or writing a children's book, she may cancel workshop time in the last week of the unit to provide continuity.

Of course, her workshop and units are not discrete; they merge all the time. For instance, Joanne's *Roll of Thunder, Hear My Cry* discussion leads to journal writing about hate and family, and many of the public writings she receives are based on her *Roll of Thunder, Hear My Cry* unit. When her students read, discuss, and write short stories, much of the reading and writing is done in the workshops. Joanne's class formats blend together and complement each other.

Joanne plans for more units than she can teach, and with her writing workshops, she has a very full class. She remembers her first year of teaching, when she thought she had planned enough but ran out of things to do. Joanne prefers that she not have enough time to carry out all her ideas, rather than have too much time on her hands. When she hears a teacher complain about too little time to get everything in, Joanne knows she is hearing a veteran with a strong repertoire of classroom activities.

Joanne's class is eclectic, having many units on several different topics. She even includes a unit on test taking, which she feels she must provide to help her students survive an increasingly test-oriented educational system. In this unit, Joanne provides her students with a great deal of practice rehearsing standardized test-taking techniques. Her students may not love this unit, and it is very different from anything else Joanne does in class, but they understand and appreciate why she does it.

Although Joanne's units and teaching methods vary, her philosophy is consistent. She provides her students a rich variety of language-creating activities. Her class centers around listening, speaking, seeing, writing, and hearing texts in meaningful contexts. Except for her survival unit on test taking, Joanne keeps her activities centered on meaningful language situations.

Weekly and Daily Plans

Although Joanne builds the structure of her class ahead of time, much of what she does on a daily basis depends on the students who are in the class. For instance, the books she recommends most strongly in her reading workshop will be based on her students' preferences. The grammar and error work that Joanne selects for class analysis is based on student needs. And, of course, all of the writing topics are student-selected, with Joanne's help if needed.

Joanne's daily plans are made relatively easy by her structure for the semester and her grading plans. Her workshops need no daily plans other than her set of rules. Organization is more important for workshop days than daily plans.

Joanne's most difficult plans are for her special units, such as her *Romeo and Juliet* unit or her *Roll of Thunder, Hear My Cry* unit. For these, she uses an outline format. For instance, Joanne often selects *Roll of Thunder, Hear My Cry* to teach. This book, written by Mildred Taylor, is about an African-American family of sharecroppers and their struggle to maintain their land and dignity in the racially hostile South of the 1930s. The central character is Cassie, a fourth-grader, who is proud, tough, and willful. The book is an account, both historical and emotional, of what it was like to be black in the South in the 1930s. Joanne's unit plans for this book look like this.

Day One—Introduction: Tell story of Ku Klux Klan rally and cross burning in a small Pennsylvania town, as told to me by my father.

- Read author's note to *Roll of Thunder, Hear My Cry*, which begins, "My father was a master storyteller..." One note tells how Mildred Taylor's father told her the stories that became this book.
- Tell class what book is about.
- Begin book by oral reading.
- Have students read silently until end of period.

Day Two—Talk about 1930s South

- Racial atmosphere.
- Depression.
- Segregated schools.
- Voting rights.
- Have students read silently in class.

Day Three—Silent reading

- Check to see progress of students.
- Help students read through Chapter 6, p. 105, for next day.
- Discuss in-class writing, critical responses.

Day Four—In-class writing assignment; use any of these topics if you wish

- Tell me about the book.
- What happens through Chapter 6?
- What do you think of the book so far?
- Tell me about Cassie.
- How will the book end?
- Discussion of family members.
    - Parents—David and Mary.
    - Stacey—seventh grade.
    - Cassie—fourth grade
    - Christopher John—second grade.
    - Little Man—first grade.
- What are characters' opinions, attitudes, ideas, habits, likes, and dislikes?
- Make list on board.

Day Five—Return and discuss critical response writing

- In-class reading. Assign book to be finished.

Day Six—In-class reading

- Discuss in-class writing.

Day Seven—In-class writing/critical response; you may use these topics if you wish

- How did the book end?
- What happened to the family?
- What did you think of the book?
- Reader-response discussion.

Day Eight—*Roll of Thunder, Hear My Cry* workshop day

- Do one of the following or make up your own idea.
- Write a letter to Mildred Taylor telling her what you thought about the book.
- Write a letter to one of the characters, such as Cassie. Tell how you feel about her or him and why.
- Script a section of the book. Write this script with a friend.
- Rewrite the ending.
- Write a character sketch of Cassie. What made her so strong?
- Tell a story about your own family or a family you have known that has had similar experiences.

Day Nine—Continuation of *Roll of Thunder, Hear My Cry* workshop

Day Ten—Performance day

- All students will share selections from their workshop projects.

Day Eleven—Performance day

These brief daily descriptions give Joanne a sense of her plan. They provide her a sense of continuity and direction. She knows where she will start and where she will end up. Because her class periods last about 50 minutes, Joanne usually plans several varied activities to keep students' attention.

Joanne's daily plans give her the detail she needs to carry out her lesson but are not word-for-word scripts. Much of Joanne's daily planning is mental and cannot be seen in what she puts down on paper. Like most teachers, Joanne thinks lessons all the time—in the car, in the shower, before she goes to sleep, when she wakes up. She mentally rehearses. Joanne enjoys these rehearsals; they help her feel prepared for her classes. What she writes down are the bare-bones outlines of what she will be doing. She uses her daily plans for reference points, generally to help trigger her memory. For instance, for Day 1 and Day 2 of the *Roll of Thunder, Hear My Cry* unit, her outline for the week has enough detail that she does not need a more extensive daily plan. Joanne knows the story she is going to tell very well and she does not need to write any more

figure ◊ **12.1**

Discussion Questions for *Roll of Thunder, Hear My Cry*

What did you think of the book?

Who were your favorite characters?

Who were your least favorite characters?

How does your school differ from the school in the book?

Are there similarities?

How is T.J. different? What went wrong with T.J.?

Do you respect Cassie? Why?

Do you think David and Mary were good parents?

Is this family like your family at all? Why?

What did the fire accomplish?

Was this family ever happy? If yes, when?

Are these kids realistic?

Is the family realistic?

Have times changed? How?

Would you recommend this book? Why or why not?

down. However, on the day she plans to lead a reader-response discussion on the book, Joanne likes to have a multitude of questions available. For instance, Joanne has these questions written down for her *Roll of Thunder, Hear My Cry* discussion (Figure 12.1).

Although Joanne always has a plan for her class, she is capable of changing it based on what she senses the needs are. Basically, Joanne walks into a classroom with a repertoire of ideas and can use one of several procedures she deems appropriate. For instance, she may decide to read parts of *Roll of Thunder, Hear My Cry* out loud to the class, or she may have students read selections out loud, or she may ask for silent reading of parts. Joanne may tell stories, with pictures, about segregation in the rural South of the 1930s, or she may lead a discussion on how to get along in a multiethnic world, or she may do parts of both. She may show a tape of Richard Wright's short story, *Almos' a Man*, or she may show a tape of *Shopping Bag Lady*. She will choose one or the other based on her assessment of her students' ability to handle the more difficult and controversial *Almos' a Man* tape. Sometimes, Joanne will decide in advance; sometimes she will decide the moment before she puts the tape in the machine; and sometimes she will discuss both tapes with the class and have them help her select one.

Joanne has classes where her plans evaporate because of where her students take her. In one class, after telling her Ku Klux Klan story, a student offered a chilling story of racial hatred directed at her and her family. This story led to a powerful discussion that filled the rest of the class period. Joanne simply deferred her plans for the rest of the period to the next day. And even the next day, Joanne used a summary of the previous day's discussion as a segue into *Roll of Thunder, Hear My Cry.*

Planning, for Joanne, is a map, but it is not the territory. Her plans guide her, giving her classes structure, continuity, purpose, and direction. She knows where she is headed, but there are days she takes detours or side roads. There are days she expands or contracts her plans and changes her mind, even at the last minute. And though she never radically changes the direction of her class, she allows herself many ways of getting where she is going. She is not the kind of teacher who becomes trapped by the inflexibility of her classroom plans.

Making Plans for the Principal

Each Friday, all the teachers in the high school are required to give the office lesson plans for the following week. Although she has problems with the behavioral format required, Joanne uses it on orders of her boss. The lesson plan format dictated by the school requires teachers to prepare performance objectives, procedures, and evaluation/summary statements.

Here is an example of one of the plans Joanne turns in to the office.

   I. Performance Objective: Students will be able to show understanding and appreciation as evidenced in journal writing and class discussion of a videotape of Richard Wright's short story *Almos' a Man.*

  II. Procedures
      A. Introduction of *Almos' a Man.*
      B. Brief oral biography of Richard Wright.
      C. Showing of *Almos' a Man* tape.
      D. Journal assignment.
      E. Questions for students who need them:
         1. What did you think of the tape? Why?
         2. Why did David run away?
         3. What do you think will happen to David?
         4. Was David treated fairly?
         5. Why did David want a gun?
      F. Discussion based on journal writing.
         Opening question: What did you think about the videotape and why?

 III. Evaluation/Summary
      Student responses in journal and discussion will be used to evaluate understanding and appreciation of videotape.

IV. Materials
   A. VHS tape of *Almos' a Man*.
   B. VCR and playback equipment.
   C. Pens, pencils, and journals.

Joanne formalizes her plans and turns in a set of them each Friday. Notice all the elements of the plan are open-ended and student-centered. Usually, she prepares these plans during her planning period on Friday. Most of the teachers in the high school look upon these formal plans as just another bureaucratic nuisance, but they are helpful as evidence of an organized and effective teacher.

Goals and Objectives

Joanne remembers spending so much of her time in her training learning how to write goals, particularly objectives. The methods and procedures of writing behavioral objectives were hammered into her. Yet, when she became a teacher, she discovered she spent most of her planning time trying to figure out how to fill the 50 minutes she would be trapped with 30 teenagers, six times a day.

Joanne understands the need, certainly, for goals and, to some extent, for daily objectives. But she sees problems in overemphasizing these, particularly objectives.

Joanne feels goals are more important in English teaching than objectives. Goals are her long-term, semester-length objectives. Joanne is well aware of her goals for her students. She wants to help them become stronger readers and writers. In order to help her students accomplish this, she must provide reading and writing experiences that engage them, that challenge them to some extent, and that interest them. She sets up her classes to accomplish these goals through her reading and writing workshops, her unit plans, her class discussions, and her plays.

Joanne also wants to aid her students in their ability to understand, appreciate, and control their relationship with the mass media, so she incorporates film and television studies into her classroom. Finally, she hopes to help her students become intelligent and thoughtful. Certainly all the reading, writing, and discussions are aimed at achieving these goals.

Objectives are another matter. Joanne has trouble describing her best activities with the level of specificity that behavioral objectives require. She can always make a statement about what she expects her students to do in a class: discuss a book; free write in a journal; free read; act out a play. But to formally operationalize her objectives in strict behavioral terms would drive her crazy and may not be possible.

In the old worksheet days, it was much easier to write behavioral objectives:

- Students will be able to complete writing exercises 1 through 10 on subject–verb agreement achieving 80% accuracy.
- As a result of this course, students will be able to write a four-paragraph theme on a given topic with a thesis statement and concluding paragraph, with two supporting paragraphs in between.

Joanne has very observable criteria in mind for her students. She hopes that their writing shows style, clarity, and correctness. But she needs to build to these goals, based on each student's ability, with a variety of strategies employed over the course of a semester. Because Joanne logs all the reading and writing her students accomplish, and because she keeps a portfolio of all of their writings, Joanne has real evidence of the progress her students make. Any evaluator who took the time to look at a portfolio would also note a record of revisions, conferences, editing, and free writing—complete documentary evidence of everything a student produced in Joanne's class.

Joanne is very careful with her record keeping. She keeps her grade book up to date and well organized. Joanne makes sure all her student-maintained records are entered on her master sheet and in her grade book. Her records show a consistent program of reading and writing based on both quantity and quality. When Joanne turns in her grade book at the end of the year, she is confident that her students were given every opportunity to demonstrate practice and growth as language users. Also, she is confident she can make a case for the grades she gives based on her conscientious record keeping.

Reflections on Planning

Joanne can write behavioral statements that are often useful, but more important is the planning of activities that lead to the large goals and outcomes that effective teachers deem important. What is more important is creating an environment where readers flourish and writers may take risks. What is more important is keeping the kind of documentation that shows how students grow and develop as language users. But what is *most* important is keeping the meaningfulness of the language activities intact so that English classes remain a part of the literacy experience rather than alienated from it. Unfortunately, too much emphasis on behavioral objectives can blur the large view of teaching and promote isolated and decontextualized skills teaching. Too much emphasis on behavioral objectives can lead to the distorted view that the successful completion of a grammar worksheet is an end in itself.

Joanne can show the results of her teaching through her portfolios and record keeping. Her results, although collected on a daily basis, provide a contextual basis for evaluation and provide the big picture of her students as language users. So, even though she does not find much that is worthwhile in writing behavioral objectives, she still believes that English teachers are responsible for making a documented case that learning does occur in their classrooms.

English may not be as clear and as linear as math, but English is more than a cheap magic trick that requires a leap of faith. Effective teachers need not fear accountability, but should welcome the opportunity to strut their stuff, to show the world the power and efficacy of this teaching philosophy and approach. Not only will the direct assessments found in the portfolios and record keeping prove the effectiveness of teaching, but the indirect assessments—parents who notice kids reading more and with more pleasure, kids taking a more active involvement in writing—will provide wonderful anecdotal evidence that the techniques are working. This anecdotal evidence, even more than the direct assessments, provides the fuel that sparks the enthusiasm and commitment of the teachers.

Joanne knows that the parents and guardians of her students support her enthusiastically. Her principal knows this well, and hears from parents and guardians about the reading and writing Joanne stimulates. Joanne gets unconditional support to create her environments and her techniques. She is empowered to create English teaching in her way.

Teacher as Researcher

Questions

- Is planning a process, as this chapter suggests? What does this mean?
- Do you agree with the statements in this chapter about goals and objectives? Why or why not?
- What outcome does Joanne rely on to justify her methodologies? How can these outcomes be used to Joanne and her students' best advantages?

Activities

- React to the story. Give your impressions and thoughts.
- Interview teachers you know. Ask them how they plan for their classes. Take a look at their plans. How does what you were taught about planning relate to what real teachers do in real classrooms? What are some of the strengths and weaknesses of both approaches?
- Create a semester plan for a secondary English course. You may wish to include reading and writing workshops, unit ideas, and grading plans.

- Create weekly and daily plans based on the system Joanne uses. You may wish to base your plans on some of the case studies.
- Write several objectives for your daily plan.
- Create a set of plans to teach *Roll of Thunder, Hear My Cry* that is very different from Joanne's.
- Review all of the sections on assessment and grading in this book. Develop your own grading plan either based on the assessment sections in this book or on other plans.

Remaining Vital in the Classroom

Introduction

In *David Copperfield*, Emily in many ways was luckier than most of the other characters. That is hard to believe considering the shame of her past experience with David's despicable friend. And it is even harder to believe considering she felt it necessary to exile herself to Australia, in the 19th century a trip so long to a place so isolated that it would be impossible for the modern person to identify with the hardships involved.

So what makes her so lucky? Although she felt disgraced, on the trip to Australia she spent her time serving others.

> But theer was some poor folks aboard as had illness among 'em, and she took care of them, and theer was the children in our company, and she took care of them, and so she got to be busy, and to be doing good, and that helped her.

Through that service, as Dickens shows, Emily maintained a calm, a sense of completeness, a lack of angst or visible anger. Because of her service, Emily was able to live with herself, face herself in the mirror every morning, and sleep at night. Despite her disgrace, in modern terms, she was centered by her good works.

I often think of this passage in *David Copperfield* when I try to understand what draws people to teaching. I am convinced Dickens was right: Those who serve are in turn served. No matter how selfish, materialistic, or self-serving the world becomes, the kinder, more empathetic among us will seek the helping professions, including teaching.

Undergraduates, of course, come to teaching, but so do graduates and professionals—lawyers, engineers, business people. Nothing discourages them—low salaries, lack of job opportunities. They tell stories of why they came.

"I always wanted to be a teacher, but I was discouraged by parents and friends." "A business career wasn't for me. I couldn't worry only about the bottom line."

"Ever since I was a child, I wanted to be a teacher. I tried law, now I want to see if I'll like teaching."

Like Emily in *David Copperfield*, such people know or sense that helping others through teaching will help them. So it is possible to find good, strong, motivated people to teach. The trick is to keep teachers teaching. The trick is to remain alive in the classroom.

The realities of teaching can be quite a shock to people who idealize the profession and have no experience. Many novice teachers are not ready for:

- Large class sizes
- Six classes a day, and the paperwork, grading, and so on that this entails
- Apathetic students
- Discipline problems
- Adversarial administrators
- Lack of power and control over one's professional life

Teaching is a demanding, tough profession that requires dedication and perseverance. Because teaching conditions do not seem to improve much, despite the claims of politicians and reformers, teachers must learn to live with the conditions they are handed. Everyone with children in school knows wonderful career teachers who have remained dedicated and alive in the classroom. How do they do it?

Thinking About It

Teaching is a dynamic profession. As long as teachers constantly face new students, the profession will never be static. Teachers are always engaged in facing new problems or finding new solutions to old ones. The profession never allows a teacher to relax. In secondary schools, there are so many daily interactions, both verbal and nonverbal, with sensitive, hormonal teenagers, that problems, questions, and issues are bound to arise, all the time. No teacher anywhere has found the answer—the perfect plan, technique, or solution. That isn't even the quest. The quest is for every teacher to be his own best, most honest critic. Teachers must constantly work on problems. They must reflect on what they do in class and what impact it has, and reflect on the methods they use and keep tinkering with them. Teachers must think about these things and keep thinking about them. This reflectiveness is required in a meaning-centered classroom where so much of the learning requires flexibility on the teacher's part. And nowhere is this reflectiveness more important than when a teacher is crossing over. Change is healthy and vital for any teacher. But, nothing requires more patience and thought than crossing over to a new approach to teaching.

Bob Thinks About It

The west leg of the expressway during morning rush hour was shrouded in a deep haze, a combination of weather conditions and smoke from the logging plant. One five-car, chain-reaction collision left several minor injuries but, thankfully, none serious. It also left Bob (Chapter Four, "Discussing Books"; Chapter Eight, "Teaching of Writing") sitting in his Toyota Camry cooling his heels five miles down the highway in a monstrous traffic jam.

Ordinarily, it takes Bob about 35 minutes to drive to work. Today, his best estimate puts him there during third period. He settles in and, befitting his mood, puts in a Benjamin Britten CD. As the music thoroughly depresses him, he thinks about yesterday.

> "I can't blame my students. All semester I have promoted the need to interact, so they do it. And it is so hard to discuss anything with kids, I can't blame myself too much for not cutting it off. Maybe I should go back over the class rules that I seem to have dropped. Raise your hands, don't interrupt . . . Yeah, I am going to do that. But remember that the basic problem is that Laura and Bill just don't like Tony and are willing to gang up on him. And Tony, who constantly has his hand up, sets himself up. He can't keep his mouth shut and he says stupid things. What am I supposed to do?"

The Britten CD comes to an end and Bob puts on Springsteen.

> "I have seen this problem before, many times—the average kid who talks too much. I want kids to talk, and I don't want to discourage Tony; he's a nice, bright young man, a bit immature, but well meaning. I'm a sucker for this problem. The trick is to get Tony to talk less and get Laura and Bill to back off the bullying. But Tony has to talk less."

Bob is inching his way to work at about 20 mph.

> "I'm going to have to talk to Tony. He has a lot to say and that's great, but I'm going to tell him he can't hog the conversation. Also, I will sit next to Tony in the circle, which will lower the eye-contact factor. Meanwhile, I will tell Laura and Bill, no, I will discuss with Laura and Bill ways to improve the discussion and ways to get more kids to talk. I will also tell Laura and Bill to get off Tony's back."

Mozart Piano Concerto 23, Korchel listing 488, blasts from Bob's CD player as he climbs to his full cruising speed of 70 mph. The haze has lifted; the highway has cleared; and Bob has a plan to improve his fourth-period discussions with just a little bit of tinkering.

Bob is a career teacher. He loves the challenge. Bob knows teaching is never fully mastered; he must continually learn how to do it and he enjoys this. He is always thinking over situations and tinkering-attempting to improve them, stabilize them as was the case with his "Tony" problem. Whenever Bob has "reflection" time, he works on his classes. His best reflecting time comes in the shower, or when he is working out. But his overall favorite time to think about teaching is in his car with his music blaring, particularly to and from work. Bob is an active teacher with an active mind, constantly working on his profession.

Doing Something New

It is easy for Bob to adjust classroom activities he is comfortable doing, activities he has been doing for years. It is quite a different mental task for Bob when he is trying a classroom activity he has never done. When Bob thinks back on starting his writing workshop, he shakes his head and sighs. It was a rough time that took a lot of mental discipline.

Bob got the idea of doing a writing workshop from reading, conferences, and university classes. Nancie Atwell's book (1987), *In the Middle*, greatly impressed Bob and much of his workshop structure was adapted from Atwell. Bob spent a great deal of time planning and preparing the summer before he started the workshop. When school started, Bob felt ready, and he was. The problems he would run into were difficult to predict, so he thought about them and handled them as they occurred.

At first, some of his students wouldn't write. "Why not? I give them credit for it," Bob thought. "What can I do? I give them many ideas to write about. Maybe I'll show them how." Bob decided to free write for his students because of this problem. Since he made this decision, he has developed a full-scale model writing for his kids. Although Bob's writing has become one of his classroom presentation highlights, it has not completely solved his problem.

Nothing, really, will solve this problem. But Bob tends to think about it now in terms of:

> "How can I get Lafreeda to tell her stories? I know she has them. I'll get Georgeanne to listen and write what Lafreeda tells her. I'll do this tomorrow.

and

> "I better not press Dominic too much. I can't win them all, and there is nothing more I can think of to get Dominic to do anything. His anger and denial run too deep."

and

> "If Timothy and Ruth don't stop chatting during writing time, I am
> going to lose it. My rules allow interaction, but they bend my rules
> enough to make me crazy. Since talking to them doesn't seem to work,
> should I separate them? Give them detention? What?"

and

> "One more day of writing. They loved writing about cliques and gangs. I
> will definitely use this theme next year, and I'll keep expanding the book
> list. Even Dominic wrote."

There is no end to the surprises and problems Bob encounters the first year
he tries the writing workshop. But Bob is resolved to keep going, and he tries
to think them through when he encounters them.

- Students take writing home and do not return it.
- Students have problems learning to read each other's writing.
- It is difficult convincing students that they must write more than the teacher
  must grade or even read.
- Some students question the idea of quantity grades for writing.
- It is much tougher to teach his students to revise than Bob thought it
  would be.

And on and on.

Bob, determined to keep the writing workshop a part of his curriculum,
spends much of his drive time on these problems.

Bob makes two basic adjustments in his classes to overcome these problems.
First, he adds more explanation and introduction. He explains the purpose of
free writing, the reasons for quantity grading, the concept of the workshop. He
includes a stronger, more informative introduction to his writing workshop. In
other words, there are days Bob stops the process and has his students reflect
on it. During these sessions, Bob gives reasons for the techniques he uses in the
workshop.

Of course, teaching means never-ending problems, and his reflection days
often lead to student challenges that sometimes border on the rude and disre-
spectful, a price Bob has found that open, democratic teachers often have to
pay. But he handles these challenges with diplomacy and will make changes
based on conscientious and constructive student suggestions.

The second adjustment Bob makes is to greatly expand the modeling sessions
in his classes. Bob has always used models; he models free writing, revision,

and peer editing. But now Bob models a procedure two times if he feels it is necessary. He free writes twice for his workshop and revises twice. Bob holds two peer-editing model sessions using two different students as partners. The modeling program is very effective in showing his students how to go about their workshop tasks.

Bob has an ongoing, internal dialogue with himself about the problems he encountered during his first writing workshops. After his third or fourth writing workshop, Bob improved them immensely, but because teaching is an imperfect art, Bob had to continually work on them, as he does all his classes and techniques. Now that his workshop is no longer new, however, his tinkering is on a much smaller idiosyncratic scale.

Keeping Motivated

Bob loves teaching high school and plans to do it until his retirement. He has worked his way into a good schedule; his pay will never be great, but with his master's plus additional coursework, he is almost at the top of the pay scale. Bob has the routine down pat—he can monitor a large study hall, sponsor a fund raising drive for a school event, handle discipline without any serious problems. He can do the job. But Bob is not on automatic pilot. He is a concerned, dynamic teacher who tries new classroom techniques and deeply cares about his students and his subject. How does Bob maintain his love and enthusiasm for teaching after 15 years in the classroom? Obviously he reflects on what he does a great deal. But that isn't his only secret. Bob remains alive in the classroom through several venues.

A Mentor

Bob has a teacher friend. Her name is Sue Blakemore, and she is in her fourth year. Although Sue teaches in his department, Bob and Sue never really talked until they attended a drug education seminar together in Sue's second year. After the seminar, Bob and Sue had dinner together and began talking about English teaching. They discovered they basically had the same philosophy of teaching, and, from that conversation, they became professional friends, true kindred spirits.

Now, they are completely comfortable in each other's classrooms, which they visit all the time. Bob and Sue are so trusting of each other that they can critique each other's teaching in an honest and helpful way. They share curriculums; they plan together; they make conference presentations on writing workshops and reader-response discussions; and they have adopted a first-year teacher, Molly Kalopodis, who has come out of the university with ideas compatible with Bob's and Sue's.

Bob feels that much of his classroom life is related to the freshness and vision Sue provides. And for Sue, Bob's experience provides much guidance.

Faculty Development

Bob's school has a faculty development program that gives him various options. This program is far better than Bob's early experiences. He remembers the time all the high school teachers were ushered into the auditorium and shown a film, *The Destruction of the Saltwater Marsh*. The administration called this faculty improvement.

Nowadays, Bob gets leave time to visit schools and teachers who have programs Bob wants to see. He initially learned about portfolios on one of these visits. Also, Bob gets time to serve on faculty visitation teams that evaluate schools for organizations such as the North Central Association of Colleges and Secondary Schools. This is another outstanding way Bob gets to see other teachers, classrooms, and students.

Of course, the school still holds its one-shot days, but many of the presentations are made by colleagues, and this often leads to interaction and communication among the staff. Some of these in-service days, during which teachers teach other teachers, have been helpful.

Conferences

Funds for faculty development come and go, and Bob has seen almost every monetary policy possible. In flush times, one English teacher is sent, all expenses paid, to the National Council of Teachers of English Convention. Three additional teachers are given money to cover their rooms and fees for the state conference. In economic hard times, no one goes to the national convention unless it is next door, and three teachers may go to the state conference, but they will have to pay their own way. Fortunately for Bob and his colleagues, it has never gotten as bad as in a neighboring district, where teachers may attend the state conference if they pay for their own substitutes.

Regardless of the economic variables, Bob loves to go to the state English teachers conference. Often, he and Sue make presentations at this conference, sharing their favorite techniques and classroom strategies. He feels he has made friends with English teachers from all over the state, people he sees only once a year, but teachers he feels a stronger philosophic attachment to than many of his colleagues at home.

Bob's attitudes and ideas about secondary teaching have been, in part, formulated at these conferences. Many of Bob's heroes have appeared here, people like Kylene Beers, an expert in teaching difficult readers; Bob Probst, with his reader-response ideas; Donald Graves and Lucy Calkins, speaking about children and writing; and, of course, Nancie Atwell, with her ideas about writing workshops and teachers as researchers. He has met authors of young-adult novels such as Gary Paulson *(Hatchet, Dogsong)*, Christopher Paul Curtis, and Paul Zindel. Teachers do not absolutely need to go to these conferences to be great teachers, but it helps to move out of the chaos and uncertainty of the classroom and to reflect with other adults about this vital profession.

Reading

Another benefit of the conferences Bob attends is the book displays. English teachers, who are readers and lovers of books, are like kids in a candy store, with shopping bags filled with catalogs, journals, and books. English teachers at these book displays are at risk, like compulsive gamblers, but instead wiping out on books rather than slot machines. At these displays, Bob not only browses the latest professional materials, but also gets a chance to see the newest young-adult novels.

Bob belongs to the National Council of Teachers of English and receives the *English Journal.* State organization membership provides him with the state journal. Bob's professional reading is one of his major sources for stimulation and new ideas that influence his professional life. Invariably, he will read about ideas he encounters at a conference or in conversation with colleagues. Reading allows Bob to process ideas in a logical and thoughtful way.

University Connections

Bob, like many of his colleagues, has his master's degree. He was certified to teach English in 1972 and took his master's several years later. He completed most of the coursework in the evening and in the summer. After hard days of teaching, he found the evening classes brutal. He usually walked into class angry, frustrated by lack of parking. Taking courses in the summer was more pleasant and even a better learning experience. All in all, earning a master's was a good experience for Bob. He met colleagues who became friends, grew professionally and personally, and met his wife, a chemistry teacher.

From time to time, Bob continues to take university courses and workshops. Bob's first experience with new writing approaches came in a university workshop, taught by teachers and university faculty, that required all participants to write.

Bob's favorite relationship with the university is with the teacher education program. Bob loves to have university students come into his classes as observers, aides, tutors, and student teachers. He developed a relationship with the local university English education professor, which has led to a great deal of work without pay for the university. Bob loves to do it, and the university person is very grateful because he considers Bob one of the best state-of-the-art English teachers he knows. On holidays such as President's Day, when his school is closed and the university is open, Bob visits a university class and shares his expertise with future English teachers. The university students, in turn, visit Bob's school and watch him teach.

What Bob likes most of all, however, is sponsoring a university student in a prestudent-teaching field experience. Often this relationship leads to a student teacher/cooperating teacher partnership. This system is the only way Bob takes student teachers anymore because he wants to get to know them ahead of time. If their personalities mesh and they bond in a prestudent-teaching experience, fine; it should work out well in student teaching. But Bob is no longer willing to risk meeting a student teacher the first day he or she reports for work. For Bob and the student, there is much to gain by having the relationship established before student teaching begins. So far, Bob's success rate with student teachers (those who achieve a high pass) under this system is 100%.

Although Bob gets paid very little for his services to the university, his rewards are great. He gets to work with young people who want to be just like him. The future teachers he grooms are in awe of Bob's skills and knowledge. They are starry-eyed apprentices to a true master teacher. Bob enjoys the appreciation, but he gets more out of this than worship. The university students are sources of all kinds of new ideas for English teaching. Much of what Bob initially learned about reader-response techniques came from university students. Also, Bob's first experience with young-adult novels came a long time ago from a student teacher who brought him *The Outsiders*.

The university students supply him with another service: They provide an indirect critique of Bob's teaching. A respectful university student will ask, "Why did you do that, Bob?" and he will have to think about it. "I don't know. Why *did I* do that?" Bob reflects until he figures out what he did, why he did it, and if he could do it better a different way. A principal is a lot more threatening, and, therefore, not as effective an observer as a grateful, intelligent, and well-meaning student teacher.

Also, university students come to Bob with new techniques they want to try out. Some of them work; some of them need to be modified. These students bring Bob new ideas from the university in a more powerful and effective way than a direct exchange between Bob and the university. In a real sense, Bob's student teachers are his best teachers.

Bob gets a great deal out of his relationship with the university. He gets almost as much as he gives, and Bob gives a great deal. He helps a new generation become the best possible English teachers.

Reflection

Bob remains a vital force in the classroom. No one can point to him as a burnout, a teacher who does not care. Bob remains alive and keeps professionally healthy through a process he has developed over his career.

Much of his reflectiveness is a talent he has developed and honed through trial and error. Also, early teacher-training experiences and conversations with the best of the supervisors he has known have helped Bob develop his talent for successful and productive introspection.

The external help he gets in remaining alive in the classroom comes in several forms.

- Friendly and nurturing relationships with his mentor and colleagues
- A staff-development program that provides the opportunity to visit other teachers and schools, as well as experience educational opportunities such as workshops, courses, and seminars
- Participation in, and attendance at, national, state, and local conferences
- Continuous professional reading
- Collaboration with a university as a teacher instructor, mentor to pre-teachers, and student-teacher supervisor

All of these pieces, when put together, create a vital and active career. Bob was able to grow into an excellent secondary teacher because of his access to them. And he remains alive in the classroom partially because of so many activities outside the classroom. Bob cannot even imagine what his life would be like as a teacher if he were isolated and alone in the classroom, without any outside support systems. Bob pities the isolated teachers he knows, but even more, he worries about their students, some of whom are Bob's at different times in the day. Many of these isolated teachers hate teaching but do it anyway. And all of these isolated teachers never change, never grow. Some teach as they did 25 years ago, despite the enormous change in the nature of students. "How can any professional remain static?" Bob wonders, grateful that he loves teaching and that he has found multiple ways of enriching his career.

He is also grateful for all the teachers he knows who remain alive in the classroom, who grow, change, and work at solving the intriguing problems that teaching produces. He is happy that he knows teachers who love the challenge, the kids, and the classroom, and he feels lucky to be among them. Bob also feels lucky to be helping produce the next generation of teachers who will remain alive in the classroom.

Teacher as Researcher

Questions

- Do you agree that teaching is a never-ending challenge that you must constantly work at?
- What are the advantages and disadvantages to having peers visit and critique you in the classroom?
- What would you ask a teacher friend to look for in an English class as you teach?
- If you were going to try a new kind of activity in the classroom, what would you prepare yourself to encounter?
- What would you tell a despondent teacher who is about to give up on a writing workshop, because s/he sensed failure?
- Should you take risks in the classroom? What does this mean? What are the benefits/problems?
- Are mentors as important as this chapter indicates?
- What is the best prestudent-teaching field experience you have had or hope to have?
- How can universities and secondary schools maintain a friendly, collegial, equal, collaborative relationship?

Activities

- React to the story. Give your impressions or thoughts.
- Write a monologue reflecting on yourself in a classroom experience. Develop a plan to improve the quality of the experience if you were given a second chance at it.
- Develop a plan on how to train a new teacher to reflect on himself/herself in the classroom.
- Ask teachers to define good in-service experiences and bad in-service experiences.
- Design a faculty improvement plan you would hope to see in a school you teach in.
- Develop a realistic plan of how you can attend conferences when you become a teacher.
- Make a list of all relevant conferences that may be possible for you to attend.
- Borrow a National Council of Teachers of English Conference (NCTE) proceedings book. Browse through it. Make a list of the sessions you find most intriguing.
- Apply to make a presentation at a local or state conference.

- Find two or three articles you find intriguing from past *English Journals*. Read them and explain why they are or are not helpful.
- List the journals you think would be most helpful as a teacher. Explain why you selected them.
- Give an English teacher friend a list of your favorite professional books. Explain why they are your favorites. Talk about it.
- Have your English teacher friend give you a list of his or her favorite professional books. Read them and talk about them.
- Describe an ideal student teaching experience and develop a plan to achieve it.
- Describe an ideal supervising teacher.

Recommended Readings

Bauer, A. M., & Sapona, R. H. (1991). *Managing classrooms to facilitate learning.* Englewood Cliffs, NJ: Prentice-Hall.

This is an extensive view of secondary classrooms and how to structure them for optimal learning.

Borich, G. D. (2000). *Effective teaching methods.* New York: Merrill.

This is a standard methods text with coverage of most issues a beginning teacher needs to know.

Charles, C. M. (1989). *Building classroom discipline: From models to practice.* New York: Longman.

Charles gives readers a description of eight basic models of discipline such as the neo-Skinnerian model, the Cantor model, and the Glasser model. Many of these models are highly student-centered.

Clift, R., Houston, R., & Pugach, M. (Eds.). (1990). *Encouraging reflective practice in education: An analysis of issues and programs.* New York: Teachers College Press.

The authors make a strong case for reflective teaching. They make it very clear what reflective teaching is and how the approach contrasts with other views of teaching.

Hayes, I. (Ed.). (1999). *Great beginnings: Reflections and advice for new English language arts teachers and the people who mentor them.* Urbana, IL: National Council of Teachers of English.

This book presents 31 essays with helpful advice for new teachers. The readings in this book often deal with reconciling the "real world" with the "ideal world" of teaching.

Kowalski, T., Weaver, R. A., & Henson, K. T. (1994). *Case studies on teaching* (5th ed.). New York: Longman.

This text illustrates with case studies the first-year experience of teachers. Stories range from finding the right job to coping with a negative faculty.

Kronowitz, E. L. (1992). *Beyond student teaching.* New York: Longman.

This book is a guide to becoming a reflective practitioner during the difficult first year of teaching. It includes a section on the first day of school.

MacDonald, R. E. (1991). *A handbook of basic skills and strategies for beginning teachers: Facing the challenge of teaching in today's schools.* New York: Longman.

This text is a practical nuts and bolts guide to teaching that provides a great deal of useful information for the novice.

McCracken, N., & Appleby, B. C. (Eds.). (1993). *Gender issues in the teaching of English.* Portsmouth, NH: Heinemann.

This book is a useful collection of essays about how gender issues impact the teaching of English. The book offers suggestions on how to shape a gender-balanced English class.

Mosston, M., & Ashworth, S. (1990). *The spectrum of teaching styles: From command to discovery.* New York: Longman.

This book provides an overview of several teaching styles with the hope that each teacher "will use as many styles as possible." Many of these styles fit the interactive, student-centered classroom.

Palonsky, S. B. (1986). *900 shows a year: A look at teaching from a teacher's side of the desk.* New York: Random House.

This is a portrait of a year of high school teaching. The book provides many contextual insights into secondary teaching, although it is limited to one setting.

Savage, T. V. (1991). *Discipline for self-control.* Englewood Cliffs, NJ: Prentice-Hall.

This is a basic overview of how to handle classroom management. The last chapter deals with serious behavior problems.

Wilen, W., Ishler, M., Hutchinson, J., & Kindsvatter, R. (2000). *Dynamics of effective teaching* (4th ed.). New York: Longman.

This is a basic introduction to teaching text. The latest edition has sections on constructivism and authentic assessment techniques.

SECTION TWO: Resources: The Fundamentals, Plans, and Terms

Three Sample Unit Plans

Introduction

This chapter contains three unit plans for activities that are described in earlier chapters. The first plan is for the performance based teaching of *A Midsummer Night's Dream* described in Chapter Five. The second plan is based on the teaching of poetry found in Chapter Six. Finally, you will find here an extensive unit plan for the teaching of *To Kill a Mockingbird* found in Chapter Seven.

Although these plans are similar to the activities found in the stories, they are not identical. These plans vary from the stories because plans and teaching are two crafts of a profession and they seldom match completely. However, what you have here are the professional statements that teachers prepare to describe the act of teaching.

Each of these plans begins with goals and objectives that state their purpose and the student learning that will take place. Each of these plans has the outlines of activities that describe what will go on in the classrooms. Also, each of these plans explains how students will be evaluated.

All of these plans describe varied and complicated language arts activities. Therefore, each unit contains large amounts of reading, writing, speaking, and, in at least two plans (*To Kill a Mockingbird* and *A Midsummer Night's Dream*), viewing.

Each unit ends with a description of how the plan fulfills the CORE Strategy: **C**onnections, **O**wnership, **R**esponse, **E**xtensions.

As with all of *Crossing Over*, this section is meant as a baseline illustration of how teachers plan, but in no way represents your final or only option. These plans are here to serve as models for you to reflect on and as scaffolds for you to consider when you build your own classroom plans.

It has been my experience that the plan is not important. What is important is the act of planning. During the activity of planning, I internalize my goals and my strategies. The act of teaching allows me to evaluate the plans effectiveness and based on my reaction and my students' reactions and the performance of my students, I revise my plans. These units are revised units, plans that have been activated in many classrooms. Yet, they are not your plans. So they serve you as guidance, perhaps. But it's doubtful you can teach the lessons designed here without creating anew your plans. So read them, react to them, and use them as baselines for your planning.

A Unit Plan for Teaching Drama: *A Midsummer Night's Dream*

Performance-Based Teaching of *A Midsummer Night's Dream*: The Plan

Goals: Students will

- read with understanding a complex literary work;
- appreciate a complex literary work;
- gain confidence as readers;
- gain an understanding and deep appreciation of a work by William Shakespeare.

Objectives: Students will

- perform with understanding selected scenes from *A Midsummer Night's Dream*;
- understand and appreciate the complete work;
- understand and appreciate a professional production of *A Midsummer Night's Dream*;
- write with clarity and understanding journal entries about selected characters and scenes from the play;
- write with clarity and understanding a review of the classroom performance of the play.

Written Assignments

Daily journal entries

Assignments given daily

Summary of experience and review of performance

Activities

1. Model Shakespeare Insult Sheet
   Have students insult each other using Shakespeare insults.

2. Select Cast for "Kwickie" Rehearsal
   Pass sheets out with Act I, scene ii on it; cast each page and have students read.

3. Select Cast for "Kwickie" Performance
   Have performers get up and perform scene in front trying to act it out; change cast for each third of scene.

4. Tell Story of Play Using Students to Mime the Parts
   Tell the story. Bring students up front and place character name tags on them to demonstrate who is who in the play.

5. Read Selected Parts from Entire Play; Clarify and Help with Language
   Demonstrate a dramatic reading and explanation of part of Act I, scene i and Act II, scenes ii and iii, and Act V. Use students to help do the reading.

6. Casting the Play
   Give students parts from the Acts and Scenes referred to above.
   Go over the rules:
   - Know your part well;
   - Be enthusiastic and work hard;
   - Cooperate with your group members.

7. Rehearse the Play
   Eight rehearsal stages:
   - Read through
   - Group discussion about scene
   - Language changes, cutting with permission of teacher
   - Read through
   - Block and read
   - Block and act
   - Block and act—finalize costumes and set
   - Dress rehearsal

8. Perform Play for Class
   - Show "Brush Up Your Shakespeare" song from the movie, *Kiss Me Kate*.
   - Give "Tootsie awards" (Tootsie pops) based on Dustin Hoffman movie where he dressed as a woman to get an acting job.
   - Congratulate students on their ability to read and understand a difficult work.
   - Show select scenes from the movie *A Midsummer Night's Dream*.

■ Discuss play, the characters, the themes, and the difficulty of performance.

Evaluation

1. Enthusiasm	20 points
2. Cooperation	20 points
3. Preparation Efforts	20 points
4. Debriefing Discussion	10 points

Written Evaluation

Journal Entries	100 points
Summary Statement and Play Review	50 points

A Midsummer Night's Dream Core

Connections

The Shakespeare insult sheet
The kwickie performance
Storytelling
Class reading of selected parts

Ownership

Rehearsals
Journal writing

Response

Performance
Summary statement and play review
Discussion of play and performance

Extensions

Tootsie awards
Viewing of the play on video

A Unit Plan for Teaching Poetry

The Plan: Poetry Soup (a class collection of poems gathered by teacher and students)

Reading Poems with Students: A Response-Based Young-Adult Poetry Activity

Goals: Students will

■ Respond to poems discussed and read to them;

■ Select, read, and discuss poems to the class.

Objectives: Students will

- Actively listen to poems and responses made by teacher;
- Participate in discussions about poems;
- Select poems to read and discuss with class.

Activities

- Give students Poetry Soup Packets (packets filled with young-adult poems) and discuss methods of collecting poems.
- Give methods for student-generated poetry collection.
- Read and tell stories of the writing of poems teacher has written:

  Jane at Jacob's Field
  Sun Tea
  Man in a Gray Suit
  To Dave

- Read and lead a response based discussion on *My Papa's Waltz*.
  Divide class response into categories:
  Those who feel poem is about child abuse;
  Those who feel poem is about a loving father;
  Those who feel poem is about both, neither, or something else.
- Read and lead response-based questions on a few other Poetry Soup entries.
- Have students select one or two poems from the packet.
- Have students lead response-based discussions.

Evaluation

Listening and responding	30 points
Selecting and reading	50 points

The Plan: Writing Poetry

Goal: Students will

- develop sensitivity to words and phrases through the writing of poetry.

Objectives: Students will

- write a poem for each activity;
- share their poem with the class.

Activities: Students will write a poem or poems based on the following activities:

- a copy change poem;
- a found poem;

- a concrete poem;
- a pattern poem;
- a poem any time, any way.

Evaluation

Each poem is worth	20 points
Each sharing is worth	10 points

Poetry Core

Connections
Students experience teacher's relationship to poems.
Ownership
Students select poems to share with each other.
Response
Students read poems and explain their responses to the poems they selected. They explain why they selected the poems.
Extensions
Students write poetry based on scaffolding provided by teacher.

A Unit Plan for Teaching the Novel: *To Kill a Mockingbird*

The Plan: *To Kill A Mockingbird* Unit
Tenth Grade—Three Weeks

Goals: Students will

- understand and appreciate Harper Lee's novel *To Kill a Mockingbird*;
- develop an awareness of the moral dimension of the novel;
- understand the significant themes of the novel;
- relate the themes and characters to their lives;
- extend the themes of the novel into other activities;
- understand the similarities and differences of the film *To Kill a Mockingbird*;
- appreciate the film *To Kill a Mockingbird* as a separate and discreet work of art.

Objectives: Students will

- read with understanding as measured by class discussion and by written responses to sections of the book, which show applicative and thematic understanding of the book as evidenced through specific references to the text;

- appreciate the moral and thematic dimensions of the book by completing an extended activity that uses specific textual thematic references;
- understand the similarities and differences of the book and film by developing a movie storyboard based on scenes from the written text and compare this storyboard to scenes from the film;
- appreciate the film of *To Kill a Mockingbird* as evidenced in an open-ended response-based discussion of the movie.

Activities
Day One—Introduction

A. A memory activity. Tell a story from your childhood, preferably about a brother or sister. Begin the story by teasing us with information about the ending, but do not give the entire story away. I will begin with a story of Terry on the day he was killed. Read aloud foreshadowing opening of *To Kill a Mockingbird*.

B. What position are you in your family and how do you think it made a difference. I am the middle child. I will tell you how it may have made a difference in my life.

C. Setting the novel—A Discussion of the 1930s.

Discussion Questions

- What were the 1930s like in America?
- What was the South like in America?
- What were homes like?
- What were roads like?
- What were cars like?
- What were the methods of communication?
- What did kids do to have fun in the 1930s?
- What were schools like in the 1930s?
- Write your own question about the 1930s.

Each student must have two answers for at least two of the questions.
Reading the novel.
This book is a memoir (explain); a memory book set in the 1930s.
Begin in-class reading.

Day Two—Reading Workshop

- Read *To Kill a Mockingbird*.
- Record readings on record keeping.

- React to reading in journal.
- Status of class report.

Day Three—Reading Workshop

- Read *To Kill a Mockingbird.*
- Record readings on record keeping.
- React to reading in journal.
- Status of class report.

The Story of Harper Lee, Author.

Day Four—Part One of Novel Due, Chapters 1–11

- Critical Response Writing.
- Respond to Part One by telling what happens.
- Consider the major characters you meet.
- Tell about them.

Response Questions

- What are the major themes of the book?
- What do you know about them so far?
- What are the relationships like? For instance, How do Jem and Scout get along?
- How do the kids relate to Atticus?
- How do the kids relate to their neighbors?
- What do you know about Boo Radley?
- What do you know about Maycomb?
- What is school like, particularly for Scout?
- Convince me you have read up to this point.

Characters in the Book

In your journal do the following:

For Each Character

Who are they? What do I know about them?

Atticus
Jem
Scout
Dill
Calpurnia

Miss Maudie
Boo Radley
Walter Cunningham
Aunt Alexandra

Day Five—To Chapter Fifteen Due
Respond to the following:

- Compare Aunt Alexander and Calpurnia.

- Why does Aunt Alexander want Atticus to fire Calpurnia?

- Describe what takes place at the jailhouse.

Continue characters in the book
Add the following:

Tom Robinson
Reverend Sykes

Day Six—The Trial, Chapters Sixteen Through Twenty-One Journal Questions
Respond to the following:

- Describe Judge Taylor.

- How does Bob Ewell describe himself as a witness?

- Is Mayella a sympathetic character? Why or why not?

- Why does Tom help Mayella move the chifforobe?

- Why do you agree with Atticus's closing argument? Why or why not?

- Why were Dill and Jem more upset with the verdict than Scout?

The Theme of Racism
A History of the Scottsboro Trials
Discussing the Trial and the Racial Theme of the Novel

- What do we learn about the nature of race in the Thirties from this novel?

- How do you feel the racial aspects of this novel have been handled so far?

Day Seven—Finish the Book
Writing workshop day
Critical response: Respond to the following:

- What did you think about the book?

- Did you like it? Why or why not?

- How does the book end?

- How does the ending tie in all the themes of the book?

- What are the themes of the book? Support your answer.

- Why doesn't the book end with the trial?
- What is the Boo Radley story and why is it so important to the novel?
- Are the racial issues in the book well handled and still relevant?
- Why is this book seen through the eyes of a child?
- Why the title?

Day Eight—Reader-Response Discussion

An open ended discussion of *To Kill a Mockingbird.* Discussion rules apply.

Days Nine, Ten, and Eleven—Compare Select Scenes of the Book with the Movie.

Storyboard the following:

- The Opening
- Jem on the Radley Porch
- The Jailhouse Scene
- The End of the Trial
- The Attack on the Kids
- The Last Scene

In groups you are to do the following:

Each group will draw a cartoon of the scene to present to the class. You will receive a grade based on the following with every student in the group doing one of the following activities:

- Drawing the scene (up to three illustrators with each panel signed)
- Describing the drawing under each panel based on the book (up to two describers with each description signed).
- An outline of the storyboard (up to two contributors dividing the storyboard in half).

Each group will present its storyboard. After each storyboard is completed, we will watch the Academy Award-winning movie of *To Kill a Mockingbird.*

Days Twelve and Thirteen—Extended Activities Selection and Preparation Days

Activity choices:

Racism and prejudice

- Dramatize a scene that reflects the townspeople's prejudices.
- Hold a panel discussion on whether Tom would have been found guilty in a modern court.
- Use quotations from the novel to create a collage of images representing racism.

Justice vs. Injustice

- Write an article for the *Maycomb Tribune* summarizing Tom's trial. Then write an editorial in which you express your opinion of the jury's decision.

- Design a book jacket illustrating the novel's condemnation of injustice.

- Present an opening argument in defense of Boo's actions on Halloween night.

Courage

- Write an essay describing the most courageous character from the novel.

- Write a letter to Dill from Scout in which you describe the events of Halloween night.

Coming of age

- Interview Scout and Jem twenty years after the close of the novel.

- Create a mural illustrating Jem's coming of age.

Grades for *To Kill a Mockingbrid*

Journal Writing	10%
Critical Responses, Reading	25%
Storyboard Activity	20%
Extended Activity	20%
Class Participation and Cooperation	25%

From Scaffolding to Response: *To Kill a Mockingbird* Core

Connections
   Setting the Themes
      The Memory Activity
      Discussing Siblings
      The Scottsboro History and Discussion

   Setting the Setting
      Viewing the 1930s
      Learning About the Author

   Learning the Characters
      The Character Activity
Ownership
   Opening the Book
      Class Readings
      Reading Workshops
      Critical Responses
      Journal Responses

Measuring the Reading
   Critical Responses
Response
Growing an Awareness
   Critical Responses
   Journal Writings

Responding to the Reading
   Open-ended Reader-Response Discussion
Extensions
Extending the Experience
   Storyboarding Scenes
   Viewing the Film
   Developing and Sharing the Final Project

Teacher As Researcher

Questions

- What do all of these plans have in common?
- What is the purpose of the CORE Strategy?
- What gave you more information about the strategies, the stories, or the plans?
- What would you add to the plans?
- What would you eliminate?
- What is the purpose of planning in outlines?
- What is the difference between goals and objectives?
- Do teachers really plan like this for most of their classes? Explain.
- What are the advantages of having these plans?
- Are there any disadvantages? Explain.
- What would you do differently in creating unit plans? Why?
- What do you like about these plans?
- What don't you like about them?

Activities

- Create unit plans based on these for other lessons.
- Write daily lesson plans for the lessons described in these units.
- Write out plans for reading and writing workshops.
- Prepare a lesson on planning to present to new teachers.

chapter FIFTEEN

Glossary: What Every English Teacher Needs to Know

Introduction

This section is devoted to issues, ideas, trends, and strategies that are important for all English-Language Arts teachers. You will find here the specialized vocabulary and tools of the practice of English teaching. Most of the information in this section runs throughout this book. However, here you will find an organized compendium of this important information. For most entries, you will encounter a reference to the specific location in *Crossing Over*.

Reading

In traditional instruction, reading is broken into two categories: decoding and comprehending. This is a false dichotomy because the purpose of all reading instruction is to comprehend written texts. However, opinions differ on the place of decoding activities in the development of readers.

Decoding

Decoding is the ability to name words or to get the intended meaning of words by context, phonics, or structural analysis (e.g., prefixes or suffixes) (Cooper, 1997, p. 14). In *Crossing Over*, although the word decoding is never mentioned, the strategies to help readers with dialect and vocabulary in Chapter Seven in "Teaching the Novel" are decoding skills as is the help in *A Midsummer Night's Dream*.

Phonics. Phonics is a strategy of sounding out words to be able to name them. The place of phonics instruction in the curriculum has created some controversy with differing opinions about the need for systematic phonics lessons. Critics of phonics say that phonics is about naming words and not about understanding texts. Proponents of phonics claim a reader needs word attack strategies to make sense out of a text. Probably the best approach is to incorporate all strategies in a reading program. Certainly, the sounds of words are important parts of many books for young children, such as the Dr. Seuss books or poetry by Shel Silverstein. However, word attack skills can lead to comprehension problems if a reader spends too much time trying to name words and loses the meanings of the groups of words that come before and after.

In *Crossing Over*, phonics is not dealt with in any detail. A 16-year-old would have a short attention span with traditional phonics exercises that require sounding out words and sound families. Yet, Chapter Six, "Teaching Poetry," describes several ways of teaching poetry where the sounds of words are important issues. Poetry writing is an excellent place to help older students obtain the ear required to sound out words.

Comprehension

Comprehension is the ability to elicit meaning from a written text. This is the sole purpose of reading, and all reading skills need to be addressed at helping readers comprehend texts.

In *Crossing Over*, every chapter on literature, and even writing, is about making meaning from texts. The heart of this book is about comprehension, keeping this as the primary goal of all language instruction.

Levels of Reading:

Independent Level. At this level, readers need no help with texts. They can comprehend the text by simply reading it. Leisure reading is mainly at the independent level.

In *Crossing Over*, Chapter Three, "Teaching the Reading Workshops," is about setting up a program of independent reading with the idea that so much of learning to read requires practice reading and the love of books.

Instruction Level. At this level, readers can comprehend the text, but need to employ several strategies in order to do so. In some cases, these may be technical texts, difficult poetry, or prose.

In *Crossing Over*, "Teaching Drama," Chapter Five, is a good example of how to help students with a text at this level. Also Chapter Seven, "Teaching the Novel," gives examples of instructional level reading.

Frustration Level. At this level, the text is just too difficult for the reader and will create frustration.

In *Crossing Over*, some students are frustrated by any text. No matter what teachers do, there will be some students, for whatever reason, who will not read. Our goal is to decrease that number. Reading instruction remains, to some extent, a human mystery. *Crossing Over* reflects the reality of teachers who face problems they cannot solve.

Literature Circles

These are literature discussion groups. There are many ways of formatting these. It may be best if each student has a specific discussion assignment involving an in common reading. In *Crossing Over*, examples of literature circles can be found in Chapter Three, "Teaching the Reading Workshop."

Directed Reading Activities

Activities that tap into students backgrounds and connect them to the reading also provide a purpose for reading. These lessons may be called Directed Writing Activities for Writing. I refer to these lessons in a broader context as *Scaffolding*. In *Crossing Over*, every chapter in this book provides examples of Directed Reading and Directed Writing Lessons.

Scaffolding

J. David Cooper (1997, p. 34) defines scaffolding as the support teachers provide students in reading and writing. I would add it is the support in all English/Language Arts endeavors. Cooper goes on to extend this metaphor (that's what it is) by suggesting that the teacher removes this scaffolding bit by bit until the student takes over. This metaphor for learning is the theme of this book, and it is stated several ways here, including the following:

Build a Bridge. This is a metaphor. Teachers build bridges for students to cross over, which extends the metaphoric title of this book. I like this one. Students are Crossing Over into independent literacy. That is, they have achieved our goals. They can read, write, speak, listen, and view independently, thoughtfully, critically, with enthusiasm and passion.

KWL. This is a well-known strategy for helping students use prior knowledge to interpret texts. This strategy has three large steps:

1. Students are asked what they know about a subject. This brainstorming activity should be recorded on a worksheet and is the K(now) step.

2. Next, students are asked to brainstorm a series of questions or statements about what they want to learn. This too should be recorded and is the W(hat) step.

3. Finally, after reading the work, students write answers to the questions they brainstormed in step 2. Also, they may have additional questions. This is the L(earn) step (Cooper, 1997, pp. 112–113).

CORE

CORE, is a scaffolding acronym that defines the process from the scaffold to independence and beyond. The acronym stands for:

Connections
Ownership
Response
Extensions

Crossing Over has examples of scaffolding throughout. That's what this book is about—building the scaffolding and slowly removing it. Every chapter deals with helping students make connections with language so they can achieve ownership.

Perhaps the best example of the CORE method is in the steps in teaching *A Midsummer Night's Dream*, Chapter Five. The acronym CORE is used in the teaching of *To Kill a Mockingbird* in Chapter Seven on teaching novels. All of the sample unit plans in Chapter Fourteen use CORE. This acronym was designed by Kylene Beers and myself at a workshop on teaching literature.

Workshops

On workshop days, students are actively engaged in reading and writing. Often, during reading workshops, students read self-selected books, sometimes from approved teacher lists. In Writing Workshops, students are engaged in the various stages of the writing process. These activities require maintenance and monitoring. In *Crossing Over*, workshops are described in Chapter Three on reading workshops and in Chapter Eight on writing.

Writing

The Writing Process

The writing process is old new news. Popularized in the seventies by teachers like Peter Elbow (1998) and Ken Macrorie (1984), the process soon became standard practice. The process breaks writing into several distinct parts, including *prewriting* or *studio writing*.

Students are allowed to write without fear of evaluation or grading. Sometimes, topics are given and sometimes they may write whatever they feel like writing about. Often, this writing is kept in journals. Grades may be based on quantity (filling two pages) and/or sticking to the topic. The point of this phase in the process is for students to gain the ability to write fluently without always fearing evaluation.

Drafting, Revising

Drafting and revising is the step in which students begin to shape the writing. Perhaps students will take a piece from their prewriting and begin to develop this writing for an audience outside themselves.

Editing

Editing is the final stage. Here students are concerned with final proofreading elements: punctuation, spelling, grammar. At this stage, teachers find out what skills students are missing as individuals, and what skills need reinforcement for the entire class.

Writing Process in General

The writing process differs from traditional approaches in several ways. First, the process breaks writing into sections that the traditional never did. Second, the process is more descriptive about correctness and grammar, whereas traditional approaches see grammar as a separate and discrete set of skills. Writing process teachers are more diagnostic with grammar instruction, often basing it on the writing students give them.

New Issues in the Teaching of Writing

Audience. In the writing process, the audience the student addresses is often a key issue in how a piece of writing is undertaken. For instance, rough drafts or prewriting is most likely student-centered writing. In other words, the audience for this kind of writing is the student writer and perhaps the teacher who may comment on issues raised or perhaps suggest sections that can be developed into public writing. Public writings are all the pieces students will take to the final stage of editing.

Many writing teachers feel that the writing process is unnatural in its progressive nature. Many believe that writers move in and out of stages without following a prescribed formula. It may depend upon the writing task. For instance, a work memo may be quickly drafted in its final form with little editing and no prewriting.

However, a complicated essay may follow the process but not linearly. For instance, I am editing this as I prewrite, yet I will rewrite and draft. However, the simplicity of the process steps, for some teachers, makes an easy teaching paradigm, particularly for novice writers.

Social Considerations. Some teachers feel the writing process is heavily weighed toward personal writing, which they see as a flaw. What these teachers recommend is purposeful writing with a stance specified (you are a child of a victim of lung cancer who smoked all his life), and an audience in mind (write to a lawyer seeking justice against tobacco companies who you feel killed your parent). This writing is more in sync with the complicated world our students live in today. However, purposeful social topics do not deny the need for drafting or revising.

Rejection of the Process as Too Vague and Student Centered. Some critics of the process feel the lack of formula ill suits students. Many of these critics prescribe topics and traditional five paragraph themes. The most prescriptive of these systems is called the Touleman System, which has a complete logical structure for students to develop a sentence by sentence argument based on a triple topic sentence. Teachers who believe in this system probably believe in prescriptive grammar as well and would grade students severely based on grammar mistakes.

Beyond Personal Writing

Personal writing is a way of ensuring that beginning writers have something to say. Many examples in *Crossing Over* deal with personal writing. Personal topics allow students to bring in a myriad of details and experiences. Yet, English/Language Arts teachers can offer students additional writing options. For instance, Tom Romano (2000) suggests students take different stances, place themselves in many positions or characters to write from. He also suggests that students write from different genres, such as poetry or drama.

James Moffett (1968) recommends that moving out of personal writing is developmental. That is, moving out of personal writing to impersonal essay is moving from concrete to abstract. Of course, much personal writing may be abstract and much impersonal essay may very well be concrete.

Social educational theorists see a need to write from a social or political context such as feminism or social justice.

In *Crossing Over*, there are many different kinds of writing such as book responses found in the reading workshop chapter (Chapter Three) or Shakespeare responses (Chapter Five). Also, students write a newscast (Chapter Nine), which is multigenre, and write poetry (Chapter Six). In Chapter Seven, students create and write dialect, dialogue pieces that are also multigenre.

Personal response writing can be found in Chapter Eight. Most state proficiency tests give personal response prompts.

Grading—Composition

There are two main ways teachers grade. A point system allows for giving credit for many activities in the classroom and gives a teacher a specific and seemingly objective criteria for grading. The problems occur in managing the point system and in the opportunity for students to quibble over points.

The other method is a percentage system. This divides activities into categories, with each category worth a percentage of the final grade. The system allows for flexibility, and it is harder for students to quibble over their grades, but it lacks the seemingly objectiveness of the point system. It also lacks the rigor and fine tuning the point system will allow. There is no perfect way to give grades in an English classroom. In *Crossing Over*, all of these issues on writing are addressed in Chapter Ten, "Grading and Assessing."

A new terminology centering around grading has developed in recent years.

Prompts

Prompts is the official name for topics. Prompts are most commonly used with proficiency testing, but many teachers now call their topics prompts.

Rubrics

This is the official term for a method of grading writing. Rubrics refer to the specific scoring sheet used to measure or grade writing. Most likely a rubric falls into one of the three categories: holistic, analytic, or primary trait. These forms of assessment are often labeled Direct Assessment because they require a writing sample. Indirect Assessment refers to multiple choice tests that purport to diagnose writing ability.

Holistic. Holistic rubrics tend to be pass/fail grading procedures. These rubrics are used for gross discrimination between students who are considered capable writers and those that are considered to have problems. Holistic scoring may be:

> High pass
> Pass
> Fail

Analytic Scoring. Analytic scoring uses a more discriminating scale with criteria. This scoring approach gives teachers a reason for the score placed on the paper. For instance:

5 strong voice, arguments clear with good examples, organization excellent and clearly written

4 voice evident, well organized, writing is clear, few mistakes with little meaning lost

3 organization evident, writing is clear, mistakes detract only somewhat from meaning

2 serious flaws in the paper such as lack of clear organization, systematic grammar, and punctuation problems that detract from the meaning.

1 no discernible meaning or clear intent of the writing.

Primary Trait Scoring.   This method of scoring is a way of selecting specific traits in the paper. For instance, if the essay is about a work of literature, a teacher may require quotes from the text and look for these traits. Or, if the teacher is concerned about supporting detail, these specific traits can be required.

Portfolios

For many teachers, the writing process encompasses a system of gathering and keeping student work in portfolios. On the simplest level, portfolios are folders where students keep their writings so they can see progress and the accumulated totality of their work. However, a portfolio system can be more than just collecting writings. For one thing, it can be a system of cataloguing writings and it also can be a system of reflecting on writing. Also, portfolios can be divided into two or more classifications. Work portfolios can be a way of keeping all the writing in one place and cataloging the work. Show portfolios can be the culmination of the semester or year by a careful selection and display of writing that shows the progress of the year. Often show portfolio selections are a combination of teacher and student input. Also, show portfolios contain a sheet for cataloging, describing, and reflecting on the writing. Chapter Eight describes both kinds of portfolios.

Proficiency Testing

Most states require high school students to pass high stakes proficiency tests. For English teachers, this usually means a reading and writing test. The reading test is more often than not a computerized traditional reading test. The writing test often requires a writing sample that is scored analytically, and sometimes a computerized grammar and language test. Different states do have different tests. In *Crossing Over*, Chapter Nine is devoted to the issues of testing and proficiency.

Planning

Although planning is a complex skill requiring a high level of professional knowledge, lesson plans are somewhat standardized into the following format.

Goals

These are long-range statements that are not included in every daily plan, but are mostly found in unit plans that are plans for a long-term project, such as teaching a class novel like *To Kill a Mockingbird*.

A goal may state that students will read and appreciate *To Kill a Mockingbird*, or that students will write critical responses about *To Kill a Mockingbird*, indicating a reading and comprehending of the book. Thus, goals are long term and large targets for students.

Objectives

Objectives, on the other hand, are specific targets that are stated for every class on every lesson plan. Objectives, often short for behavioral objectives, give a very specific, observable, and measurable target for each class. Behavioral objectives are the operational statement of the behaviorist theory of teaching, which postulates that all learning is observable and quantifiable. The view of this text sees behaviorism as reductivist and simplistic, undercutting the critical elements of English teaching such as appreciation and enjoyment. Yet, it is important for English teachers to know how to state specific objectives in order to keep English teaching from becoming too vague, drifting, into ambiguity.

> An objective for *To Kill a Mockingbird* lesson may be as follows: Students will be able to identify the historical roots of the trial in *To Kill a Mockingbird* by participating in discussion of the Scottsboro Boys after the teacher tells the story.

A behavioral objective requires that the teacher give a multiple choice quiz based on her class presentation about the Scottsboro Boys. The nonbehavioral objective allows the teacher to gauge the learning of her students by discussion afterward. One is very specific and the other is not quite as specific. You decide which is more effective. A teacher can argue either way.

Activities/Procedures

This is the next part of a lesson plan that describes what the steps are in carrying out the lesson. This is often done in outline form and sometimes has a timeline designating how long each of the parts will take.

Evaluation/Summary

The last part of the lesson plan designates the way the lesson's success will be measured.

A colleague of mine prepared a format for instructional planning that represents an ideal. I am including this format here as an example of what the highest level of planning would approach. As you will note, this format includes a section for planning for "students with special needs" and a reflection section at the end. This format makes an excellent training model that can be adapted for real classroom conditions (Figure 15.1)

In *Crossing Over*, Chapters Twelve and Fourteen concern planning.

figure ◊ **15.1**

Instructional Plan and Reflection/Rationale

Instructional Planning

What problem/situation have you identified/What problem/situation are you addressing? Why does this problem/situation need to be addressed? Is instruction/training the only/best alternative?

Lesson title:

Subject area(s):

Grade level(s):

Time allocation:

Objectives

What are your specific objectives for this lesson?

- Tie to specific state Proficiency Outcomes, specific national standards, or your school district's course of study
- Attach copy of the portion of the outcomes/standards/course of study that support your objectives

Why have you chosen these objectives?

figure ◊ **15.1** | *(Continued)*

Grouping

How will you group students for instruction?

Why have you chosen this grouping?

What are other students doing when you are instructing a small group?

What do you do if the groups get done early?

What does the student do if she/he finishes before the rest of the class?

Prior Knowledge

List the prior knowledge students must have to be successful in this learning experience.

How did you obtain information about prior knowledge students must have?

How does this information help shape your instructional plan?

Do you need to find out if your students have necessary prior knowledge?

If so, how will you find out?

Learner Analysis

What specific characteristics of your target learners impact this instructional plan?

Are learners developmentally capable of being successful in this learning experience?

How do you know these factors about your learners?

Students with Special Needs

How are you modifying the instruction for students with special needs?

Model of Instruction/Instructional Strategies

Identify the instructional model you will use for this instructional plan:

- teaching for conceptual change
- learning cycle
- problem-based learning
- inquiry-based learning
- discussion
- demonstration
- etc.

Why have you chosen this model of instruction?

Why do you think it will be effective with your learners?

figure ◊ 15.1   (Continued)

How have you accommodated different learning styles?
Have you used this instructional model previously? If so, how did
it work? What was successful? What needed to be improved?
How will you use a classroom assistant (parent volunteer,
preservice teacher, teacher assistant, technology resource person)?

Materials
What materials will you use?
Are these materials suited to your students?
Do the materials match your instructional strategies?
Have you evaluated the materials?

Activity
What activity have you planned?
Outline the activity
Is the activity consistent with the model of instruction?
How does the activity help students achieve the objectives?

Evaluation/Assessment
How will you evaluate/assess students?
Describe and attach your concrete assessment instrument.
When do you plan to assess students?
How does this instrument measure achievement of the objectives?
Will students participate in defining measures of achievement?
How?

Reflection/Rationale

To what extent did students learn what you intended? How
do you know?
How effective was the grouping? Would you change
the grouping? Why?
In what ways was the model of instruction effective?
Was the lesson safe for all students?
Was modification for students with special needs effective?
In what ways did you modify the lesson for students?
In what ways were instructional materials effective? Would you
make other choices? Why?
In what ways were activities effective? What would you change?
How did students perform? What aspects of your assessment
would you change? Why?

Performance-Based Teaching

This method of teaching requires plans with specific student performances tied to them. The strategies in *Crossing Over* do make performance-based teaching possible. The section at the end of each chapter on the IRA/NCTE Standards for English Language Arts documents how the strategies can be defined as performance-based.

Benchmarks

These are specific learning outcomes that a teacher plans to accomplish as a result of units and plans. Benchmarks are specific goals a teacher can use in a performance-based classroom. For instance, a benchmark for *To Kill a Mockingbird* may be a series of responses that show an understanding and appreciation for the novel. A benchmark for writing may be at least one essay that is for a public audience and shows a strong voice, strong organization, purpose, and correctness.

In *Crossing Over*, benchmarks are dealt with specifically in the references to the IRA/NCTE Standards for English Language Arts.

Thematic Units

Thematic units involve themes such as ethnic diversity. A variety of literature, including films, may be used to help illustrate the theme.

Teacher as Researcher

Questions

- What are additional ideas and strategies English teachers need to know?
- Which of these strategies are the most important? Explain.
- Which of these strategies are the least important? Explain.

Activities

- Use one or two of these strategies in a teaching plan you are developing.
- Create your own list of what every English teacher needs to know.
- Write *Crossing Over* style stories incorporating some of these strategies.
- Rank these strategies in the order of importance.

Appendix

Crossing Over: A Guide to Personal Writing

Introduction

Use this section as a way of discovering through writing your direction as an English teacher. Do you see yourself as a meaning-centered teacher? Or do you approach English in a different way? You might benefit by writing your own *Crossing Over* if:

- You are training to become an English teacher and are beginning to develop a viewpoint and need to see in writing what you feel, know, and need to learn.
- You are a new teacher and would like to know where your early experiences in teaching are leading you.
- You are a veteran teacher and would like to have a written review of where you came from and, perhaps, a plan for where you are going.

Where This Book Began

It is October 8, 2:55 Pacific Time. I am in the outdoor eating area of Vista Grande Elementary School in El Cajon, on a beautiful, sunlit, California day, waiting for Lizzy and Jane to end their school day. As I begin the writing of whatever this will become, I need to reflect a little on immediate past events and some not-so-immediate past events. I think I know the subject and know it well, for the subject is me, like no other piece I have written before, and it is about these kids in front of me as I await my daughters, and it is for their teachers. It is about books, magazines, records, newspapers, television, videos, telephones, and computers, and talk, listening, and thought processing. It is about the very new and very old, and very, very complex web of communication and story and art and excess.

These random thoughts were the first words written for this text. About a year earlier, I had developed an outline for a fairly traditional text that would deal with changing literacy patterns and their relationship to English teaching. Three books in particular influenced my initial thinking, represented in that outline. I felt that Wayne Booth's *The Company We Keep* (1988) painted an interesting portrait of how readers form a moral bond with books. Robert Coles' *Call of Stories* (1989) presented a view of the paradigmatic and mythical importance of stories-printed, oral, visual-in everyone's lives. Finally, Robert Scholes' *Textual Power* (1985) reaffirmed my sense that literacy has shifted away from print exclusively and that all texts need to be studied as potentially powerful and manipulative change agents.

So, for the year before I wrote these first words, I spent much of my free time in a library studying all the various loose ends of ideas I had in relation to this book. For years I have been influenced by Frank Smith. And Louise Rosenblatt has, in my opinion, defined reading in the most productive way I have ever known. The proliferation of reader-based theories and concurrent practice is one of the finest developments I have encountered in English teaching.

My time in the library ended when my reading became repetitive. I felt it was time to write, but I wasn't sure how to start. It was only after I picked up a copy of Mike Rose's *Lives on the Boundary* (1989) that I realized how I was going to write this book. Rose taught me that no amount of library research alone would answer the questions I had about literacy and English teaching. I had to write this book about my experiences, which, after all, span one of the periods of greatest change in literacy and communication in history. I realized that I could only find part of the story in the library. This book had to be about my "crossing over."

So I put away my research and notes and began writing *Crossing Over*. I wrote and wrote and wrote. I wrote at desks in libraries, on benches overlooking the Pacific Ocean, in airplane seats, in cars, and at picnic tables. And it was working. I had taken my own advice. Writing is discovery, I saw, as *Crossing Over* evolved. And then, after numerous drafts, I had it. The book told my story. The loose ends were gone. I learned so much about myself as an English teacher and my ideas and beliefs that I highly recommend that those of you who will be or already are English teachers try it.

Creating Your Personal Profile

No one prescription will fit all writers; what I offer is a step-by-step guide based on the way I wrote this text. I hope you will be able to adapt this guide to your writing style and that you will be able to use this as an aid in creating your personal profile.

Step 1: Thinking It Over

Discuss Part 1, *Crossing Over*, with your class, your friends, or your writing group. You may use the following questions as guides:

- How do you feel about *Crossing Over*? Explain.
- What are the premises of Part 1?
- Do you agree with the description of the shift in literacy? Explain.
- Are young people like the description in *Crossing Over*? Explain.
- If you read *Catcher in the Rye*, how does it hold up by today's standards?
- Do you believe there are other films that deserve mention because of their influence? What are they? Explain.
- What do you perceive as "super media"? Explain.
- Is "super media" a whole new way of viewing literacy? Explain.
- Do you agree with my definitions of effective teaching? Why or why not?
- What will literacy and literacy skills be like 20 years from now?

Writing It Down

You may find it beneficial, when you begin writing your personal profile, to have some notes on your discussion of *Crossing Over*. Why don't you spend some time writing down some of the ideas, concerns, and questions that this discussion provoked in you.

Step 2: Gathering of Materials

I describe for you some of the theorists and books that influenced my writing. Make a list of some of your influences. You may wish to consider the following:

- Theorists and professional books
- Novels, short stories, poems, plays
- Teachers: elementary, secondary, college
- Colleagues
- Friends, particularly those who support your career decisions

- Family
- Experiences such as camp counseling, Sunday school teaching, field experiences in schools, teaching experiences
- Experiences particular to you
- Teenagers you know
- Popular media-film, television, music, newspapers, magazines

Before I began the initial writing, I took notes on my sources on file cards. I recommend you devise a system for retrieving specific texts, pages, and stories that you may weave into your profile.

Step 3: The Draft

There comes a time in every writer's life when writing is unavoidable; no notecards, preparation, or computer screen will write for you. So, you may wish to do what I did. Forget all the work you have done up to this point. Take whatever writing instruments you are most comfortable with—a pen and pad, newly sharpened pencils, a typewriter, or computer keyboard—and begin your story, your *Crossing Over*.

I would recommend that you do not spend too much time with your pen in the air. If you have to, begin the way I did: "It is _____ a.m./p.m. I am in _____ on a _____ waiting _____. Once you begin writing, the ideas will come and you will discover your *Crossing Over*. Do not worry about editing yet. Spelling and punctuation *do not count here.* Just keep the writing going.

Although I did not work with written-out questions, here are some you may wish to use if you get stuck. Remember, use these questions carefully. This is your *Crossing Over* and these are my questions.

- How did I learn to read?
- How did I learn to love reading?
- When did I watch television, growing up?
- What did I watch on television, growing up?
- What are my favorite childhood and young-adult books?
- What are my favorite films from youth?
- What classes and teachers, good and bad, had an influence on me as a child and young adult?
- What kind of literacy experiences did I witness in my home?

- What changes have I seen in reading, writing, and seeing since my youth? How have books, magazines, newspapers, television, and film changed since I first encountered these media?
- What are my most memorable classroom experiences—as a student, teacher trainee, teacher?
- Where did I learn how to write?
- How did I get my current writing system?
- How do I believe teachers help teenagers learn to read and write?
- How do teenagers grow as readers and writers?
- Does modern communication technology—computers, fax machines, telecommunication improvements, new television technology (high-definition television)—have an influence on me as a teacher?
- What are the characteristics of teenagers whom I know?
- What do the teenagers I know like most or least about school?
- Do the teenagers I know read?
- What do they read and why?
- What do teenagers watch on television?
- What do teenagers do in their spare time?
- What are the differences among teenagers?
- What do teenagers spend money on?
- How do teenagers get their money?

Step 4: Rewriting

My first draft ended when I ran out of things to write. I had written my first draft by hand on a yellow legal pad, single spaced. My handwriting was awful; it was obvious I was to be the only reader of this draft. For my second draft, I took the first and began rewriting it. This time I wrote every other line and slowed down my writing to make it readable for others. My second draft began this way.

It is October 8, 2:55 p.m. Pacific Time. I am in the outdoor eating area of Vista Grande Elementary School in El Cajon on a beautiful, sunlit, California day, waiting for my daughters to finish school. As I watch the children leave their classrooms and as I see their teachers say their goodbyes, I realize I am writing about them—for the teachers to help those children navigate and interpret their tricky and complex world characterized by a sophisticated and multifaceted communications web. This is about teaching English and language arts in the new world—the world that includes talk and print but also includes television and film. A world where talk can occur between people 10,000 miles apart connected by telephone receivers and a microdish; a world where print may be as fresh as the instantaneous thought of the writer and the microseconds the fax machine requires from sender to receiver; a world where something can occur at 10:00 p.m. in New York that can be read about in a newspaper in California the following morning; a world where television provides 100 choices not including videos for the VCR.

Notice the changes between draft one and draft two. Some are very small— "waiting for Lizzy and Jane to end their school day" (draft one) becomes "waiting for my daughters to finish school" (draft two). Some are larger changes, such as the differences between the sentence in draft one that begins, "As I begin the writing of whatever this will become. . ." and the sentence in draft two that begins, "As I watch the children leave their classrooms and as I see their teachers say their goodbyes. . . ."

As the writing progressed, I discovered I had more to say as well as better ways to say what I already had written. The second draft was twice as long as the first one. I recommend you write a second draft as I did, word for word. When you are finished with your second draft, you will have to make a big decision.

Step 5: Drafting Again and Bringing in Sources

The decision you face concerns another rewrite. I rewrote word for word again and found that my *Crossing Over* became even better, as well as longer. Compare these two sections. The first is from the original draft and the second is from the third rewrite.

If the book was spread by means of the Old World to the cross over generation, the messages received from the book were certainly new generational. The book took us by the hand and crossed us over. The text my generation created from *The Catcher in the Rye* was the text that still covers our society. It taught us that the elders can be wrong, corrupt, stupid, vacuous, sad, phony (draft one).

The Catcher in the Rye may have become known by means of the old world, but the messages received were all new generational. My generation may have grown up in a world reminiscent of the nineteenth century, but we were going to be the cross over generation, defining the new parameters of popular culture in America. The following generations would refer to what we did and so much of what we did began with the world of Holden Caulfield in *The Catcher in the Rye*, the book that took us by the hand and crossed us over (draft three).

Notice how some of the seeds of draft one are in draft three, but the changes are big. Also notice how the "crossed us over" idea buried inside the draft one paragraph became the focus in draft three, the destination of the entire paragraph.

You may feel that rewriting your *Crossing Over* again is too much work and not worth the effort. Whatever you decide, you may want to do what I did next. Remember those sources that I recommended you write down? I went back to my notes, arranged them by subject and integrated sources that I felt most enhanced my story into my text. However, an editor informed me that I had used too many quotes in the text, particularly long, stylistically out-of-place quotes. So be careful. This is *your Crossing Over.* Don't try to protect yourself with footnotes. Be brave.

Step 6: Finding a Reader

This was one of my hardest moments, allowing my statement to go public. Actually, what you need to find is a conscientious reader, a knowledgeable friend who will read your statement and will offer you real advice. You may wish to use the following questions to guide your friend, but be careful because, once again, these are my questions and this is your statement.

- Am I logical and consistent?
- Is my voice evident?
- Is my voice the same throughout?
- Do I make sense?
- Are my arguments strong and my reasoning clear?
- How can I make the stories I tell more interesting?
- If I have to shorten this, what would you recommend I cut?
- Do I need more or fewer subheadings? Are they appropriate and helpful? Have I left out anything that should be included?
- Tell me what you like and dislike about my statement.

Step 7: Editing

Take your friend's suggestions and go at it—cut, rewrite, and add. Once again, this is yours, so you need not do everything your friend suggests, but readers are very helpful in pointing out things that writers have difficulty seeing. Because of readers, I added new chapters, created new sections, cut quotations, made the tone less strident, took out several irrelevant sections. In many ways, the editing was much more difficult than the original writing.

Step 8: Final Editing/Copyreading

This is the last editing. It is time to cross the t's and dot the i's. Ask:

- Is everything spelled correctly?
- Is my punctuation accurate?
- Should I cut or add anything?
- Is my bibliography in a standard format?
- Are my pages numbered accurately?
- Any typos?

Step 9: Publishing

Get it out and give it up. You will collect your share of critics, but look forward to some sympathetic readers. No matter how careful you were, expect someone to find embarrassing mistakes. But with any luck, this will become an important statement for you, a personalized view of your ideas about English teaching and where they came from. In the long run, your typos won't matter. However, your honesty and insights, your voice and style, your ideas and empathy may count for a long time. If you feel like sharing ideas or thoughts about your *Crossing Over*, or mine, write to me at:

134 Zook Hall
University of Akron
Akron, OH 44325-4205
E-mail: hfoster@uakron.edu

References

Atwell, N. (1987). *In the middle: Writing, reading, and learning with adolescents.* Portsmouth, NH: Heinemann.

Beary, M., Salvner, G., & Wesolowski, B. (1977). *Newscast: A simulation of a TV news team's coverage of present or historic events.* Lakeside, CA: Interact.

Bleich, D. (1988). *The double perspective: Language, literacy, and social relations.* New York: Oxford University Press.

Booth, W. (1988). *The company we keep: An ethics of fiction.* Berkeley, CA: University of California Press.

Brown, K. M. (1992, April 15). Writing about "The other": New approaches to field work can end the colonial mindset of anthropological research. *The Chronicle of Higher Education, 38,* A56.

Carey, J. W. (Ed.). (1988). *Media, myths and narratives: Television and the press.* Newbury Park, CA: Sage Publications.

Chomsky, N. (1975). *Reflections on language.* New York: Pantheon Books.

Coles, R. (1989). *The call of stories: Teaching and the moral imagination.* Boston: Houghton Mifflin.

Cooper, J. D. (1997). *Literacy: Helping children construct meaning* (3rd ed.). Boston: Houghton Mifflin.

Cullinan, B. E. (1990, July 1). And some words for the children. *New York Times Book Review,* p. 17.

Cunningham, P. M. (2000). *Phonics they use: Words for reading and writing* (3rd ed.). New York: Longman.

D'Angelo, F. (1983). Literacy and cognition: A developmental perspective. In R. W. Bailey & R. M. Fosheim (Eds.), *Literacy for life: The demand for reading and writing.* New York: Modern Language Association of America.

Davis, J. E. (Ed.). (1979). *Dealing with censorship.* Urbana, IL: National Council of Teachers of English.

Dickens, C. (1966). *Hard times.* G. Ford & S. Monod (Eds.). New York: W. W. Norton.

Dickens, C. (1980). *David Copperfield.* New York: Signet Classic.

Dunning, S. (1975). *Teaching literature to adolescents: Poetry.* Glenview, IL: Scott, Foresman.

Dunning, S. M., Eaton, J., & Glass, M. (1975). *For poets.* New York: Scholastic.

Elbow, P. (1998). *Writing without teachers* (2nd ed.). New York: Oxford University Press.

Emig, J. (1983). *The web of meaning: Essays on writing, teaching, learning, and thinking.* Upper Montclair, NJ: Boynton/Cook Publishers.

Farrell, E. (1991). Instructional models for English language arts, K-12. In J. Flood, J. Jensen, D. Lapp, & J. Squire (Eds.), *Handbook of research on teaching English language arts* (pp. 63–84). New York: Macmillan.

Fitzgerald, F. S. (1925). *The great Gatsby*. New York: Scribner Classic.

Foster, H. M., & Newman, I. (1990). Error analysis for high school teachers. *Language and Education: An International Journal, 2,* 222–239.

Foster, H. M. (1979). *The new literacy: The language of films and television.* Urbana, IL: National Council of Teachers of English.

Freire, P. (1985). *The politics of education: Culture, power, and liberation.* South Hadley, MA: Bergin and Garvey.

Freire, P., & Macedo, D. (1987). *Reading the word and the world.* South Hadley, MA: Bergin and Garvey.

Gere, A. R., Fairbanks, C., Howes, A., Roop, L., & Schaafsma, D. (1992). *Language and reflection: An integrated approach to teaching English.* New York: Merrill.

Gonzales, R. D. (1990). When minority becomes majority: The changing faces of English classrooms. *English Journal, 79,* 16–23.

Goodman, K. (1977). *Miscue analysis: Applications to reading instruction.* Urbana, IL: National Council of Teachers of English.

Graff, H. J. (1986). *The labyrinths of literacy: Reflections on literacy past and present.* New York: Falmer Press.

Hamilton, V. (1968). *House of Dies Drear.* New York: Collier Books.

Hinton, S. E. (1967). *The outsiders.* New York: Dell.

Hirsch, E. D. (1987). *Cultural literacy: What every American needs to know.* Boston: Houghton Mifflin.

Koch, K. (1970). *Wishes, lies and dreams.* New York: Chelsea House.

L'Engle, M. (1962). *A wrinkle in time.* New York: Dell.

Lord, B. B. (1986). *In the year of the boar and Jackie Robinson.* New York: HarperCollins.

Macrorie, K. (1984). *Writing to be Read.* Upper Montclair, NJ: Boynton/Cook Publishers.

Mayer, R. E. (1987). *Educational psychology: A cognitive approach.* Boston: Little, Brown.

McLuhan, M. (1964). *Understanding media: The extensions of man.* New York: McGraw-Hill.

Moffett, J. (1968). *Teaching the universe of discourse.* Boston: Houghton Mifflin.

Newman, J., & Church, S. M. (1990, September). Commentary: Myths of whole language. *The Reading Teacher, 44,* 20–27.

Olson, D. R., Torrance, N., & Hildyard, A. (Eds.). (1985). *Literacy, language and learning: The nature and consequences of reading and writing.* New York: Cambridge University Press.

Paterson, K. (1977). *Bridge to Terabithia.* New York: Crowell.

Pattison, R. (1982). *On literacy: The politics of the word from Homer to the age of rock.* New York: Oxford University Press.

Paulsen, G. (1987). *Hatchet.* New York: Bradbury Press.

Peck, R. N. (1972). *A day no pigs would die.* New York: Dell.

Piaget, J. (1959). *Language and thought of the child* (3rd ed.). M. Gabain, trans. London: Routledge and Kegan Paul.

Probst, R. (1988). *Response and analysis:* Teaching literature in junior and senior high school. Portsmouth, NH: Heinemann.

Purves, A., Rogers, T., & Soter, A. O. (1990). *How porcupines make love. II. Teaching a response-centered literature curriculum.* New York: Longman.

Real, M. (1989). *Super media: A cultural studies approach.* Newbury Park, CA: Sage Publications.

Robinson, J. L. (1983). The users and uses of literacy. In R. W. Bailey & R. M. Fosheim (Eds.), *Literacy for life: The demand for reading and writing.* New York: Modern Language Association of America.

Romano, T. (2000). *Blending genres, altering style: Writing multigenre papers.* Portsmouth, NH: Heinemann/Boynton Cook.

Rose, M. (1989). *Lives on the boundary: The struggles and achievements of America's underprepared.* New York: Free Press.

Rosenblatt, L. (1978). *The reader, the text, the poem: The transactional theory of the literary work.* Carbondale, IL: Southern Illinois University Press.

Rosenblatt, L. (1983). *Literature as exploration.* New York: Modern Language Association of America.

Routman, R. (1996). *Literacy at the crossroads: Crucial talk about reading, writing, and other teaching dilemmas.* Portsmouth, NH: Heinemann.

Salinger, J. D. (1951). *The catcher in the rye.* Boston: Little, Brown.

Scholes, R. (1985). *Textual power: Literary theory and the teaching of English.* New Haven, CT: Yale University Press.

Scholes, R. (1989). *Protocols of reading.* New Haven, CT: Yale University Press.

Shakespeare, W. (1961). A midsummer night's dream. In H. Craig (Ed.), *The complete works of Shakespeare.* New York: Scott, Foresman.

Shaughnessy, M. (1977). *Errors and expectations: A guide for the teacher of basic writing.* New York: Oxford University Press.

Smith, F. (1992, February). Learning to read: The never-ending debate. *Phi Delta Kappan, 73,* 432–441.

Smith, F. (1983). *Essays into literacy: Selected papers and some afterthoughts.* Exeter, NJ: Heinemann Educational Books.

Smith, F. (1982). *Understanding reading: A psycholinguistic analysis of reading and learning to read.* New York: Holt, Rinehart and Winston.

Solomon, C. (1990, October 7). It wasn't always magic. *Los Angeles Times,* pp. 3, 92–93.

Speare, E. G. (1986). *The witch of blackbird pond*. New York: Dell.

Strickland, J. (Ed.). (1991, February 13). *English Language Quarterly*.

Sussman, H. S. (1989). *High resolution: Critical theory and the problem of literacy*. New York: Oxford University Press.

Taylor, M. D. (1976). *Roll of thunder, hear my cry*. New York: Bantam Books.

Tchudi, S., & Mitchell, D. (1989). *Explorations in the teaching of English* (3rd ed.). New York: Harper and Row.

Thornburn, D. (1988). Television as an aesthetic medium. In J. W. Carey (Ed.), *Media, myth and narratives: Television and the press*. Newbury Park, CA: Sage Publications.

Tompkins, G. E. (2000). *Literacy for the twenty-first century: A balanced approach*. Upper Saddle River, NJ: Merrill, Prentice Hall.

Twain, M. (1970). *The adventures of Huckleberry Finn*. New York: Washington Square Press.

Van Deweghe, R. (1982). Spelling and grammar logs. In C. Carter (Ed.), *Non-native and nonstandard dialect students: Classroom practices in teaching English*. Urbana, IL: National Council of Teachers of English.

Why Johnny can't write. (1975, December 8). *Newsweek*.

Winterowd, W. R. (1989). *The culture and politics of literacy*. New York: Oxford University Press.

Zindel, P. (1968). *The pigman*. New York: Bantam Books.

Author Index

Subject Index